EMPIRE *of*
INFIELDS

EMPIRE *of* INFIELDS

Baseball in Taiwan and Cultural Identity, 1895–1968

JOHN J. HARNEY

University of Nebraska Press | Lincoln

Library of Congress Cataloging-in-Publication Data
Names: Harney, John J., author.
Title: Empire of infields: baseball in Taiwan and
cultural identity, 1895–1968 / John J. Harney.
Description: Lincoln: University of Nebraska Press,
[2019] | Includes bibliographical references and index.
Identifiers: LCCN 2018047890
ISBN 9780803286825 (cloth: alk. paper)
ISBN 9781496215338 (epub)
ISBN 9781496215345 (mobi)
ISBN 9781496215352 (pdf)
Subjects: LCSH: Baseball—Taiwan—History. |
Baseball—Taiwan—Political aspects. | Group
identity—Taiwan. | Sports and globalization—Taiwan.
Classification: LCC GV863.795.A1 H37 2019 |
DDC 796.3570951249—dc23 LC record available at
https://lccn.loc.gov/2018047890

Set in Lyon Text by Mikala R. Kolander.

For my family

Contents

Note on Transliteration and Choice of Team Names

This book follows the standard practice in the field of utilizing Hanyu Pinyin transliterations for Chinese-language words, names, and places. Exceptions are made for certain Taiwanese individuals known predominantly in English by names using other transliterative methods—for example, Chiang Kai-shek. Furthermore, Chinese-language terms are preferred when possible. For example, the city of Hualian is referred to using its Chinese-language name when both the colonial and postwar periods are being discussed, rather than the Japanese form, Karenkō, for the period prior to 1945. When citing team names, I have sought to utilize either the contemporary usage or usage that has become common in the present historiography. For example, the Jiayi Agriculture and Forestry Institute team is regularly referred to in Chinese-language sources by the Japanese name Kanō rather than the Chinese title, Jianong.

Acknowledgments

I have many people to thank, and I have been extraordinarily fortunate. This project has lived in some form as I studied and worked at the University of Texas at Austin, DePaul University, and Centre College. At all three institutions, at various conferences, at archival locations, and at the University of Nebraska Press I have benefitted enormously from the generosity of colleagues and friends.

My adviser at Texas, Li Huaiyin, was an excellent mentor for any developing scholar. My plans shifted and changed throughout graduate school as they tend to do; he encouraged the initial version of this project with enthusiasm and examined it under demanding standards. John Traphagan, also at Texas, was a very important person for me, without whom I am not sure this project would have got going at all. He will be very glad the book has finally arrived. I also benefitted from the help and assistance of our graduate program coordinator and will never forget it. Thank you, Marilyn Lehman.

I thank everyone at the DePaul University History Department for being a welcoming and supportive group during my short stay, though I would be remiss not to mention a few for conversations and feedback on this project or just general guidance on writing and scholarship. Thank you, Tom Foster, Kerry Ross, Warren Schultz, Lisa Sigel, Roshanna Sylvester, Amy Tyson, and Benton Williams.

Centre College similarly hosts a lot of wonderful people. Tara Strauch's summer writing boot camp helped fuel an important summer of writing. Steve Beaudoin, Jonathan L. Earle, Sara Egge, and Amos Tubb have helped me understand how the relationship between teaching and research flows in two directions to the benefit of both. God bless Stacey Peebles, without whom the dissertation would never have become a book.

I extend the same gratitude to Rob Taylor at Nebraska, who as an editor gave good advice, always sought to understand my viewpoint on the project, and never hesitated to confront problems in need of solving. I am also indebted to Courtney Ochsner, Bojana Ristich, Anna Weir, and Joeth Zucco. Thanks to them and the rest of their team. Thanks also to those anonymous readers who reviewed this manuscript before it moved on to become a book. I am extremely grateful, and of course all remaining mistakes remain my own.

While conducting research I benefitted from the help of a number of people, including Chris Jhou of the Taiwan Resource Center at George Washington University in Washington DC, the staffs of the National Central Library in Taipei and the National Taiwan Library in Zhonghe, the staff of the Special Collections Research Center at the University of Chicago, and Taku Chinone at the Baseball Hall of Fame and Museum Library in Tokyo. Yu Junwei very kindly agreed to meet me in Taipei to discuss my work and offer his own advice and viewpoints. Lin Ting-kuo, at Academica Sinica in Taipei, was particularly supportive, both of the project as a whole and in encouraging me to make the best possible use of the archival materials at his institution. Jonathan Martin at the Irish Newspaper Archives in Dublin was also very helpful.

The list of those who have helped this project in ways big and small, ranging from offering expertise in depth to a kind word over a cup of coffee or following a conference presentation, is long but must include the following: Yvonne Sung-Sheng Chang, Robert Fitts, George Gmelch, Madeline Hsu, Mark Metzler, Ryan Noriega, Robert Oppenheim, Jess Shore, Trey Strecker, John Thorn, Bob Whitaker, and Dan Wold.

I have been very fortunate to receive the support of a number of talented and generous people. Nina Wu, Ana Lu and her husband Wang Wei-ta, and my good and dear friend Graham Lee all made my research trips less lonely and keenly offered suggestions. My parents, Lorcan and Grace, will be thrilled to see this in print and deserve my eternal thanks, as do my sisters Deirdre and Claire. Thank you, Jen, for putting up with me and for supporting me, for always encouraging me and never letting me off the hook. Thank you, Ryan and Saoirse, for not using up all twenty-four hours of daddy's day.

One last thank you, for Jared Diener, who one day outside his office in the Religious Studies Department at Texas turned to me and asked, "So, why do they play baseball in Taiwan?" I consider him utterly to blame.

Introduction | NATIONAL GAMES

Games capture the imagination and, when expanded to wider communities, take on grand ambition. A Boston Red Sox fan participates in a narrative recently characterized by a return to greatness, easily taken on by commercial interests, and channeled into a commercially palatable depiction of the "Red Sox Nation." The Bostonian looks back to Ted Williams, Carlton Fisk, even Bill Buckner or Sam Malone, as part of a national story. The fortunes and more welcome misfortunes of the New York Yankees are no small part of that. To be a Red Sox fan is to express one's identity as part of a larger tale, a larger shared experience.

The Red Sox are not the only sports team to embrace a "nation" moniker, but the effectiveness of the concept is elevated further only when attached to an existing example of the more traditional usage of the term. A national game can be, as baseball is in the United States, a reflection of a collective self-image within a community aspiring to a specific communal view. The American Pastime reflects a commitment to history, a now obscured commitment to a pastoral idyll as a metaphorical national value. The concept truly takes flight when differing national ideas rub up against each other and international sports teams compete for supremacy. In some cases, as for the English national soccer team, such competition becomes an opportunity and obligation to uphold some sense of national ownership. Association football is an English national game in the domestic sense and one of the better examples of national and nationalist sporting competitions on the international stage. English sports teams can claim to be representatives of the home of many modern popular sports and equally become "the Yankees" to more than a few opposing nations.

The international stage plays host to many dramas, not least of which include great moments for national communities unlikely to command attention in more traditional political arenas. As Allen Guttmann puts it, "In sports, more often probably than in any other domain, the initially dominated have turned the tables on their erstwhile dominators."[1] Modern popular sport emerged in large part thanks to the urbanization of countries experiencing the Industrial Revolution, particularly Britain, and soon set off across oceans on the ships produced by the same factories that let their workers out on Saturday just in time to attend soccer matches. Soccer, cricket, and rugby traveled across the world and soon provided arenas for the various jewels in Britain's empire to strike back. Famous victories and rivalries on playing fields have outlived most of the more dangerous animosities, just as they continue to provide the echoes of old grievances. Liberation from the imperial grip often does little to dilute popular interest in the sports of the colonizer. When Janaki Dass, secretary of the Indian Cycling Federation, lamented in 1946 on cricket's popularity in India as a "blackspot stamped by British Imperialism on the face of India," his hopes that his own beloved import, cycling, and the indigenous sport hutu-tu (kabaddi) would become dominant in Indian sport were dashed as, to quote Ramachandra Guha, "the black spot grew blacker, and spread alarmingly." Indian cricket fans greeted their national side's first test victory over England in 1971 with a reaction so hysterically gleeful that Prime Minister Indira Gandhi had the players' flight home redirected to New Delhi so that she could welcome them personally and share a photograph.[2] Scottish football fans famously took to the field at the spiritual and national home of English football, Wembley Stadium, in 1977 to congratulate their players on winning the Home Championship, only to lose the run of themselves and take various souvenirs for the trip home, such as the goalposts, much to the chagrin of their hosts.[3]

The phenomenon is not restricted to the echoes of British empire. A 2001 exhibition football match between France and its former colony Algeria had to be canceled due to pitch invasions and rioting. French international and French-Algerian global superstar Zinedine Zidane had received death threats.[4] The United States, hardly an international minnow, nevertheless found its great underdog moment in 1980, when a team of amateur ice hockey players defeated a powerhouse Soviet Union side in the "Miracle on Ice," a medal round game in that year's Winter Olympics. Language of imperialism of course saturated propaganda on both sides during the Cold War, as evidenced famously by Ronald Reagan's casting of the Soviet Union as an "evil empire" in 1983. Baseball's home, the land of the free, in theory stands in opposition to such imperial ambition.

Nevertheless, imperialism has played an important role in baseball's development as an international sport. Baseball arrived in Taiwan not directly from the sport's practical and spiritual home in the United States but on ships bearing Japanese engineers, teachers, and bureaucrats traveling to expand the borders of Japan's empire. Yet animosity toward the Japanese struggled to find its way on to baseball fields, even after the rapid increase of local Taiwanese involvement in the sport from the 1920s onward. Kanō, a multiethnic team of the 1920s and 1930s that enjoys pride of place as perhaps the most famous youth team in a country replete with adolescent baseball legends, stands as a great victory for Japanese players alongside their local counterparts. The greatest victory for Taiwanese baseball *against* the Japanese remains the victory in 1968 of the Hongye team, whose excellence paved the way for the small island's domination of the Little League World Series in the 1970s. It was this latter victory that signaled a shift for the sport's role in Taiwan, finally, into a national game.

Still Taiwanese baseball failed to take up the mantle of a sport of protest against Japanese colonialism. Instead the game quickly became an arena for an entirely different type of national contest: to determine whether or not Taiwan was, in fact, a nation. Any role the sport

may have played as a vessel for colonial and postcolonial mixtures of antipathy and closeness toward Japan evaporated. The sport finally assumed the mantle of a device through which the targets of a nationalizing project both received and resisted cultural ideology, but that device operated as a conduit between an undemocratic state bent on reinforcing the norm of eventual Chinese reunification and those who sought an identity peculiar to Taiwan, independent from its Chinese past. Japan hovers between the role of bystander in this dynamic between competing Chinese identities and that of a benevolent historical agent in assistance of forming a unique Taiwanese society rather than thwarting it. Identifying a Taiwanese national game is immensely challenging, even if baseball is the strongest candidate for such a title. Then again, finding a Taiwanese nation has not proved simple either.
***

In the 2014 Taiwanese film *Kanō*, a grim-faced but stoic manager leads a team of young men to a victory of which they had never dreamed, let alone thought possible. The film has all the ingredients of a rousing sports film: athletes learning to come together, cooperating just as the music becomes more and more dramatic until our heroes fall at the very last. Their loss, to a superlative team playing on its home field, is the most enriching of moral victories. The Taiwanese—for that is what this collection of ethnic Japanese, ethnic Chinese, and aboriginal children are—return home in triumph. The biopic leans hard on the fact it is based on a true story for emotional impact. The Kanō team, a collection of youths from different ethnic and socioeconomic backgrounds, traveled in 1931 to the famous Kōshien Stadium in Nishinomiya, Japan, where they lost in the final of the Japanese national high school baseball tournament. They had overcome their differences to forge unity through discipline and to respond together to adversity on the greatest stage. Kanō had journeyed from the edge of Japan's empire to its heart.

So far, so good. In recent decades Kanō has accrued a remarkable amount of importance in Taiwan's historical narrative as a team that essentially proves a number of contentious arguments about Taiwan during its colonial period. Kanō provides, on the one hand, evidence of the ideological and economic success of Japan in uplifting and assimilating its colony; on the other, it is testimony to the existence of a unified Taiwanese spirit and collective social self-recognition. In other words, this team of teenage boys proves both that Taiwan became a successful component of the Japanese imperial corporate body and that the island celebrated a unique, complex identity specific to the people living there. That the team accomplishes both of these things at the same time is remarkable, if not a little confusing. In Taiwanese popular memory, and in Taiwanese historiography, Kanō represents the complexity of the colonial period and provides evidence that Taiwan enjoyed some sense of cohesive identity independent of a province shorn from the mainland, awaiting recovery. Thus the victory of the Kanō team is a victory for a united vision of Taiwan far more than it is a victory against colonial overlords. Indeed in the film and in much Taiwanese writing it is not presented as a victory against colonial overlords at all.

In this respect an anticolonial message has proven less imperative than arguments in favor of a cohesive, extant Taiwanese national idea. Local cultural practice continues to trump the homogenizing effects of any supposedly uniform sense of globalism.[5] In India, where cricket has had considerably more success in gaining a foothold as the nation's favorite sport, if not a "national game," British authorities frowned on locals playing their game, just as the Japanese initially sought to restrict local Taiwanese involvement in the colonial game of baseball. In both cases such limits collapsed in the face of each sport's capacity to attract widespread interest. The Indian love of cricket is riddled with ambiguity but singularly dedicated in its intensity, a gift from British authority over the subcontinent but an experience that has long since moved beyond a binary relationship of oppression and resistance.[6] It has moved beyond that relationship, yes, but the relationship is not eclipsed: the game retained its imperial inheritance as England shed, one by one, its old possessions. On a cricket field if nowhere else, as C. L. R. James wrote of so beautifully in *Beyond a Boundary*, the dispossessed, the colonized, and the nonwhite can feel equal.[7]

In recent years the historiography of Taiwanese baseball has reached out toward this unifying aspect of modern sport with a more determined effort to interrogate and further enshrine baseball's status as a "national game" for the Taiwanese people, representing and sustaining a contiguous sense of Taiwaneseness that predates the advent of postwar Guomindang (GMD) rule under Chiang Kai-shek. Taiwanese baseball is now over a century-long endeavor, spanning across traditional lines of demarcation to highlight the existence of Taiwanese celebration of identity that expands beyond the far more recent political movements that helped to draw the territory out from Chiang's postwar era of martial law. The achievements of Taiwanese baseball during the colonial period thus represent long-standing evidence of Taiwanese unity and the validity of Taiwanese interactions with the world not defined by relationships between governments in Taipei and Beijing.

This concept of Taiwaneseness manifests in popular works focusing on Kanō.[8] The Chinese-language scholarship goes beyond these popularized accounts of Taiwanese victory, emphasizing in considerably more sophisticated analyses the importance of baseball in crafting a common social and communal consciousness on the island that exists beyond rigid definitions of Chinese identity rooted in Taiwan's pre-1895 status as a constituent part of the Chinese dynastic state. Chief among these is the work of Xie Shiyuan, who argues for the recognition of the birth of Taiwan's national game within the colonial era, recognizing the central role of colonial Japanese in creating the framework for Taiwanese baseball that would live on past the island's retrocession in 1945, and argues cogently for recognition that this enabled rather than stifled a common Taiwanese identity empowered by baseball.[9] This Japanization of Taiwanese baseball thus effectively marks the Taiwanization of Taiwanese baseball: by placing the development of the sport on a historical narrative line that includes—in fact celebrates—aspects of the Japanese colonial period, Taiwanese historians have created a metanarrative that would have been unacceptable, at least in public discussion, only a few decades ago.

This line of analysis continues in English-language scholarship. Yu Junwei has focused on the division of Taiwanese baseball into distinct periods, with an amateur postwar Golden Age ultimately succumbing to external cultural and capitalist pressures that have led to the sport struggling as a modern enterprise. His work *Playing in Isolation* focuses on baseball in postwar Taiwan and the subsequent double-edged sword of a popular game that has brought joy to millions of Taiwanese and is at the same time beset by the more questionable ethics surrounding the eligibility of child athletes sent to Pennsylvania to compete in the Little League World Series and the gambling scandals surrounding professional Taiwanese baseball in the 1990s. Yu, though hopeful for the game's future, ultimately depicts a national game thwarted or perhaps hollowed out from within, but a national game nonetheless. Andrew Morris's *Colonial Project, National Game* succeeds in further complicating this concept, situating Taiwanese baseball within an analysis of the game as an example of "glocalization," the adoption and implementation by Taiwanese of globalized cultural practice. For Morris this "glocalization" goes beyond analyses otherwise built on an assumption of an American cultural imprint onto East Asian consciousness, recognizing the agency of the Taiwanese in interacting with the world around them. Morris's approach relies on a sophisticated reading of an existing Taiwanese social identity recognizable through the practice of baseball, one shaped by considerably varied political and ideological impulses during the colonial era and the postwar period. The idea fits into a narrative of baseball as a uniting force in Taiwanese consciousness across the breadth of the twentieth century, albeit one contextualized primarily within discussions of global dynamics.

In the case of Taiwanese baseball the regional trumps the global in terms of immediate importance: Japanese expansionism was one facet of a broader globalizing wave, to be sure, but it must be taken on its own merits. The increased popularity of baseball, an American game introduced by Japanese colonizers and not one that enjoyed popularity on the Chinese mainland, created a sporting community that proved flexible to the changing political currents in Taiwan, as well as the changing expectations of individuals resident on the island. The formal organization of sporting events, itself a modern phenomenon closely tied to nineteenth-century concepts of individual participation in a healthy nation-state, brings new perspective to the development of national consciousness in small players in the global nation-state system. Taiwan's emergence from the colonial period led not to an independent state but an incorporation within a Chinese nation-state of which it had never been part, with former subjects of the Japanese empire now subject to an "initially overwhelming dominant émigré state" in the form of the ROC government driven by the GMD, the Nationalist Party.[10]

Because of the incongruity of postwar GMD leadership of the local Taiwanese population, it took time to dilute the importance of Japanese cultural influence. In this case Tokyo operated as the center of a cultural sporting sphere that emphasized uniformity within through example but diversified significantly from its own American model. That cultural sphere outlasted the policies that bolstered it and the broader strategic goals that underpinned it. If the study of modern sporting cultures in multiple communities is an exercise in the examination of globalization, then this book offers further proof that globalization can now be seen to produce diversity in addition to uniformity.[11] The global dissemination of a modern concept of sporting culture developed in Western Europe has not inexorably led to the mimicry of Western experience or the homogenization of native social development. In Taiwan, baseball does not fit neatly into dichotomies of Japanese assimilation and anticolonial resistance. The sport persisted as an extension of Japanese sporting tradition in the years following the end of Taiwan's colonial status in 1945, diluted only after a belated great national moment in the 1968 Hongye victory.

We are left with a complex relationship between an Asian metropole and an Asian periphery. Emulation of the British example provided Japanese imperialism with its impetus, the "orientalization" of the empire of Japan's new peripheries that emanated from Tokyo and other swiftly developing Japanese cities resembling the Western model in form and use of historical interrogation and selection, but the process remained resolutely one within an Asian context—an Asian context, albeit never freed from the central problematic of a Japanese narrative, dependent in some ways on Eurocentric antecedence, that focused on the relationship between Japan and China. The Chinese subcontinent offered the Japanese intelligentsia its clearest point of comparison, and twentieth-century discussions for the most part sought to move beyond the long-standing dilemma of China's production and translation of Japan's cultural foundations toward an active explanation of Japan's recent successes as an avatar of modernity in contrast with China's recalcitrant adherence to outdated political and cultural forms. Japan's orientalism focused not on the positioning of the Japanese nation but of the East Asian region, now a hierarchy of locations at the summit of which the Japanese comfortably sat in dominion.[12] This repositioning immersed Taiwan, Japan's first colony, in a modernizing mission that sought to share Japan's ascension into modernity with its expanding empire, through the replication of modern Japanese life in the colonies where possible.[13]

It was under Japanese leadership that Taiwanese education, print culture, sporting culture, and numerous other elements of public life developed into modern forms. Colonization divorced the island from China's own advances in modernizing projects of the 1910s and 1920s, which, if not comprehensive in their establishment of fundamentally democratic institutions, did effect the beginning of significant changes in Chinese civic identities.[14] Taiwanese baseball emerged and flourished within a Japanese imperial context. Colonial Japanese brought the sport to the island. The development of Japanese touring university teams, aimed squarely at series with prestigious American opponents, saw the expansion of Japanese baseball further outward and the cementing of connections between baseball in the metropole and baseball on the periphery. Taiwan received Japanese tourists and soon sent touring teams of its own to Japan, perhaps most notably the all-aboriginal Taiwanese Nōkō team of 1925. Kanō's adventures followed in 1931. Postwar GMD efforts to ignore the legacies of these events and the structures and culture built around them, to draft Taiwan back into a specifically Chinese narrative from which the former colony and newly recovered province had been forcibly excluded, finally gave way to the practicality of channeling public enthusiasm for the game in 1968. Even then Japanese legacies remained implicit background to GMD-approved narratives of victories for a culturally and politically legitimate China.

The shared cultural sphere centered on baseball that stretched across the Pacific offers a promising glimpse at the potential of sporting ideologies and sporting communities to transcend national borders and entrenched animosities. Taiwanese baseball's origins as a Japanese game and the persistent reliance of the community's cultural definitions on Japanese example for over two decades after the fall of the empire of Japan offer a stark contrast to Indian glee at the defeat of the English or Algerian vitriol directed against the French. Baseball has struggled to offer the Taiwanese avenues of retribution against Japan, the sport both referencing and reinforcing a general lack of antipathy among Taiwanese toward their formal imperial masters. In the years since the final fading of a clear Japanese domain over Taiwanese baseball diamonds in the late 1960s, the sport has become an arena for contestation and dispute over the nature of Taiwanese identity.[15] Even for those Taiwanese who would see the People's Republic of China (PRC) as a figure of opposition, the general lack of interest in the game among mainland Chinese somewhat reduces the potential for moral victories for Taiwanese sides. Taiwanese baseball is unique in similar ways to those in which Taiwan itself is unique. Rather than persisting as a postcolonial hangover or carrier of resentment against Japan, baseball has become subsumed into the complex politics of irredentism in Taiwan, where debate over reunification with the mainland is colored by the frustrations of those who feel the GMD is the one guilty of dispossession. It is therefore thoroughly representative of Taiwanese postcolonial experience, and like that experience, it offers us a clear departure from narratives of assimilation and resistance toward alternatives to our existing taxonomy of national games.

EMPIRE *of*
INFIELDS

1 | A Japanese Sport in the Colony

In 1895 the Qing Empire (1664–1912) was forced to agree terms after a debilitating and humiliating loss to the forces of imperial Japan in the Sino-Japanese War of 1894–95. The Treaty of Shimonoseki, in addition to granting Japan the right of most-favored-nation status in negotiations with Beijing, forcing the Chinese recognition of Korean independence, and imposing a massive war indemnity of 200 million taels, ceded the island of Taiwan to Japanese control.[1] The Japanese empire, after almost three decades of reform modeled after the Western example following the Meiji Restoration in 1868, had established itself as the predominant power in the region and gained access to its first colony. The impetus behind such access was rather vague, itself based on jumbled European ideas of colonization caught between the gradually outmoded concepts of mercantilist expansion and increasingly influential interpretations of Social Darwinism and the advantages of creating external, controlled markets for the purpose of facilitating continued industrial growth. However, one thing was clear: Japan had arrived as a major global power according to the standards set by the Western powers that had sought to subjugate Japan and China economically only a few years before.[2]

Faced with immediate practical issues of colonial governance, the Japanese political leadership struggled to reach consensus on how to best incorporate Taiwanese society into the Japanese imperial civic order in the years following colonization in 1895. On the ground, faced with the practical concerns of creating a functioning administration, Governor-General Kodama Gentarō and his chief administrator, Gotō Shimpei, set precedents during Kodama's term of office, 1898–1906, in the colonial governance of Taiwan that would be upheld by succeeding administrations until the late 1910s.[3] Their approach, driven largely by Gotō's own appraisal of how best to incorporate Taiwan into the empire, was highly pragmatic. There was no concerted effort to transform the average Taiwanese person into a Japanese citizen in the sense that he or she would *feel* Japanese; to walk, talk, and think as Japanese did, thereby making Japanese political administration more straightforward, would be enough. Gotō, with the full support of Kodama, concentrated on policies that encouraged Taiwanese coexistence with their Japanese colonial masters. Integration, in any sense of an overarching plan to reach the hearts and minds of Taiwanese and plant the seed of Japanese identity, was not the intention of early Japanese administrations in Taiwan. Gotō's approach earned him criticism in Tokyo, but he was ultimately in little danger of suffering direct interference from outside the colonial government.[4] Gotō and Kodama had a simple goal for Taiwan—namely, to make it a model colony to confirm Japan's arrival into the elite of the geopolitical world order. Gotō himself was unequivocal in this regard, dismissing his critics in Japan as poorly informed and clearly stating that the failure or success of the Japanese administration in Taiwan would have a "marked influence" on the future of the Japanese expansionist project.[5] Still, as Peter Duus has pointed out in reference to Korea, the colonial leaders of the Japanese empire formed one part of an "imperialist coalition."[6] Gotō's practicality reigned supreme in the creation of localized colonial policy but did not go unchallenged in the wider imperial discourse.

Japanese intellectuals such as Izawa Shuji instead looked to methods for including the Taiwanese in a collective Japanese identity, making Taiwan an extension of the imperial homeland, or *naichi*.[7] Izawa's chief role in the Japanese development of Taiwan as an imperial colony derived from his success in Japan as an innovative force in the continued evolution of universal education. His dreams of applying a Japanese model to the education of all Taiwanese fell victim to the colonial administration's desire that the education system be self-sufficient financially, but he nevertheless succeeded in establishing the curriculum for a primary school system that served the majority of all Taiwanese children, not just the children of colonial Japanese resident on the island. This curriculum, which focused on a mix of Japanese language, arithmetic, classical Chinese, and physical education, served as the core of the student experience at "common schools," the Japanese nomenclature for primary schools in Taiwan. Common schools proved a successful compromise between Izawa's ideological goals and Gotō's preferred approach to governance. The colonial administration established firm boundaries for the education of non-Japanese students in Taiwan that emphasized the common school experience and restricted post-secondary educational experiences outside of medical training, something considered by the colonial leadership as immediately vital, until at least 1915.[8]

In the broader sense Izawa and Gotō labored under the same umbrella of Japanese imperial aims; Gotō's inclinations toward coexistence at the expense of assimilation did not preclude the importation of state-building measures from Japan to Taiwan. Education had proved an important state-building tool in Meiji Japan, if an imperfect one, shaping in the late nineteenth century a model for universal education that sought to navigate the contending influences of Western texts (from Samuel Smiles's *Self-Help* to Aesop's *Fables*) and Japanese conceptions of morality while leading Japanese society forward on an aggressively ambitious path to industrial-economic development and geopolitical relevance.[9] Japanese administrators now turned their attention to applying lessons learned at home to this wild and untamed Chinese colony with the added authority of the imperial imprimatur. The colonial administration promptly promoted physical education in Taiwanese schools as part of a wider Meiji-period philosophical view of education that actively copied the Western example. The Japanese placed athletic ability as a premium objective, although Taiwanese suspicions that their children were being militarized ran deeper than any desire on the part of Japanese colonists to specifically utilize sport to alter Taiwanese minds. Japanese educational policy possessed clear and central objectives that reflected Gotō's practicality more than any ideological framework for transforming Taiwanese culture. Simply put, the colonial education system's treatment of native Taiwanese was centered specifically on winning support for the new regime, producing enough Taiwanese professionals to support the colonial government, and remaining as economically self-sufficient as possible.[10]

Japanese educational policy also served to undermine an elitist imperial Chinese ethos among the Taiwanese privileged class that traditionally eschewed physical activity and thus inevitably impacted the popularity of sporting activity and physical culture in general among local Taiwanese. However, Japanese colonial education policymakers were mindful from the beginning of colonial rule of the contrasts between their general educational goals and the existing practice of education in Taiwan. The practicality and direct nature of Meiji-period goals for the education of the Japanese people and the entrenched imperial Chinese attitude toward the role of schooling in the lives of Chinese at differing levels within society were completely at odds. Taiwan may have been a relative backwater in 1895, but it remained in the eyes of the Confucian literati living on the island (and crucially their Japanese conquerors) a fully integrated part of the Qing Empire and its enormous administrative system.[11] The Chinese education system focused on rote memorization of classical Chinese texts and the composition of poetry and prose that displayed excellence in reproducing the structure and syntax of the central texts in the classical Chinese canon.

After 1895 the path to participation in the civil service of the empire no longer existed for the sons of Taiwanese elites, but the principle remained, and those Taiwanese who could afford to do so continued to send their children to *shufang*, privately run Chinese schools that continued the tradition of a classical Chinese education and gave young Taiwanese the appreciation of and expertise in Chinese culture that their parents desired.[12] Regardless of the depth of Japanese interest in fully incorporating Taiwanese society into a Japanese imperial identity, the policies in place to drive up support for the colonial regime were clearly at odds with significant and influential sections of the Taiwanese population being educated as effective subjects of the Qing Empire and continuing participants in the Chinese cultural sphere. Absenteeism in the common schools set up by the Japanese government for Taiwanese children was rampant.[13] Parents from Taiwan's wealthier social classes simply did not care about their children's common school attendance so long as they attended to their studies at the *shufang*. Families further down the socioeconomic ladder showed limited interest in sending their children to classrooms for extended portions of the working day.

The Japanese government tolerated such attitudes as part of a long-term view toward the development of the educational system in Taiwan. An impetus to abolish the *shufang* was put aside in favor of effecting a gradual erosion of Taiwanese attendance at these schools and the replacement of classical Chinese educational principles with an educational ethos of which the Japanese approved. The gradual approach had merit, as the Japanese were in a position to offer young Taiwanese students a completely different educational experience. The Japanese education system was driven to be more practical, to prepare the Taiwanese for specific professional roles within the colonial administration. It also contained pleasures of a different sort to those provided by a classical Chinese education. Classes in music and physical education, and the facilities to make teaching these classes possible, proved popular with Taiwanese students; tennis courts and musical instruments were among the chief attractions of a Japanese education.[14]

Such progressive courses directly contradicted the more conservative curricula of the *shufang*, the principles of which brooked no engagement in organized physical activity at all for young people, seeing it as profoundly detrimental to their development and to society as a whole. Chinese culture had encouraged intellectualism and been predominantly biased against the celebration of the body for centuries, a complex position described succinctly by Susan Brownell as a "long history of intellectual antagonism" encapsulated in the Chinese proverb *zhong wen qing wu*: to esteem literacy and to despise martiality.[15] Taiwanese parents were far from enthusiastic about their children's participation in physical activity at Japanese-run schools. For their own part Japanese administrators focused on wrenching Taiwanese children away from the intellectual and cultural grasp of the *shufang*. As attendance improved alongside the pacification of Taiwanese violent resistance to Japanese rule, young generations of Taiwanese students grew up in a system designed to shape more effective citizens of a modernized nation-state. Efficiency included exposure to sporting activity, which included baseball.[16]

The colonial government's approach began to pay dividends in an increased interest among local Taiwanese, particularly as it became clear that their children would be at a major disadvantage to those of the colonial Japanese. The upper classes of local Taiwanese society pushed for expansion of education in the colony throughout the 1910s. Middle schools already existed in Taiwan in limited number, and the Japanese Department of Education granted accreditation on a case-by-case basis. Japanese authorities, mindful of the increasing flood of children of affluent Taiwanese families traveling to Japan for post-primary education, relented to Taiwanese demands for the establishment of the Taizhong Middle School in 1915, an institution that aimed to provide Japanese standards of middle-school education in Taiwan, one hundred students at a time.[17] In 1919 Taiwanese Governor-General Akashi Motojirō introduced broad reform with an education rescript that dramatically extended the reach of the Japanese educational framework on the island. This expansion beyond the basic common school system collected all of the colony's public schools for local Taiwanese into a single coordinated system for the first time and provided Taiwanese children with scholastic opportunities beyond the primary level, although the availability of such opportunity quickly narrowed as students moved upward from the broad common school base. The educational reform also saw to it that Taiwanese were funneled into avenues that would make Taiwan a more efficient colony rather than an intellectually vibrant complement to the Japanese empire.[18]

The colonial educational system was refined and standardized, funneling Taiwanese students into a mixture of post-primary educational opportunities. The higher ordinary school offered Taiwanese boys a course of education one year shorter than that of a Japanese middle school and focused more on the Japanese language, classical Chinese, and vocational training than its Japanese counterpart, with significantly less time devoted to chemistry and physics. Taiwanese girls could attend the girls' higher ordinary school, where students devoted more time to the Japanese language and handicrafts but less time to mathematics than their counterparts in Japanese vocational higher girls' schools. Akashi Motojirō had crafted a systematized framework of post-primary schooling in Taiwan to replace the haphazard array of individual institutions that had popped up across the island in response to the emergence of a generation of young students graduated from the common schools established early in the Japanese colonial reign. He had also greatly improved and increased educational opportunities for the average Taiwanese child.[19]

The systematization followed the basic pattern of primary- and secondary-level education established by Mori Arinori in Japan in 1886, with multiple educational tracks extending from a universal and compulsory primary educational tier into varying types of secondary-level and subsequently third-level institutions.[20] Physical education formed an important component of Japanese educational principles in the Meiji period after visits by prominent Japanese intellectuals, including Mori, to the United States in the 1870s. One of those intellectuals, Tanaka Fujimaro, had developed an intense interest in all things Western in his own ideas for educational reform in Japan. In particular he became fascinated with the physical education program conducted at Amherst College in Massachusetts, and in 1878 he hired an Amherst graduate, Dr. George Leland, to introduce American-style physical education to Japan. Leland ignored militaristic approaches to physical education in schools, instead promoting calisthenics and the construction of gymnasia on school grounds. Leland's involvement in Japan came at the end of a short period of intense borrowing from the West led by Tanaka, who was removed as minister of education in 1879.[21] However, the physical component remained in the Japanese educational system and became an important component of a broader cultural modernizing mission.

The rise of Japanese baseball came in the context of Meiji-period Japan's intersections of state building, the resulting growth in the imperial project, and the inclusion of Western ideas in such development. Horace Wilson, famed originator of the Japanese game, lectured at the Kaisei Gakkō, an institution first founded in 1857 as the Bansho Shirabesho, the "Institute for the Study of Barbarian Books." While there, Wilson introduced the game to some of his students, and from these meetings sprang the beginning of a national game that in its early days took equipment, rules, and modes of competition wholesale and untouched from the existing system of organized baseball in the United States. Wilson's meetings with students, beginning in 1873, render the American a kind of foreign Abner Doubleday in Japanese baseball. His role in the introduction of the game to Japan is more concretely identified than that of his compatriot's oft-purported role in inventing the game wholesale, but his relevance to the current historicizing of the sport is similarly ambivalent.

Wilson's role in the origins of Japanese baseball is both enhanced and somewhat complicated by his ethnicity and so is supplemented in Japanese baseball's origin story by the presence of a Japanese parent of the game, or perhaps co-parent: Hiraoka Hiroshi, a young Japanese engineer who spent several years in the United States studying railroad technology. Hiraoka fell in love with baseball and returned to Japan in 1877 with physical equipment and guidebooks, taking the idyllic picture of Wilson and his students batting a ball around on a leafy campus and developing the reality of an organized popular sport. He founded Japan's first baseball team, the Shinbashi Athletic Club, soon after his return. Hiraoka's vision of a baseball team was heavily informed by the American example, and he dressed his Shinbashi players in appropriate uniforms and sent them on to the field with authentic (that is, as fitting the American standard) bats and gloves. Hiraoka was a central figure in the beginning of a heavily structured approach to the amateur game in Japan, the "father" of Japanese baseball in a way that Wilson is not, a Japanese baseball man so in love with the game that he played catch on the long journey by ship home from America.[22] Wilson and Hiraoka together personified the easiness with which Japanese baseball embraced its American roots and the need to clearly define a distinct Japanese experience.

The complicated relationship between the spread of the game in Japan and its origins in the United States often played out at Japanese educational sites. In the 1890s the First Higher School of Tokyo, Ichikō for short, fielded a team that embroiled itself in rivalries with foreign-affiliated teams, most notably in a series of famous contests with the Yokohama Country Athletic Club in 1896. The country club teams, filled with Americans, lost in short order to the drilled and intense young Japanese athletes on the Ichikō side by devastating scores: 29-4, 35-9, 22-6. The Americans' pride and confidence, borne of their self-assured racial superiority, lay in tatters.[23] Baseball soon emerged as an elite collegiate sport too, particularly on the campuses of Tokyo-based Waseda University and Keiō University, which began to play series of exhibition games against each other following their first recorded meeting in 1903.[24] Within two years the Waseda team had made the first of many trips by Japanese collegiate baseball teams to the United States to play American teams. By 1926 Waseda and Keiō were joined by Hōsei University, Rikkyō University, Meiji University, and the Imperial University in Tokyo to form what would become known as the Big Six League.[25] Japanese baseball flourished in the opening quarter of the twentieth century on university and high school campuses, attracting large crowds to games and receiving significant exposure in the Japanese press.

Japanese attitudes to the development of public participation in sport in Taiwan potentially mirroring the evolution of public physical culture more broadly in Japan were conflicted. Baseball arrived in Taiwan shortly after colonization in a manner similar to that in which it had arrived in Japan: informally and spread by enthusiastic individuals. Japanese professionals in Taiwan grouped together in loose meetings of baseball enthusiasts who pitched, hit, and fielded without the formal trappings of organized sport, often without separating into distinct teams on the field. The sport spread throughout Taiwan with the great influx of Japanese professionals and military to the island. Still it was not until 1906 that the first organized game of baseball was played in Taiwan. The Taiwan Colonial Government High School and the National Language Normal School played to a 5-5 draw at High School Sports Field. The two schools were joined by the Taipei East Gate Night School in the formation of a three-way rivalry over the next couple of years. The principal of East Gate Night School even hired a pitcher from Japan to move to Taiwan and coach his team. In the autumn of 1908, however, the new principal of the Taiwan Colonial Government High School called an end to the rivalry. Honjō Taichirō, no enthusiast of the sport, feared that such competition held the potential to stir up a passion in the crowd watching the event that could manifest in violence, not to mention the possible negative effects on the local Taiwanese.[26] In this man's mind at least, baseball had the potential to cause issues for Japanese attempts to manage the local population and raised more serious ethical questions of how to manage the moral standards of public behavior in the city.

Honjō's concerns reflected a wider belief in the Japanese administration that potential unrest in Taiwanese society would present obstacles to Japanese goals that would prove difficult to overcome. The approach to colonial governance pioneered and modeled by Chief Administrator Gotō remained supremely practical. The spread of organized sport in Japanese society throughout the educational system had been a Japanese development. It was not inevitable, or desirable, that such a spread occur in Taiwan. The educational system in Taiwan as a whole was designed to contain local Taiwanese within a role set for them by the Japanese administration. The common school system gave most participating Taiwanese just enough education to continue with the trades that their families practiced. A chosen few were in a position to further their education, and those students filtered into practical professions the Japanese considered acceptable, such as medicine and teaching. Interest in the humanities was not encouraged beyond the Japanese concessions in teaching Chinese languages and literature. Gotō, his sponsor Kodama, and Kodama's successors as governors-general of the colony had little interest in training Taiwanese colonial subjects in rhetoric or in encouraging Taiwanese to attend sporting events en masse where their emotions could potentially become enflamed.

Still the role of sport in the modernization of the island as part of imperial development was muddled. Gotō himself, an enthusiastic admirer of the British success in empire building, set up a school for Japanese boys in 1908 to emulate the British public school system. Here young colonial Japanese were encouraged to develop their character in intellectual activities and the physical disciplines of labor and team sports, including baseball. The school struggled to receive any encouragement from Tokyo, earning accreditation only in 1911. The Tokyo-based Ministry of Education then used the increased power over the curriculum granted by accreditation to gradually erode all of the school's distinctive character.[27] The failure of the school, despite Gotō's reputation, highlighted the Ministry of Education's determination to maintain a strictly homogenous educational system in the colony. Gotō's school saw its baseball team dismissed in 1914. The rapid rise in popularity of the sport among Japanese in Taiwan in the 1910s came against a background of frequently unconvinced gatekeepers of the education system who saw the sport as a possible distraction for students, at the very least.[28] Opportunities to engage with the imperial superstructure were limited. The first Taiwanese to play in organized tournament play did not take the field until 1919.[29] Taiwan's public sphere featured baseball specifically in the context of visiting teams from Japan and the subsequent effect on local troop morale.[30] Baseball in Taiwan in the 1910s was an outlet exclusively for Japanese colonists in the practical senses of participating on the field and associating together in formal organizations.

Such formal organizations thrived thanks to the colonial administration's goal to win support among the Taiwanese population beyond the educational system. Japanese authorities established "Military Ethics Association" branches in Taipei in 1900 and proceeded to construct military parade grounds in Taipei, Taizhong, Xinzhu, and Gaoxiong.[31] The parade grounds hosted gatherings of artists and military personnel from around Taiwan in the promotion of Japanese goals as part of engaging the Taiwanese populace and promoting a militaristic general ethic. In 1903 the government-general police department director Oshima Hisashi established a "sports club" for the same purpose.[32] Games between school organizations and private clubs were common occurrences by the end of the decade.[33] Slowly the colonial government was constructing an apparatus throughout the island to promote Japanese ideals through participation by the Taiwanese in group activities, either exclusively military in character or primarily sporting but occurring in public places created by Japanese authorities for specific Japanese purposes.

By the late 1910s sporting activity, particularly baseball, was popular throughout the island, with participation running at high levels among the Japanese colonial community and growing. The popularity of baseball continued to thrive in the face of muddled signals of resistance and encouragement by Japanese authorities to the spread of participation by Taiwanese in organized sport. The success of the sport in teaching colleges established to spread the growth of Japanese as a national language churned out baseball enthusiast teachers in a prime position to influence young Taiwanese minds.[34] The popularity of the game continued to grow despite administrators' reservations regarding the risk that large groups of Taiwanese associating together at a sporting event or any other public gathering would mitigate the development of a model colony, one characterized by order and efficiency in service of Japan's role in Taiwan as a civilizing force.[35] The *Nichi Nichi Shimpō*, a predominantly Japanese-language newspaper published in Taiwan with the support of the colonial government that ran from 1898 until 1944, carried an increasing number of reports on various baseball-related events throughout the island. In June 1914 the sport was already considered worthy of a spot on the paper's front page, featuring a photograph of a baseball player sliding into third base in formal tournament play.[36] On a day with a surfeit of news related to the sport, a single page could carry multiple articles, including the tournament results of the previous day, a photograph of a young man in uniform throwing a ceremonial pitch, and relevant information for the paper's readers on the baseball game to be played on the day of that issue's publication and the fireworks planned for just before the opening pitch.[37] Yet for all of this clear enthusiasm, which local Taiwanese would surely have been unable to completely ignore, baseball developed as a link between the Japanese colonists and their native land. The tournament play that began to grow in the 1910s mirrored similar developments in Japan. All of the athletes playing the game were Japanese.

The baseball community in the 1910s was thus an exclusively colonial Japanese affair. Young men established clubs based around public- and private-sector workplaces. In the years 1910–11 teams of financiers, railroad company workers, law professionals, restaurateurs, and others sprung up throughout the island. Teams formed to represent branches of Japanese banks or factories.[38] In 1914 the Taizhong branch of the Taiwan Bank hosted a baseball game that pitted the bank's married employees against their unmarried colleagues. The players drew squares on the ground to represent the bases and afterward gave onlookers lessons on the rules of the game and some basic playing skills.[39]

As the 1910s began, a fledgling baseball community in Taiwan began to take shape. The Takasago Club, named after the Japanese-language term for the aboriginal Taiwanese ethnic group, began to play games in Taipei, often against the ever-present Taipei High School Association.[40] The club struck up a relationship with the school system, with a game between the two sides forming a central attraction in an intramural high school competition in 1910. The adults competed in a single game while teams composed of students from various grades competed for first place. A team composed of third- and fourth-year students successfully defeated the fifth-year team, and posed for a photograph for the newspaper.[41] This tournament, although earning significant space on the *Nichi Nichi Shimpō* pages compared to other baseball-centered events—with full box scores and descriptions of the games—was the exception rather than the norm. Organized baseball was predominantly the field of adults, and by 1914 the game had spread to the public sector with representative teams playing in the name of the Post Office and the Railroad Departments.[42] Organized tournaments between high school students, as opposed to teachers employed by the High School Association, did happen during this time, but the adult baseball scene took precedence in media coverage.[43] Although it is extremely difficult to ascertain the part that baseball played in the physical education of young students in Taiwan during this time, we know that the boys' teachers and teachers in training were frequently playing the sport.

In 1915 Japanese baseball enthusiasts, led by Kafuku Kinzō and Iseda Gō, proposed the establishment of a single organization to administrate the increasing number of games in northern Taiwan. In January 1915 the Northern Baseball Association was formed with a membership of over twenty teams.[44] Similar organizations in the south and in Taizhong soon followed.[45] These organizations directly followed Japanese examples in the proliferation of administrative associations to arrange play and prepare tournaments. In 1915, only a year after the formation of the Northern and Southern Baseball Associations in Taiwan, the *Asahi Shimbun* newspaper in Japan sponsored the creation of a nationwide baseball tournament for high school teams that would quickly become extremely popular across the country. The paper, previously a strident critic of the earlier development of the sport, now actively sought to capitalize on the popularity of the game.[46] In 1914 the baseball teams of Waseda, Keiō, and Meiji Universities agreed to create a regular three-team tournament, born of the rivalry of the first two schools dating back to 1903.[47] Mimicking developments in Japan, the new Taiwanese associations had been set up primarily to organize and regulate tournaments among the numerous teams in the colony. All-star games to commemorate the beginning of a new season, featuring star athletes decked out in colorful uniforms, were common, both among adults and in schools for the children of Japanese colonials.[48]

Baseball as a spectator sport had arrived in Taiwan, acquiring sufficient public support among the colonial Japanese community for the hosting of a large baseball tournament to celebrate the twentieth anniversary of Taiwan's becoming Japan's first colony. Sixteen of the prominent adult teams throughout the colony merged into two all-star squads that competed against each other as Red and White teams over the course of the two-day tournament.[49] However, youth baseball was still virtually nonexistent on the pages of the Japanese-controlled press. In fact, as more and more adult baseball clubs began to form across the colony, the former powerhouse High School Association took a lower profile role in the formal organization of the game.[50] Baseball teams with various connections to educational institutions persisted, but the late 1910s became the province of adult male baseball teams centered on private- and public-sector organizations.[51] Mentions of high school teams populated by actual high school students are fleeting, though games featuring school employees drew passionate reactions from students in attendance, particularly the "hundreds of youngsters crying tears of regret" due to their team's narrow loss.[52]

Governmental disapproval of Taiwanese involvement in organized baseball was never seriously tested in the 1910s, as the plethora of locally arranged matches and the organized tournaments that succeeded them from 1914 onward featured Japanese players and were reported prominently in officially sanctioned Japanese-language publications. Nevertheless, baseball was a component of a spectrum of Japanese cultural influence that infringed on the Taiwanese cultural model, itself a small-scale encapsulation of traditional Chinese imperial culture. The sport occasionally made an appearance in the brief Chinese-language section of the *Nichi Nichi Shimpō*, as it did in a brief report in October 1914 on the seventh annual government-general sponsored Autumn Competition, where participants of all ages competed morning and evening in a variety of athletic activities, including baseball, in Danshui and Jilong.[53] At this time, despite the lack of opportunity for local Taiwanese to actively participate in the official baseball tournaments that had sprung up, the paper was reporting events such as picking the player of the year and celebrating the achievements of other athletes during the previous year. The precolonial elitist disdain for physical exertion appeared well on the way to dissolution.

The barriers between colonial Japanese and local Taiwanese participation in the game did not remain entirely ideological, nor were they born directly of policies that sought to divide the communities. Socioeconomic barriers played their part as well throughout the colonial period. Former Tainan No. 2 Common School player Li Changsheng recalls the popularity among local Taiwanese of "soft ball," a variant of baseball played with a softer ball and with fewer of the trappings of organized baseball, citing financial constraints as the chief reason for a lack of participation in the game by the Taiwanese. It is tempting to imagine the existence of a popular street game played by relatively poor local Taiwanese alongside the expensive trappings of organized baseball as practiced by the colonial Japanese, though Li grew up mostly in the 1920s, following the expansion of the popularity of baseball and its variants.[54] In the 1910s baseball was still developing as a highly organized and structured amateur emulation of the sport's structures in Japan, themselves highly organized emulations of the original American example. Baseball tournaments and all of their trappings, from the appropriate uniforms and equipment to the use and maintenance of public and private spaces, required significant investment from those participating.

It is fascinating that baseball in Taiwan dovetailed with other Japanese policies in the use of public space. The military parade grounds and public parks established by the Japanese government in cities across the island became sites for the holding of games and tournaments.[55] The Japanese colonization of Taiwan effectively wrenched the island away from Chinese cultural hegemony at a time when China was about to enter serious cultural and philosophical change. The Treaty of Shimonoseki, so vital to the increased interest among the Chinese in reforming the governance of their nation and the philosophical underpinnings of the state, excluded Taiwan from all these developments. Sun Yat-sen's drive for a Chinese state based on centralized political power lying with a Han Chinese race, the transition of imperial China into a modern nation-state, even the May Fourth Movement, all exist on a time line outside that of the historical path followed by Taiwan during the same period. In Taiwan, Japanese influence was paramount. The Japanese interpretation of Social Darwinism reigned, with specific form in Gotō Shimpei's "scientific colonialism," investigated in the laboratory of Japan's first colony.[56] Thus for the first twenty years of Japanese rule on the island, local Taiwanese were reduced to bystanders, observing cultural processes on their own island that formed part of a Japanese transnational experience.

Systematic expansion of secondary schooling in Taiwan and the regularization of what secondary schools existed in 1919 heralded baseball's further penetration into Taiwanese society. The rescript in 1919 was the final death knell for the *shufang* schools (though secondary schools in Taiwan continued to include classes in classical Chinese), and every Taiwanese schoolchild was now attending classes in physical education that well-to-do Taiwanese parents in the pre-1895 Qing Taiwan era would have considered unacceptable.[57] Instruction in calisthenics and stress on the importance of physical fitness, long a staple of the Meiji-reformed Japanese education system, was now fully implemented in Taiwanese colonial education. However, the stark divide between schools educating the children of Japanese colonials and those educating Taiwanese children, regardless of their class background, remained. Den Kenjirō, successor to Akashi and the first civilian governor-general of Taiwan, swiftly made public his intentions to end this situation upon his appointment in 1919. Den was an avid supporter of the assimilation of the Taiwanese population, supported in this by Prime Minister Hara Kei in Tokyo; the two men had served together in the Taiwan Affairs Bureau, established in 1895. Assimilation, or *dōka*, involved numerous ambitious measures, including the employment of Taiwanese in senior colonial government posts and the dissolution of a law banning marriages between Taiwanese and Japanese.[58] Den and Hara were both motivated by a desire for Japan to govern Taiwan and Korea in much the same way it governed its home islands, falling in line more directly with a broader approach advocated by Izawa Shuji and his contemporaries that used linguistic and cultural assimilation to embrace Taiwan into the imperial core.[59] In 1922 Den further advanced the reforms of the 1919 rescript by removing the restrictions in admissions to government schools on the basis of race. The 1922 integration rescript, although retaining competence in the Japanese language as a prerequisite for entrance to educational institutions, represented a solid commitment on behalf of the colonial government to the assimilation of the Taiwanese population.

Assimilation faced numerous challenges in Taiwan, not least in the attempted integration of the school systems that would become legislated in the 1922 integration rescript.[60] Compulsory education remained a goal and not an official educational policy, with attendance in the otherwise successful common school system a virtue neither prized by students and their families as paramount nor within the ability of the school administrators to control. Furthermore, Japanese families in Taiwan expressed dismay that their children would be educated alongside Taiwanese students, who would clearly struggle with the language barriers in the classroom and thus hinder, in their view, the development of the Japanese primary school students already present. Ultimately the integration rescript integrated schools from the secondary level upward, choosing to divide the common school and primary school systems on the basis of language. The primary schools were open to all who could satisfy Japanese language requirements while the common schools were designated as institutions for children who lacked fluency in Japanese.[61]

The compromise that the integration rescript became was a sign of political issues within Taiwan, specifically the ongoing differences of opinion among politicians such as Den, who championed the ideals of assimilation, and local Japanese officials and members of the professional classes. Ultimately the rescript resulted in a further limitation of educational opportunities for the Taiwanese, as the Japanese colonials in positions of power exercised their considerable control to reject applications on various bases of failure, such as language competency or academic achievement. Nevertheless, the integration rescript was important for more than ideological reasons: it succeeded in bringing two disparate strands of the island's education system closer together, and the measures introduced by the rescript also represented a fresh commitment to improve attendance among the Taiwanese population. Compulsory attendance would not be legislated in Taiwan until 1943, but the integration rescript of 1922 resulted in the construction of more common schools and further expanded the penetration of the education system into Taiwanese society after the expansion and systematization of the schooling system brought about by the education rescript of 1919.[62]

The integration rescript of 1922 is directly pertinent to an examination of baseball's role in Taiwanese society in the twentieth century in two ways. First, the rescript continued the expansion of the common school system in Taiwan. More and more Taiwanese children were exposed to Japanese educational methods, which included physical education and the introduction of team sports, primarily baseball. Second, the significant opposition to the rescript within the Japanese colonial community rested on a pronounced fear among a privileged class of losing certain hitherto guaranteed social advantages and genuine concern on the part of Japanese colonials that linguistic issues would cause a lowering of the standards of education in Japanese primary schools that were forced to accept Taiwanese students. Japanese parents did not voice concerns about the ideological impact of more Japanese-styled education for local Taiwanese; this was already happening across the island. There was no systematic opposition to the continued Japanese acculturation of Taiwanese children or any meaningful acknowledgement such acculturation was in any way unnatural or illegitimate, just as there was little appetite for the integration of schools that would bring alleged simplifications and lowering of standards in language and instruction that the Japanese community feared. Those in opposition to the rescript were fully focused on the potential for immediate problems in the education of their children. The question of baseball and other forms of physical education in schools lay clearly within the domain of this specific debate, which the colonial Japanese were losing. By the early 1920s press coverage of students engaged in games of baseball and bouts of sumo wrestling reflected the extent to which Taiwanese public life mirrored features of Japanese public life.[63]

Such public life was defined by Japanese parameters. As society on the Chinese mainland entered a process of renovation that would soon translate into years of sociopolitical upheaval, the local Taiwanese person's experience of cultural change was dominated by Japanese concepts imported from the colonial homeland to replace the imperial Qing worldview. Taiwan was excluded from Sun Yat-sen's theoretical re-imagining of China as a modern nation-state dominated by the Han and the multifaceted May Fourth intellectual movement in 1919 that gave birth to, among other things, Chinese communism. From 1895 onward, the development of the social identity of being "Taiwanese" was separated from the Chinese social consciousness with which it had previously been united, although it was not yet voiced or specifically identified.[64] The paramount influence was Japanese, and the differing approaches by Japanese colonial administrations to the inclusion of the Taiwanese into a Japanese imperial identity were dominant in the initial evolution of a sense of being "Taiwanese" as opposed to being "Chinese" (in either an ethnic or a civic sense). Traditional Chinese forms of physical activity, such as martial arts or qi gong, were enveloped in a highly Western-influenced Japanese conception of the role of team sports in public society and further marginalized by Japanese attempts to promote sumo wrestling.

The cultural transformations in Taiwan manifested in the growing popularity of baseball were the result of Japanese colonial policy that had oscillated between aiming for coexistence between the Taiwanese and colonial Japanese populations and assimilation of Taiwanese society and culture into a pan-Asian imperial civic identity led by Japan. Throughout these oscillations the aims of Japanese educational policy remained constant.[65] The Japanese educational infrastructure provided universal education at the primary level and funneled academically successful children into professional and technically oriented educational tracks at second and third levels. A small portion of local Taiwanese had the opportunity to join colonial Japanese in institutions similar to those of a Western-style liberal arts college, but in general the Taiwanese population was given the skills to improve the island's material infrastructure and supplement Taiwan's productive capacity. Rhetoric and historical criticism that might upset Japanese superiority were not encouraged.[66]

In Japan itself the concept of "nation" had moved on from more straightforward Social Darwinist competitive impulses, although those impulses had served the modernized state well in its military victory of 1895. Japanese imperialism initially rode on the confident wave of a "virus of racial assertiveness" to deliver a humiliating blow to the once great Chinese empire and establish Japan as the predominant regional power and chief emulator of European military success.[67] Domestic intellectual conceptions of Japan's role in the world soon turned to recognition of a natural Japanese state, and Japanese children were taught to contribute to the national family, an eternal nation-state both "natural and transcendent" that required the subjugation of personal interest to communal advancement.[68] Taiwanese children were similarly included in an educational system that aimed to promote communal advancement, although the goal remained the advancement of Japan, the fountain and embodiment of imperial concepts of the broader community. Throughout the 1910s Taiwanese children attended classes at common schools, the system encouraging universal education, but only to the completion of the primary level. Scholastic opportunities in Taiwan for young Taiwanese were extremely limited. Baseball was neglected, neither promoted as a tool by the colonial government to Japanize the Taiwanese populace nor targeted as a possible avenue for Taiwanese national self-consciousness by indigenous politically aware classes. Baseball's earliest appearances in Taiwan came in sporting competition among school teams organized independently by young professionals and students in 1906.[69] There was no encouragement of formal competition among sporting teams composed of Taiwanese children during this period, and even among the Japanese colonials baseball was a game for adults.[70]

Despite the tailoring of Japanese educational principles to narrow horizons for young Taiwanese, the objective of enhancing Taiwanese productivity while leaving social and cultural development to stagnate into some form of neutral pro-Japanese identity proved impossible. Educational policies strove to alter Taiwanese society from the beginning of occupation in 1895. Confucian principles of filial piety were adjusted to incorporate civic duty and loyalty to Japanese governance.[71] The children of the scholar-official caste were pried away from the *shufang* teaching classical Chinese texts and encouraged to learn the Japanese language. Japanese language policy was defined by its singular legitimacy as the only language of the Japanese nation and thus the Japanese race.[72] The definition avoided the issues of "dialect" that plagued the Chinese sociolinguistic landscape and would affect Taiwan for decades to come.[73] The educational system gradually strove to have Taiwanese children put down their pens for a small portion of their class day and participate in physical education, divided into basic calisthenics and team sports.[74]

Baseball served as an important ingredient in the ongoing expansion of a cultural project devised to fulfill the relatively recent Japanese dreams of a pan-Asian empire to rival those of nineteenth-century Europe.[75] However, it was also a key cultural practice in the lives of the Japanese colonists, and it evolved as Japanese practice in both Taiwan and Japan. Informal Japanese social activity accompanied the pervasive effect of an educational system that incorporated modern concepts of physical exercise in exposing local Taiwanese to this specific aspect of Japanese culture. Baseball, fully appropriated from the original introduction by Americans to Asia, entered Taiwanese public life as a striking example of Japanese life. Baseball associations, mirroring the formation of similar organizations in Japan, held tournaments among teams with specific identities, normally linked to the players' place of employment. Playing fields across the island became the local sites expressing a Japanese cultural phenomenon. Japanese played the game as they had learned it in Japan. They formed organizations to formalize tournament play among the various teams at the same time that such organizations took root in Japan. The Japanese played baseball in Taiwan for the fun of the game. The colonial Japanese who brought equipment and rule books to Taiwan (just as Hiraoka Hiroshi had done on his journey back to Japan from the United States), who organized amateur competitions, and who founded baseball associations within a handful of years of similar institutions being founded in their homeland were creating a community that extended out from Japanese cities toward the edges of the Empire of Japan, the post-1868 Japanese state now an increasingly adventurous ideological project encompassing territories from the Japanese homeland to colonies in Taiwan and Korea and eagerly eyeing territory in China itself. They were not missionaries of the newly established Japanese national game but its furthermost sentries, and for them Taiwan became a satellite in the Japanese orbit within a wider baseball universe.

That baseball universe reflected the creation of a Japanese sphere of modernity that sprang from multiple, competing sources rotating around the consolidation of a modern Japanese state in the late Meiji period. The expansion of the Japanese education system to its first colony relied heavily on the utilitarian benefits to be reaped, with the arguments between supporters of Gotō's coexistence and Izawa's assimilation somewhat repeating concerns in Japan as to the function of a universal education system immediately following the creation of the Ministry of Education in 1871.[76] These questions were existential in nature regarding the composition of and future pathways available to Japanese modernity, and in the case of Taiwan the additional question was raised as to how Japan's colonies would be plugged into such formulations. The dispute of course also rested heavily on long-standing ideological and intellectual paradoxes regarding the cohabitation of Japan's modernist and traditional exceptionalism with its intellectual Chinese foundations. The widespread adaptation of Western concepts and practices exacerbated the problem. The solution, emerging in vigorous debate in the late Meiji and early Taisho periods, ingeniously argued both that Japanese tradition had been separate from Chinese experience for centuries and that Japan's successful emergence as a modern power using Western methods was testament to the innate adaptability and progressive nature of Japan and its people.[77] The education system thus operated as a vessel of transformation, certainly within Japan itself. Baseball's introduction to Taiwan came as part of that transformation, though by no means a central plank in a cohesive Japanization project. Even within the contested aims between coexistence and assimilation, baseball took a back seat to the promulgation of the Japanese language and the crafting of productive colonial subjects.

The limitations of assimilation prior to the 1922 rescript helped ensure that the game operated primarily as connective tissue between Japanese in colony and metropole. The practice of baseball, in both the act of physical participation on the field and the formation of administrative organizations to bring teams together, very much functioned as an execution of ritual that reinforced the relationship between Japanese in Japan and Taiwan, undiluted by geographical distance. This relationship flourished not merely in the colonial emulation of a growing national pastime at home, but also thanks in large part to visits by prominent Japanese teams to the edge of empire. In 1914 colonial Japanese in the metropolitan Tainan area arranged a competition among teams representing the local post office, law and medical students, *ronin* students, "masterless samurai" students waiting to retake university entrance exams after an unsuccessful first effort, and featuring ballplayers with experience on the vaunted Waseda University baseball team.[78] It was one case of many in which colonial Japanese who had played the game at a high level found themselves in demand and worthy of note. Formal tours from the university side itself and other major Japanese teams soon followed, not to evangelize the game but to tend to the fire already lit by the emissaries of Japanese empire.

2 | Waseda Baseball and Japan's Place in the World

In 1911, Amos Alonzo Stagg, director of the University of Chicago's Department of Physical Culture and a legendary figure in American collegiate athletics, issued a small postcard to be distributed among the alumni of the university. The card itself was simple: a bright white background with blue text and two red flags at the top and center crossed in amity, bearing the names of the University of Chicago and Tokyo's Waseda University. Stagg appealed to each alumnus to take advantage of the opportunity to welcome the first Japanese baseball team to ever visit Chicago and called on all "interested in the development of a closer relationship between the United States and the Orient."[1] The card was brief and to the point and broadly reflected Stagg's hopes for the upcoming games as reflected in his correspondence with representatives of Waseda University and his own man in Tokyo, Alfred W. Place, a Chicago alumnus and former football player who had served as coach for the Waseda University baseball team in 1908.[2] Stagg had gone to great lengths to organize the games in the face of opposition from the chief administrators at the University of Chicago, who fretted mostly over the expense, both to satisfy these larger ideological goals and to uphold a promise to return the favor following Waseda University's hosting of his team in Tokyo the previous year.

Stagg's counterpart at Waseda, Abe Isoo, who in founding the baseball program at Waseda and then establishing the regular home and away series between his home institution and Keiō University was himself a major figure in Japanese collegiate athletics, pushed hard for the series.[3] Both men were ambitious, and in seeking to develop sporting relationships across the Pacific, they participated in an increasingly vibrant relationship between the United States and Japan fed by the technological advances of steamship and telegraph, dispersed across a variety of points of contact between official and unofficial members of each community.[4] The Waseda tours to Chicago that followed were far from the first example of baseball serving as a domain of geopolitical and cultural exchange. Abe was furthering an already existing practice of Japanese teams visiting the continental United States, and baseball had spread across the world for decades, with communities playing the game in Cuba, Hawaii, Japan, and the Philippines. Early examples of baseball spreading in Hawaii and mainland China came alongside the work of American Protestant missionaries, and the introduction of baseball to Filipinos coincided with American acquisition of the tropical archipelago as a colony following the defeat of the Spanish in 1898. The tying together of baseball to differing forms of American imperialism, in these cases, highlighted the troubling potential of the sport (alongside other modern games) to be wielded as a civilizing force utilized by civilized whites so inclined.[5] It also created a model for Japanese experience, for ensuring the legitimacy of early twentieth-century Japan's potential for what we today call soft power. Indeed the famous Albert Spalding–led baseball tour of 1888–89 brought an all-star team around the globe in an ingenious combination of seeking to enlarge the growing international standing of the United States and developing Spalding's own commercial reach, a fitting encapsulation of the beginnings of American global dominance rooted in cultural weight and capitalist potency.[6]

Abe's interest in creating and shaping relationships between Waseda and American universities fit neatly with his own visions for Japan and its future. He was politically energetic, a prominent member of a new generation of middle-class social and political activists who had come of age in a changed Japanese political environment at the end of the nineteenth century. The 1890 Meiji Constitution committed the elite-driven government to a bicameral national assembly, the National Diet. Direct vote, albeit limited to those of significant means, elected members of the lower house. Abe, along with his peers, was a "respectable" successor to the more hectic and protest-driven politics of Japan prior to the institution of the Diet; he was older, and he earned his living in a field separate from direct involvement in politics, an example of the newly institutionalized Japanese politician of the twentieth century.[7] Still Abe and his contemporaries also occupied a space beyond the 1900s contest between reformist liberals and resolute oligarchs that came to dominate Japanese politics; he was a Christian Socialist, a central figure in the 1901 establishment of a Social Democratic Party that was swiftly banned by the government of Katsura Tarō, a military man and long-serving prime minister. He and his peers represented a new middle class in a Japanese society rapidly evolving as the country entered the new century on the back of over three decades of modernizing reform.[8]

Abe's involvement in Waseda baseball was owing to a similarly forward-thinking position as the university became a pioneer for fellow Japanese institutions in sending baseball teams to the United States in an avowed spirit of friendship that ostensibly assured both sides of the importance of creating positive relations between East and West. The tours also provided a subtle but meaningful contribution to the increased international standing of the Empire of Japan. In 1905 Abe led a Waseda team of twelve players to the West Coast of the United States to play a series of games in California and Washington against multiple American opponents. The tour featured games against Stanford University, the American institution's prestige providing a highlight for those following the tour from home. The relationship between a continued projection of Japanese influence and Waseda's travels was clear, the trip to California made possible by a massive increase in Japanese maritime transport in the final years of the nineteenth century and first years of the twentieth that saw Japan come close to reaching parity with British and American shippers. Abe performed the role of sports administrator to the letter, declaring his purpose for travel to the United States to be the improvement of his players' skills and the acquisition of the most up-to-date standards of training and preparation. He also willingly took part of the gate receipts from games played to help pay for the trip, despite criticisms of the venality of such action from established voices back in Tokyo.[9] These issues did not seem to bother Waseda's growing fan base much, with hundreds gathering to see the team members off on their trip across the Pacific. They were similarly well received by members of the Japanese diaspora living in America, who attended Waseda's games with local teams in large numbers.[10] In San Francisco Waseda met with a local group of Japanese nationals who had gathered together enough money to donate a large silver cup as a memorial trophy to the team to commemorate its visit.[11]

Waseda's returns on the field were modest: the team lost the majority of its games, recording seven victories against nineteen losses. The trip was bookended by early defeats to Stanford and late defeats to the University of Washington, though Abe and his players could at least take some solace from a defeat of the University of Southern California.[12] Still Waseda had successfully cleared a path for other Japanese teams. Waseda's burgeoning rivalry with its Tokyo neighbor Keiō University left the confines of Japanese baseball fields as the two universities began competing in a new arena of cultural exchange across the Pacific, attempting to one-up each other through trips to the United States to play American teams and inviting American teams to visit.[13] Washington University visited Japan to play Waseda in 1908; Keiō then invited the University of Wisconsin, who visited in 1909. A pattern was emerging: visiting American teams would typically play both Waseda and Keiō, with the institution that extended the invitation retaining the honor of performing as official host for the visitors. Keiō officials treated Wisconsin players to sightseeing tours and an official banquet featuring entertainment offered by "beautiful geisha girls" who successfully garnered the attention of the Americans, who went on to describe the evening as a highlight of the tour.[14] A 1910 visit by the University of Chicago baseball team, the Maroons, came formally at the invitation of Waseda University. Abe and his fellow administrators had faced an uphill task in convincing the American university's rather reluctant chief administrators to send a team, so they established clear financial terms that would see the Japanese hosts fund their visitors' travel.

Funding such enterprises soon became an important sticking point, particularly on the American side. Writing in 1910, Stagg expressed his concerns in advance of his team's proposed visit to Tokyo that autumn. Stagg was more than happy to satisfy Abe's request that the team play five games against Waseda and another five against Keiō, but he sought permission from Abe to arrange other games for the express purpose of raising funds to make the trip possible in the first place.[15] Funding was of particular concern considering expectations on the Japanese side. Waseda's administrators fully expected that the invitation would be reciprocated the following year as the completion of a home-and-away series between the two universities. Furthermore, they expressed the hope that such a series would be repeated every five years —expectations that would fail to be dampened by the Maroons' eventual successful sweep of the Tokyo side across three games upon their arrival.[16] Ultimately Chicago and Waseda were able to agree terms, with each university guaranteeing the other $3,500 toward travel expenses and hotel accommodations for the visitors provided by the hosts in future series. Stagg agreed that no games outside of the ten proposed by Abe would be arranged until those games had been completed but in turn requested that his Japanese counterpart ensure the Chicago players would not be asked to play games on Sunday in observance of the Sabbath. The two men were already looking forward to the return visit by Waseda's team to Chicago, with Stagg frankly admitting there was no hope of the University of Chicago's funding Waseda's trip unless Abe was interested in playing games against other teams, the popularity of the White Sox and the Cubs (and the attendant drag on ticket sales for the university's games) weighing heavily on his mind.[17]

Communication among representatives of Chicago and Waseda was extremely cordial. Takasugi "Frank" Takizō, the president of the Waseda Baseball Association who would lead the Waseda team to Chicago himself in 1911, was well versed in American culture and had personal experience with the city of Chicago. He had graduated from Northwestern and had met Stagg previously, so he felt moved to express his regret that they would not see each other during Chicago's 1910 visit due to Stagg's obligations in America as coach of the University of Chicago football team.[18] The men that inhabited the elite spheres of the Japanese intelligentsia saw Stagg and his fellow faculty as equals, and the immaculate English and genteel manners of Abe and Takasugi did little to undermine such a connection in Stagg's mind. At this individual level the gap between a modernizing, vibrant Japan and an American state that provided an example of the success of such enterprise seemed far from insurmountable. Negotiations passed from professor to professor across the Pacific Ocean, cultural differences neatly and politely acknowledged. Abe had no problems with refraining from games being played on Sunday, but as Abe was a practicing Christian Unitarian, this should perhaps hardly be surprising. Stagg wrote ahead to his "C" man in Tokyo, Alfred W. Place, to inquire about specific advice for the Chicago students so that they could avoid offending their hosts.[19] He was motivated by both his own cultural inclinations to avoid any possible embarrassment to the university and a desire to appear courteous and respectful to his Japanese counterparts. Letters between Chicago and Tokyo provided ample evidence for Waseda administrators that the Americans believed they were dealing with equals.

Such egalitarian fellowship was unfortunately not quite as evident in the Chicago press, where reporters and editors felt few or no qualms in presenting the "Jap" visitors as simultaneously otherworldly in appearance and nature and worthy of patronizing treatment. The *Chicago Examiner*'s Hugh Fullerton gleefully reported a successful Chicago survival in a close game against Japanese "invaders" during the Waseda team's visit in 1911.[20] Stagg was determined that the Waseda players and administrators be received with the utmost courtesy, extending invitations to alumni to attend the games, organizing a social reception for the Japanese, and demanding that his players join him in singing the Waseda University alma mater in greeting to their visitors upon their arrival.[21] The broad strokes with which the Chicago papers happily painted the visiting team stood in sharp relief against Stagg's thoughtful gesture. One cartoonist made great hay with Stagg's efforts, depicting flustered Chicago students unable to decipher which symbols on the pages handed out by Stagg represented musical notes and which conveyed the combined Chinese characters and syllabaries of the Japanese written language.[22] In truth the cartoonist was having as much fun mocking the young varsity men as he was ridiculing the Japanese, but a clear orientalist perspective remained evident. Ralph Wilder had some fun in the *Chicago Record-Herald* depicting a Waseda man in full baseball gear being introduced by a University of Chicago player to the "Chicago fan" sitting on his throne, a large crown atop his head.[23] Both the Caucasian figures in the cartoon towered over their diminutive Japanese counterpart, and examples of less sensitive portrayals of the Waseda players and their professor were not hard to find.[24]

The 1910–11 series between the two teams produced a mixed bag, then, in terms of contributing to Japan's increased standing in the world, but the Japanese had advanced their ambitions to play more games in the United States and cultivate closer relationships between Japanese universities and the American institutions they hoped to see as their counterparts. The series had also established a clear foundation for future tours, with all successive Waseda tours of the United States involving trips to Hyde Park to play against the University of Chicago Maroons. Success on the field itself, though welcome in Tokyo, tilted toward American expectations, with Waseda generally winning enough games on the wider tour to save face but struggling against prominent varsity teams. American reporters commented on the disparity between the talent of the Japanese and American players, offering scientifically dubious theories as to the issues of the former group with running based on a perceived disadvantage given their shorter legs. They similarly showered faint praise on Iseda Gō, Waseda's star pitcher, claiming him as a Japanese Hughie Jennings, the Detroit Tigers manager famous for erratic behavior at games. Jennings was a notorious character at the time, known for yelping loudly at Major League games and grabbing tufts of grass in attention-grabbing antics. Shorn of Jennings's inherent legitimacy as an American white man and a successful Major Leaguer, Iseda came off poorly as an "oriental" imitation, a crude and primitive simulacrum of a genuine American character. The course of the American narrative was clear: the visit from the Japanese was welcome, it represented a clear cultural victory for the spread of the American pastime, and the Japanese were good enough to indicate a true love for this American game but not good enough to threaten American superiority. Waseda captain Matsuda played up to such expectations, describing Japanese baseball in its "infancy" and arguing that the experience of playing against American teams and watching the Cubs and White Sox had transformed his and his teammates' playing abilities.[25]

It's not hard to believe that playing against American teams *did* help the Waseda players improve, and indeed this had been an influential motive for the trip in the first place. Still it was convenient for American observers to welcome the Japanese with open arms and magnanimously accept positive results for American teams as evidence of their own superiority in a sport of American devising. It was also no small thing that such results emphasized the superior physical gifts of Chicago's young athletes more generally. For the Japanese, who could point to the hospitality of their hosts and an enthusiastic reaction both from the Japanese press and the American fans who showed up in significant numbers and cheered "Banzai!" from packed stands in tribute, the 1911 tour offered evidence that this was a relationship between equals. The crude depictions of race in the press could perhaps be somewhat written off as more symptomatic of the crudity of early twentieth-century reporting than as evidence of a wider sapping of the legitimization of the Japanese enterprise. The home-and-away series would continue for the next twenty years, providing Waseda baseball teams cause to visit the United States to play games in 1915–16, 1920–21, and 1925–27. Waseda further visited the United States on another tour in 1936, again visiting the University of Chicago, but it proved to be the final hurrah in over two decades of intercollegiate games across the Pacific. The relationship between the United States and Japan had at that point already deteriorated significantly as Japanese military aggression in China gained momentum and World War II loomed.

The 1910–11 series in many ways gave a premonition of the shape of wider Japanese foreign policy in the two decades to come, specifically in the Japanese adoption of the "Washington system" in the 1920s following a turbulent decade. A five-power naval disarmament treaty among the United States, Britain, Japan, France, and Italy, alongside the four-power treaty for mutual consultation among the United States, Britain, Japan, and France, replaced Japan's previous foreign policy arrangements. The Empire of Japan had now transitioned away from a limited Anglo-Japanese alliance toward wider agreements that specifically included the United States. The 1911 Xinhai Revolution in China and the 1917 Bolshevik revolution in Russia had drastically altered Japan's regional geopolitics, as had the broader ramifications of World War I for the European imperial elites of the late nineteenth century. Japan's unification of its military, economic, and political concerns in foreign affairs led to a more stable relationship with Britain and the United States and more fertile ground for Stagg's and Abe's talk of uniting two cultures through the playing of a pastoral game; the Japanese seat at the top table of global geopolitics appeared secure, and baseball tours across the Pacific thrived. The 1930s saw a return in Japanese foreign policy to a distinct imbalance brought about by a military leadership never entirely satisfied with what it increasingly saw as the limitations of the "Washington system." An increasing focus on an Asianism that cast Japan as a direct rival, military and otherwise, to the preponderant influence of the Western world left little room for talk of a closer relationship between Japan and the United States. Japan's unilateral withdrawal from the League of Nations in 1933 only underscored the reality of a change in tone that permeated Japan's interactions with the rest of the world, despite the best intentions of people like Abe, Takasugi, and Stagg. Babe Ruth's famous visit to Japan in 1934 proved one of the last great baseball exchanges of the interwar period, as the sport's potential for helping to forge a relationship among equals became lost in the increased desire of the Japanese state to view relations with those across the Pacific in starkly competitive terms.

In the early years of the twentieth century, before such disintegrations between Japan and the great powers of the Western world would come to pass, Waseda's American tours set a precedent and ongoing example for relationships with baseball communities within the Empire of Japan and on its fringes. Visits to the American West Coast and Chicago were followed by trips to Honolulu and Manila, somewhat contestable, if not contested, locations on the borders between Japanese expansion and the nascent American empire. In Hawaii locals of Japanese descent had played in organized baseball games and tournaments since the early years of the twentieth century—for example, the "Seaside League," won by the predominantly Japanese Ōkwa Club in 1906. In 1907 a Hawaiian team composed mostly of players of Japanese descent won the "Hero League," defeating a team composed of American servicemen.[26] Hawaiian teams visited Japan to play in exhibition games against Waseda, which returned the favor, even setting off on an official tour of Hawaii as late as 1938, when the Japanese recorded seven wins and only one loss.[27] Waseda University led the way in cultivating relationships with these baseball communities on the edges of Japan's imperial cultural sphere, solidifying relationships with ethnic Japanese in Hawaii, who in 1940 were still making special note of early victories against ethnically white *gaijin* Americans.

Meanwhile, Chicago's visits to Tokyo were followed by visits from the University of Southern California, the University of Washington, Stanford, and Yale. Until the ascendance of the military within Japanese politics and the attendant effects on the country's relationship with the United States, baseball featured as a key element in cultural exchange across the Pacific as part of a mechanism that saw Abe Isoo and his contemporaries reach out to their American counterparts as partners in expediting the emergence of the twentieth century, presenting Japan's modern, thoroughly acceptable face to a Western world that only a few decades earlier had looked to the country as an anachronism awaiting appropriate imperial exploitation. Within the Empire of Japan but outside the borders of the home country, Waseda's baseball team and its public face functioned differently, with the world outlook reversed: the Japanese university and its touring baseball team were imbued with a legitimizing function to bestow upon colonial Japanese working toward their own expressions of a growing and expansive

Japanese cultural sphere. Abe and Stagg saw in each other kindred spirits, sharing a love of sport and a belief in the capability of sport to cultivate genuinely shared cultural experiences among communities from opposite ends of the earth. Waseda's presence in Taiwan, on the other hand, would not be that of a friendly coreligionist in the evangelizing mission of sport coming to visit but that of a herald from the center of the sporting universe.

Waseda's American tours found their way into the pages of the Japanese-language press in Taiwan as early as 1906, indeed providing the first mention of the sport in the pages of the *Nichi Nichi Shimpō*, in which an article announced an agreement between Waseda and Stanford to play an exhibition game in May of the following year.[28] In the following years, as the matches among the fledgling baseball teams of Taipei began to garner more coverage in the Japanese-controlled press, Waseda continued as a prominent feature in articles reporting on the steadily growing baseball community at home in Japan. In 1908 readers were treated to a description of the colorful procession leading to Waseda Athletic Grounds, where the university founder, Ōkuma Shigenobu, threw out the first pitch in an exhibition game against an all-American representative team.[29] In 1910 the newspaper dutifully reported the first meeting between Waseda and the University of Chicago in Tokyo, a 9–2 loss for the Japanese team before Chicago moved on to defeat Keiō University.[30] At this time a baseball article in the colony's main newspaper was as likely to cover developments in Tokyo as in Taipei, coverage of the growing intercollegiate scene in Tokyo Japanese baseball and of Waseda in particular important ingredients among many in the carefully curated collection of news from home. Although headlines specifically referring to baseball as the subject were common, word of the rivalries in Tokyo spilled past the boundaries of the sports pages. In serial newspaper bylines, such as the regular "Tokyo Miscellany," it was not uncommon for the selection of news items from home to include reports of Japanese sporting prowess across the Pacific, whether they cited Ōkuma Shigenobu's pride at the Japanese team's performance against Chicago in the fall of 1910 or the success of Japanese ballplayers in getting on with the professionals of the New York Giants. Such pieces would typically share such good news with colonial Japanese readers in the course of publicizing upcoming games between Tokyo rivals Waseda and Keiō.[31] The intercollegiate athletics scene developing around the two universities thus became conflated with the broader ideological successes of Japanese student athletes comporting themselves as perfect gentlemen in the most modern sense while traveling abroad.

The burgeoning relationship among the major Tokyo university baseball teams and American educational institutions was noteworthy news in Taiwan, particularly for the Japanese emigres who composed its political, financial, and educational infrastructure.[32] Moreover, Waseda represented the central partner in a rivalry between massive organizations in the imperial capital, idealized representations of the fledgling rivalries building between teaching colleges and professional institutions in colonial Taiwan. Waseda occupied a clear role in the colonial Japanese press as one of the defining examples of the growing success of Japanese baseball, whether it was in the developing relationships with American universities and professional teams, regardless of results on the field, or as a leading example of the evolving and ever-modernizing popular culture of the imperial capital. By the early 1910s various references to baseball became more and more common in the sports pages and beyond.[33] As the decade went on and the Taiwanese baseball scene continued to grow, major Japanese university teams maintained a significant level of prestige in Taiwan's baseball world. The United States existed as home to the game of baseball in an abstract sense, but the preponderance of Japanese involvement in the game and the definition in particular of its organizational and competitive norms eclipsed Americans' claims to singular authenticity as the gatekeepers of the sport for Japanese in the colony.

In 1917 the Waseda baseball team made its first visit to Taiwan. Invited by the Taiwanese baseball association and led by Abe Isoo himself, Waseda played a series of exhibition matches in Taipei, including one against a form of all-star Taiwanese team made of various Japanese with experience playing on teams consisting of employees from the private and public sectors.[34] The Waseda team's arrival on

December 27 was big news, the racial politics of its tours to America now inverted to reflect the balance of power between imperial core and periphery. A cartoon displaying a number of dark-suited visitors on the ship *Amerika*, led by Abe pointing with patriarchal enthusiasm at the Taiwanese coast, where locals in white baseball uniforms and caps waved welcome from among the palm trees, drew a stark contrast with the mockery handed out by the cartoonists of Chicago.[35] Representatives of colonial Taipei society met the fifteen-student-strong squad with much enthusiasm. The young visitors impressed their hosts with their "vim and vigor" and their piety, promptly visiting a premier Shinto shrine in Taipei upon arrival in anticipation of their first game the next day.[36] Abe soon sat down with the local press to discuss issues ranging from the provision of electricity to the central part of the island to the hygienic benefits of Taipei's clean city streets, doing his bit as a prominent intellectual figure in promoting the success of the Japanese colonial project.[37]

The team was lauded by the colonial public throughout the trip, demonstrations of its clear superiority over the local teams it faced doing very little to dilute its popularity. The press covered Waseda's victories with glee, the risk of the local players losing face apparently remote. The exhibitions received full coverage, with detailed box scores and large, wide-angle photographs to convey the excitement in the stadiums.[38] The Waseda team took on and defeated an all-Taiwan side as its last game in Taipei before moving south, conducting an entire program of games against various Taiwanese teams.[39] The games against local teams, and victories for Waseda, continued until the final exhibition match on January 18, 1918. Both sides dressed in opposing red and white uniforms, the *kōhaku* style common in Japan that both reflected national colors and directly referenced the Genpei Wars of 1180–1185. It was already common for all-star games in Taiwan, usually held at the end of the season, to adopt the practice. This "send-off" game was played at Taipei's New Ground, both confirming and enhancing its status as the premier baseball stadium in the colony.[40]

The 1917 Waseda tour in many ways performed as a culmination of a sustained period of growth for Taiwanese baseball over the preceding decade or so. The colony now had the resources to host the most famous baseball team in the Empire of Japan, with teams fit to take it on and stadiums in which to play the games. It also proved a capstone of sorts on a period of exclusively Japanese-driven development of the game on the island, with the gradual incursion of local Taiwanese into the game beginning at the very end of the 1910s, accelerated by the integration of Taiwanese schools in the 1920s. Tokyo rivalries, increasing beyond the Waseda-Keiō rivalry with the addition of Meiji University in 1914 and Hōsei University in 1917, continued to provide the gold standard for high-level play, however. Thanks to the Waseda tour, university students, whose exploits otherwise filled the pages of the colonial newspaper, had played at fields up and down the island, reinforcing the cultural connections between Japanese living in the colony and Japanese at home and reinforcing baseball's status as an important component in that connection. Over the following fifteen years the appeal of baseball in Taiwan expanded with a clear and related change in the role of the sport in Taiwanese society. Teams featuring local players captured the colony's imagination, though Japanese university teams continued to attract attention. Ongoing visits to the American mainland by Japanese teams, particularly Waseda, featured prominently in press coverage.[41]

By 1926 it was clear that local sporting events of various types had the potential of being deemed more newsworthy than events in Tokyo. That year marked Waseda's participation in the inaugural Big Six League university baseball competition, with old rivals Keiō and Hōsei, as well as Rikkyō University, Meiji University, and the Imperial University in Tokyo. The Taiwanese press faithfully reported on league events, with a notable focus on Waseda, but brief match reports were often overshadowed by more extensive features on local events. On September 27, for example, a Hōsei victory over Rikkyō occupied a relatively humble spot on a *Nichi Nichi Shimpō* page dominated by a large photograph and detailed article on a schoolgirls' tennis tournament.[42] The same universities were similarly overshadowed the following day by another large photograph and article on the assembled participants in the same tennis tournament.[43] The Waseda team managed to earn slightly more real estate on the newspaper's pages with a drawn game against Hōsei, but this coverage probably owed more to the rarity of such a result than any increased interest in Waseda's fortunes relative to its fellow Tokyo universities.[44] Only two weeks later another Big Six game featuring Waseda was again overshadowed, this time by coverage of an athletics meet for girls' high schools and a marathon for middle school students.[45]

The Japanese authorities overseeing the publication of the *Nichi Nichi Shimpō* would obviously have been interested in publicizing the continued development of sophisticated sporting events for Taiwanese children in the colonial educational system as continued evidence of the success of Japan's colonial enterprise on the island. Still, regardless of such political motivations, the sporting environment in Taiwan, including local baseball, now dwarfed reportage of sporting events in Japan for the most part. Coverage of Waseda had not diminished, but it had failed to keep pace with the explosion in coverage of sports in the colony. Coverage of Waseda's victory in the inaugural tournament was similarly modest in scope.[46] Befitting of the newspaper's new role, independent of serving as a form of umbilical cord between colonial Japanese and the imperial homeland, coverage of Tokyo baseball was now one aspect of a broader supply of news on sporting events in Taiwan itself. The continued interactions between Waseda and American universities, such as the University of Chicago's visit to Japan in 1930,[47] continued to be newsworthy but now appeared among ever-increasing articles on local baseball as the Taiwanese baseball community continued to grow.[48]

Waseda sent touring baseball teams to Taiwan two more times in the colonial period, in 1930 and 1934. The 1930 visit is of particular interest. The Waseda baseball team arrived in Taiwan at the invitation of the *Nichi Nichi Shimpō* publishing group itself, the visiting team's roster proudly announced in the newspaper's pages.[49] The newspaper, happy to make plenty of hay from its own role in bringing the Waseda team to Taiwan, continued with coverage reminiscent of the previous Waseda visit to the colony thirteen years earlier. The university athletes would again play games in Taipei before setting out on a tour of the island, facing a variety of opponents. However, the mood in anticipation of Waseda's arrival differed from that of 1917. The nineteen-man contingent's schedule was announced in full ten days before the team's arrival on December 30, 1930.[50] The same page of the newspaper carried further articles on a local event involving the Taiwanese Railroad baseball team and news of the planned hospitality for the incoming Waseda players.[51] As evidenced by the article on the Taiwanese Railroad team, Waseda was no longer the only game in town, so to speak. Still Waseda baseball remained big news in its own right. If anything, the expansion of baseball into the public realm, as characterized by increased media coverage and steadily improving crowds at specific games since 1917, resulted in a markedly different expression of enthusiasm for the Waseda visit in 1930. Awe was replaced by a clear air of expectation. Although local reporting clearly saw the Waseda players as practitioners of a higher standard of play, the announcement of schedules and anticipation of Waseda's trip down the Taiwanese west coast betrayed an added level of anticipation. Three days before the Japanese team's scheduled arrival, a lengthy preview of Taiwan's strongest team, Taipei CB, mused on the local side's chances against the clearly superior visitors. If CB's players could perform to their abilities, the article's author reasoned, "a result against Waseda would not be far away." The same article carried photographs of CB players Yoshitome and Horinaka, as the preview of the Taiwanese team's potential play against Waseda earned equal status alongside coverage of the university students' departure from Tokyo.[52]

The *Nichi Nichi Shimpō*, both as host organization and the preeminent paper of colonial Taiwan, covered the games themselves as major events. Local readers were treated to full previews of games, photographs of athletes in action and an excited crowd, and full box scores featuring individual statistics in at-bats, hits, walks, and strike-outs.[53] Unlike in the 1917 tour, this Waseda team proved far from invincible, as an 8-4 defeat to the Railroad team bore out. The *Nichi Nichi Shimpō*'s readers were treated to the game's events inning by inning, fully outlining in dry detail a convincing win for the local side.[54] Defeating the Waseda baseball team was a major achievement and a fillip for the sport in Taiwan, but it was no longer a miracle. Close results followed, with the Railroad team narrowly failing to repeat its achievement in the second game against Waseda and the CB team living up to the faith placed in it by the earlier reporter, if not quite able to secure the victory.[55] The Taipei side lost 12–11 in a game attended by a lively crowd whose enthusiasm and demeanor earned the approval of the *Nichi Nichi Shimpō* writers.[56]

If the 1917 visit represented a legitimization of the nascent baseball community in Taiwan, the 1930–31 visit confirmed that the colony's baseball environment now stood on its own, even capable of producing teams that could perform alongside Japan's finest. Of course the success of Taiwanese baseball was inherently a Japanese success, testament to the success of the core's assimilation of the colony. Top Taiwanese teams were composed mostly, if not entirely, of Japanese athletes. The hospitality offered by various Taiwanese baseball associations confirmed the social function of the tour as confirmation of imperial solidarity extended to Japanese visitors by Japanese hosts.[57] Four years later Waseda returned to play the same teams in another celebration of cultural unity. The games again drew large crowds and yet another thrilling contest against the CB team, this time with a narrow 12–11 victory for the visitors, belied the continuation of a central role for Waseda baseball in the development of the sport in Taiwan.[58] There was little sign of local Taiwanese involvement dwarfing the importance of continued connections between the colonial community and its sporting heartland.

Waseda and its fellow Japanese touring teams thus performed on two separate ends of the same dynamic: reaching out for recognition from a desired and claimed peer in the United States and receiving confirmation of Japanese superiority when visiting Taiwan. The university team in both cases served to preserve the legitimacy of Japanese modernity in both the country's success in reaching the top tables of global geopolitics and its dedication in reproducing Japanese modern life in its recently conquered territories. The racial problematics inherent in the U.S.-Japan relationship did not simply reverse in the case of the Taiwan tours. Japanese views of colonial subjects were patronizing, if of a different character to the resolutely orientalized viewpoints of some Americans. Furthermore, although the changing nature of Japan's interactions with the world that brought the cross-Pacific tours to an end in the 1930s would prove to have a comprehensive effect on its colonies in the imposition of still more aggressive Japanese assimilation, the impact on Taiwanese baseball would prove negated by the very domesticity of the colonial game. Beyond the ethnic composition of the average Taiwanese baseball team in the 1910s and early 1920s, the framework of the game's administration and activities, as anointed by visits from Tokyo teams, was inherently that of a Japanese model. If visits to America offered a chance to prove the viability of Japan's modernizing project to the world, Taiwan offered the laboratory within which that success could be proven reproducible. The changing roles of Japanese touring teams from alien visitors to imperial standard-bearers highlighted an important position for Japan in the creation of baseball tours as an international phenomenon rather than simply an extension of American influence and ambition.

Still, despite its potential for proving the inherent success of Japan's modernization, Taiwan offered the Japanese something savage, lying as it did at the very edges of the empire. Colonial Japanese dominance of playing fields continued into the 1930s, particularly in Taipei, but the integration of the school system brought more and more local Taiwanese into competitive play. This included aboriginal Taiwanese, whose ethnicity and cultural background proved central to Japanese racial conceptions of its first colony, avatars of pre-modernity modern imperial life so aggressively rejected. This segment of the colonial population, more or less ignored in the discourse surrounding the 1917 Waseda tour, produced a famous team in the 1920s that would offer imperial Japan a chance to see its use of the touring system reciprocated. Japanese teams, having taken their role as visitors to the United States and recast it for trips to Taiwan, would now receive a colonial and racial other as gracious hosts.

3 | Barnstormers or Emissaries of Empire?

Visits by Japanese university teams to American sites, for all their alien characteristics, fit neatly into a broad American understanding of the touring team. Touring in and of itself was not something new. The staid, patrician attitudes of Stagg and his contemporaries in Hyde Park were but one element in the culture and sociology of early twentieth-century baseball. The need to fund the trips provided another element, as the Japanese played willing novelties in local clashes with a variety of amateur teams. Dating back to its origins as an amateur game in the nineteenth century, baseball had long included such novel encounters, and the connections between the humanistic, idealized concepts of baseball as a bucolic adventure from the swiftly engorged cities of the American East Coast and a more hard-nosed capitalistic side to the game as an enterprise were numerous and complex. As the Japanese brought the concept of the traveling tour from Hawaii and the American mainland to the Japanese colonies, they soon discovered another variety of baseball tour that differed from their missions in cultural diplomacy in nuanced but crucial ways. In the 1920s Taiwan produced a bona fide group of barnstormers.

Barnstorming began as a series of domestic postseason tours in the United States, run mostly by players themselves to make extra money before the coming winter took their main source of income away. From the start these exhibitions embraced entertainment over competition, a result both of the lack of any real stakes and the reluctance of the players to risk injury. Players with significant reputations typically drove ticket sales for events, but a lack of opponents sent the teams on tour. As the nineteenth century went on, Major League club owners joined the barnstorming market, though they typically confined themselves to the domain of spring tours featuring Major League teams. These members of the American baseball establishment developed the idea of taking groups of players on tours abroad, thus creating the transpacific culture of touring teams in which Japanese universities so enthusiastically began to participate at the beginning of the twentieth century.[1] The foreign tours alternated between the more gregarious and sometimes swaggeringly onfield play of superior players against hopeful locals and theoretically higher-minded ideas about spreading the game. All the tours fed into the essential barnstorming formula that relied on a sense of outlandish entertainment not found in the more formal settings of organized league play. This formula also typically involved a healthy financial incentive too, but it was a sense of extraordinariness that drove fan interest.

The difference between a touring team such as the Waseda University squad that visited Taiwan in 1917 and a barnstorming outfit, such as the American League all-star team featuring Babe Ruth and Lou Gehrig that visited Japan in 1934, is one of degree. The dividing line comes between the traveling team's status as envoy or novelty. In the case of Waseda's visits to Chicago, the Japanese team performed as both, albeit willingly only as the former. For Abe Isoo and his contemporaries the tour clearly elevated the Japanese game and the men involved in it. Still the innate and obvious foreignness of the Japanese side was for some Americans difficult to traverse. The same was true in reverse to an extent, though it was moderated by the inherent authenticity of American baseball men and the gradual increase in frequency of trips by American players across the Pacific. Spalding's global all-star tour of 1888–89 was followed by the Reach All-Star tour of 1908, sponsored by the Reach Sporting Goods Company—which featured a far less distinguished roster than Spalding's but one that, unlike the Spalding tour, visited Japan—and the star-studded 1913-14 Major League tour led by legendary manager John McGraw and Chicago White Sox owner Charles Comiskey. McGraw and Comiskey planned their tour around a domestic leg that would then fund the East Asian section of the tour. They and their players received a rapturous reception and many curious questions from a Japanese press corps disappointed at Christy Mathewson's failure to make the trip.[2]

In 1921 an all-American team led by Herbert Harrison Hunter became the first such touring team from the United States to reach Taiwan. Hunter's team, mostly a jumbled collection of professionals from the Pacific Coast League with some Major Leaguers peppered here and there, brought a clear example of the capitalist drive behind barnstorming to the colony.[3] Gimmicky at best and craven at worst, the tour was a nakedly commercial enterprise. Led by Los Angeles manager Gene Doyle, the Americans fell into dispute over money shortly after arriving in Japan, ultimately breaking up in Kobe as Doyle led Hunter and a remaining nine athletes on to Taiwan.[4] It is interesting that Hunter's tour received slightly more visually distinctive coverage in the colonial Japanese press than had earlier tours by Japanese university teams, as photographs and cartoons focused on the clear physiological differences between the local players and their exclusively Caucasian American visitors. In one example a cartoon that illustrated a diminutive local baseball player climbing a set of steps to attempt to swing his bat at a giant foreign figure's pitches made light of local teams' chances with little awkwardness as to the Americans' complete dominance on the playing field.[5] Another cartoon featured caricatured figures in various positions on the field with accompanying descriptions, such as that of third baseman Billy Huber, whose playful antics and willingness to act the fool amused the fans occupying the nearby stands.[6] The same page of the newspaper carried a large photograph of these antics as part of a pictorial feature.[7] Despite the failure of any local team to defeat the Americans in the seven games that Hunter's side played on Taiwanese soil, the team attracted large crowds and generated much interest among the colonial public.[8]

Hunter's traveling side was not the only example of such baseball tours in Taiwan in the early 1920s. In addition to the earlier visits by Waseda in 1917 and the Hōsei University baseball team in 1918, less formal tours by representative sides fed the growing appetite in Taiwan for baseball-centered spectacles.[9] The Osaka *Mainichi Shimbun* sent a baseball team to Taiwan in 1922.[10] The team's first game, as was typical of touring sides, was against a representative all-Taipei team.[11] Taipei audiences were by now accustomed to the protocol of visiting baseball teams; both sides entered the stadium to roaring applause and began play after the declaration of "Play ball!" by the master of ceremonies.[12] The coverage of the *Mainichi Shimbun* tour was again perhaps not quite as heavy as that of the Waseda tour in 1917, but the *Mainichi* players enjoyed plenty of attention, posing for the camera in full Western-style suits and ties with overcoats.[13] The team, representing one of Japan's major newspaper publishing groups, also had accompanying journalist Kadō Tadashi participate in speaking engagements as part of the tour.[14]

Taiwan welcomed another private venture later in the year from the Keiō Star club, a touring side independent of the official university team.[15] Taiwan in the 1920s entertained an increasingly diverse collection of teams in a vibrant touring culture, hosting Japanese university teams, openly commercially driven mavericks like Hunter, and others in between. The chief weapon in the true barnstormers' arsenal in attracting a crowd was their engaging sense of novelty, which for American teams traveling to Asia (and to a certain extent for Japanese teams traveling to the United States) amounted to an obvious foreignness. Such teams offered an alternative to the standard fare available, and in the case of traveling teams, it was an exotic one.

Taiwan had long held a sense of exoticism in the Japanese imagination, providing the Japanese public with a clear vision of primitive premodern society in the form of the island's aboriginal population. In 1874 the Japanese government sent an expedition of over three thousand laborers and soldiers in an early attempt to take direct control of Taiwan, ultimately thwarted by interventions from London and Washington DC. The ostensible cause for the trip was punitive, as three years earlier aboriginal Taiwanese had killed fifty-four Ryukyuan fishermen shipwrecked on the island.[16] The massacre itself and the Japanese reaction drew significant, sensationalized attention from the Japanese press, with commercial publications regularly describing the savage habits of the aboriginal Taiwanese, willfully positing accusations of cannibalism that were not reflected in official government reports.[17]

The incidents also led to the publication of a number of books that would prove highly influential in the formation of Japanese policy toward Taiwan's indigenous tribal population; they focused firmly on the need to civilize aboriginal savagery. The brouhaha had erupted in part owing to the Chinese claim, in an attempt to avoid responsibility, that the aborigines were "beyond the realm of civilization."[18] For centuries ethnic Chinese observers had separated the peoples on the fringes of their empire into two categories: "raw" people, routinely engaged in the savagery and aggression of the uncivilized or "unworked" native, and "cooked" people, liberated from such a condition through the civilizing forces of the Chinese imperial state; the "civilizing forces" materialized in governmental control of cultural norms and the manipulation of the land itself through the spread of infrastructure and development of urban settlements. When Taiwan became a Japanese colony in 1895, Tokyo adopted the distinction before developing its own nomenclature, distinguishing between aboriginal Taiwanese from the mountains and those from the plains.[19]

The Japanese attitude toward the aboriginal Taiwanese was markedly different from their attitude toward the ethnic Chinese colonial population. Put simply, the Japanese were fascinated by the physiological and cultural differences between the aboriginal Taiwanese and the ethnic Chinese, with whom the Japanese shared historical and cultural antecedents. The Han, Hakka, and Fujianese residents of Taiwan fit comfortably within the Japanese understanding of civilized society. Traditionally Japan had lain within the boundaries of Chinese cultural universalism, characterized by writing systems, Confucian intellectualism, and shared legacies in the development of religious structures. The genesis of Japan's own quest for dominance in East

Asia lay in a Confucian interpretation of Japan's position in the world and its attendant moral obligations.[20]

The aboriginal Taiwanese, on the other hand, were cast in the role of savages before the Japanese had even arrived. Whereas attitudes toward the ethnic Chinese residents of Taiwan were considerably tempered by the significant Chinese contribution to Japanese cultural inheritance, the aboriginal tribes of the Taiwanese countryside fit stereotypical images of the Asian savage beyond the pale of the Sino-Japanese cultural demesne.[21] Furthermore, the strong resistance to Japanese colonialism that persisted among the aboriginal Taiwanese community, well beyond the resistance of their ethnic Chinese neighbors, served as a continuation of violent interactions with Japan. Various elements of the Japanese colonial machinery photographed the aboriginal Taiwanese extensively as the Japanese colonials approached the aboriginal Taiwanese community with scientific curiosity. One early image portrays an official meeting between the first governor-general, Kabayama Sukenori, and representatives from aboriginal Taiwanese tribes. The Westernized military garb of Kabayama and his associates stands in stark contrast with the traditional dress of the aboriginal Taiwanese. The visitors further reinforce an uncivilized mien with two of their number squatting at the feet of the governor-general.[22] Other photographs focused on more genial depictions of aboriginal Taiwanese life, such as that of a harvest festival dance participated in by members of the Malan tribe near Taidong.[23]

Japanese colonial authorities catalogued the aboriginal Taiwanese population with an intense academic interest that clearly placed the aboriginal community beyond the sphere of interactions between the Japanese and ethnic Chinese colonial residents. The descriptions stop just short—though perhaps only just—of treating the aboriginal communities as topological features in and of themselves.[24] Academic works of ethnography proliferated, with detailed maps illustrating the distribution of aboriginal populations and extensive diagramming of tribal relations. The ethnologists elected to use English transliterations of the tribal names alongside the Japanese.[25] The decision betrayed the predominant scientific influences in such studies, implying a correlation between the cataloguing of aboriginal Taiwanese and the analysis of natural features such as the Taiwanese alpine butterfly.[26] Both were exotic subjects recently brought within the borders of an expanding Japanese empire.

Education of the aboriginal Taiwanese population remained limited into the 1920s. Nevertheless, it was a great improvement over the initial two decades of colonial rule. Most aboriginal children who received formal education did so in education centers (*kyōiku shō*), institutions that grew from initial attempts by Japanese policemen to educate the children of aboriginal chieftains. By 1920 there were 103 of these centers educating 2,179 children. Fifteen years later 8,291 students attended classes at 183 education centers throughout the island. The standard of the education was considerably lower than that of the common school system and the extensive educational framework delivered by the education rescript of 1919.[27] Although the aboriginal Taiwanese population still received unequal treatment at the hands of the Japanese authorities, aboriginal children attended schools and participated in colonial life. They were also exposed to the growing popularity of baseball.[28]

The inherent exoticism of the aboriginal Taiwanese community in Japanese eyes and the gradual extension of baseball into aboriginal communities proved fertile ground for the emergence of a unique team in the wider imperial baseball community: Nōkō, a team of aboriginal Taiwanese teenagers from Hualian who toured northern Taiwan in 1924 and went on to visit Japan in 1925. Nōkō was certainly successful in gaining the attention of the Japanese press, albeit as the savage master of the civilized game, testament to both the success and the need of the Japanese colonial project. The team came into existence in 1921 as the discovery of Lin Guixing, a local Taiwanese, the tale of its creation oft told in terms of an enlightened Han Chinese recognition of the raw abilities of local aboriginal teenagers. Lin was a young local Taiwanese employee and member of the official baseball team at the Rising Sun construction company in Hualian, having joined his new employer's team after graduation. He had previously spent his free time during his academic studies playing baseball with the Hualian Business School and was an early player and fan of the game as it developed in Taiwan in the 1910s. He has recently been put forward as the first Taiwanese member of an organized baseball team, to replace the previously identified Li and Lin, who remain the first Taiwanese recorded as playing in an actual game; photographic evidence identifies Lin Guixing as a player on the Taidong Sugar Company team in a group portrait taken in 1915. He was sixteen years of age.[29]

Taiwanese accounts present Lin's discovery of Nōkō, one of the most prominent teams in Taiwanese history, in highly romanticized terms. One day Lin observed a group of aboriginal Taiwanese teenagers of the Amis tribe playing a game of baseball using rudimentary equipment, including makeshift wooden bats and rocklike objects for baseballs. Two of the teenagers showed particular potential. Cha Wuma was an excellent pitcher, his partner Gu Maode a phenomenal batter. Lin, thanks to his wealth of experience in the game, immediately saw the potential in these young men to both earn profit for himself and—thanks to his self-confessed and clearly stated love of baseball—help spread the game to more teenagers throughout the colony. He swiftly formed a new Aboriginal Taiwanese Baseball Team with the aforementioned young men at the core of the playing squad and himself as coach.[30] He first chose the name "Takasago," using Chinese characters in common use during the colonial period to describe all aboriginal Taiwanese, a rather complicated term that evoked both the inherent savagery of these uncivilized natives and their ethnic links to the Japanese leaders of Asian races.[31] The name had been in use in Taiwanese baseball for various teams since 1908.

Lin's supposed ambition of profiting from this situation is intriguing. Nōkō emerged in a society where the baseball community enjoyed a significant level of public exposure and where tours by foreign teams with varying degrees of notoriety were common. By June 1923 he felt that his young athletes were ready to take on more established teams on the island after steadily working on their skills in various exhibitions with teams in the Hualian area. The aboriginal Taiwanese team earned recognition through both these exhibitions and performances by athletes loaned out to local teams for exhibitions.[32] Cha Wuma attracted significant attention with one such performance for the Hualian Railroad team in an exhibition game against another local side, the Green Team. Cha, setting a record in Taiwanese baseball at the time, threw 212 pitches in 16 innings. The *Nichi Nichi Shimpō* praised the teenager's strong arm and his "gallant" performance, describing the young athlete as visibly covered in sweat and spit as his performance came to a close. The article finished with a brief notice informing the reader of Nōkō's existence, where Cha Wuma and Gu Maode (referred to in the newspaper by his aboriginal name, Komodo) plied their trade as part of an all-aboriginal Taiwanese team. It was the first mention of the moniker "Nōkō," which would soon become the definitive name for the young side.[33]

Later in 1923 local Japanese authorities took action to further develop the skills of these young athletes. Umeno Tarō, a major figure in colonial east Taiwan, authority in many of the engineering projects at that time, and head of the company where Lin Guixing was employed, joined with local magistrate head Eguchi Yoshisaburō to take control of the Nōkō side. The two men invited the entire playing squad to attend classes at Hualian Agricultural School.[34] The motive behind moving all of the players was clear. Eguchi and Umeno did not extend the invitation to the aboriginal Taiwanese players as an attempt to spread the values of modern Japanese education. They were expected to play baseball. Eguchi in particular actively sought to improve the aboriginal players' chances, bringing in Coach Yano, a Keiō University graduate and later head of the Taipei Railroad team, to coach the side, now exclusively known as Nōkō, typically presented as NOKO, in all capital letters, across the front of professional-standard baseball jerseys. At Eguchi's behest Nōkō set off in 1924 to prove its mettle against the baseball teams of the Taiwanese west coast.[35]

The tour had a significant amount of notoriety from the outset. Nōkō traveled west billed as the famous aboriginal Taiwanese baseball team of Hualian, the word "aboriginal" just as easily translated as "savage." The coverage of the team clearly relied heavily on the novelty of these young men from Hualian taking on established baseball players on the west coast. The focus on their ethnic identity makes it clear that their nature, whether "savage" or "aboriginal," provided much of the newsworthy appeal. The term "aboriginal" carried sufficient negative connotations in any event. In addition to a playing squad of thirteen, the Nōkō team brought with it an additional retinue of sixty people, including school officials and supporters. The schedule covered all of the west coast, from Taipei to Taizhong, Tainan, Gaoxiong, and Pingdong.³⁶ The initial report announcing the upcoming tour featured in both the Japanese- and Chinese-language sections of the *Nichi Nichi Shimpō*, with the Japanese account opting for a more colorful description of the team from Hualian and its entourage, one that featured "flowers and song."³⁷ The expectation for the arrival of the team in Taipei on September 21 matched that of previous coverage of the much feted visiting Waseda University baseball team. On September 18 a large team portrait greeted *Nichi Nichi Shimpō* readers as the young aboriginal men gazed proudly into the camera, adorned in their pristine white baseball uniforms.³⁸ An article on the same page introduced the team's tour dates in detail, with a list of locations and a brief comment on the fact that the team's actual ability on the field was something of an unknown quantity with the exception of star players Cha Wuma and Gu Maode.³⁹

Such star quality, added to the frisson of excitement being generated in Taiwanese baseball by the supposed innate physicality of the aboriginal players, was sufficient to generate anticipation in Taipei. Newspaper articles talked up the aboriginal players' abilities as part of the significant hype building in the Japanese-language press prior to the Nōkō team's arrival in the colonial capital. One such piece noted that the young players had honed their physical gifts since childhood by throwing stones and running around in the open. They therefore played the game as naturals, without any concerns or nervousness, avatars of sporting purity and the aesthetics of a natural state beyond the limitations of the civilized urbanism found in Taipei. The article carried the headline "The Composed Savage Player Headhunts the Ball," a play on words reflecting the morbid activity for which aboriginal Taiwanese were more widely and apocryphally known in the colony.⁴⁰ For his part as the head of the team Eguchi was happy to relate in a personal interview that the results on the field didn't matter when compared to more grand philosophical concerns. The Japanese official preferred to dwell on the bravery and valor these young men were showing to those resident on the western shores of the colony, proof of the civilizing nature of sport (and by extension the machinery of Japanese colonialism) on these once savage denizens of the east coast.[41] As far as the Japanese-language press was concerned, Nōkō players were performing as part of a popular event presented in terms of their success in modern society despite the clear handicap of their ethnocultural heritage.

Nōkō's performances on the tour did not immediately reflect Cha Wuma's record-breaking brilliance for the Hualian Railroad side a year earlier. The innate sporting abilities that Lin Guixing had witnessed in 1921 and that continued to be reported in the colonial media failed to lead to a tour of domination for the Hualian side. Unfortunately for the visiting athletes, the tour started badly on the field with a loss to the Commercial School team. Off the field, however, the occasion justified the hype, with more than seven thousand fans in attendance.[42] The *Nichi Nichi Shimpō* displayed photographs of both action on the field and the large crowd.[43] Two days later the Nōkō team lost again to the Commercial School side, and suffered its third loss to an Ensuiko Sugar team in Tainan, only a day after recording its first win of the tour in Taizhong.[44] The young men from Hualian then went on to record another victory in a game against a Xinzhu team, 7-1, after an apparently catastrophic error in the ninth inning, gathering momentum from there and going on to another victory in Jilong.[45] They returned to Hualian with a respectable record of four wins and three losses.[46]

The tour had been a huge media event, certainly while the team played in Taipei. Coverage faltered a little as the games wore on and Nōkō's schedule dragged the team up and down the west coast, but throughout the tour there was no question about the star attraction. The Nōkō team had been accompanied by a senior squad, the "All-Hualian" team. However, with the notable exception of detailed coverage of their own opening game in Taipei, the older men clearly took a back seat as the aboriginal teenagers received the lion's share of attention.[47] Throughout the tour the Nōkō team was repeatedly presented as something exceptional and alien to the rest of colonial society. A cartoon illustrated star Nōkō players in action and a group of Nōkō players showing frustration as the byline noted the regrettable incidents of the young players publicly displaying their anxiety through their facial expressions and outbursts during the game.[48] The cartoon, in addition to its admonishing tone, was somewhat reminiscent of the caricatures of the American ballplayers in 1921. The aboriginal Taiwanese players on the Nōkō squad, though regularly referred to as representing the colonial city of Hualian, were treated with the same cultural curiosity and separation from the local teams of the west coast so as to be treated as a foreign team. In October 1924 Eguchi gave an interview stressing the essentialist values of his players. Under a banner headline celebrating the "virility and innocence" of the young players, Eguchi talked about the aboriginal Taiwanese athletes' "innate strength" and refusal to succumb to injury. The tour had much historical significance for Eguchi, who related the importance of these young aboriginal men sitting at the same dinner table as himself and fellow Japanese colonial officials.[49] For Eguchi too the tour within Taiwan had been something more akin to the visiting tours by foreign teams such as the Osaka *Mainichi* team or the Waseda University baseball team, the Nōkō players just another set of alien visitors to a domestic community dominated by colonial Japanese. He happily took credit for the successful stewardship of the players as they ascended through the colonial order.

Nōkō's otherness clearly functioned as a key element in the team's appeal. A year later, in 1925, the team ascended still further, setting off on a nine-game tour of Japan. Nōkō made the trip in July, a relatively slow period in domestic Japanese baseball. After an exhibition game with the Engineering School in Taipei, a loss that perhaps did not auger well for the journey ahead, Nōkō arrived in Japan.[50] However, the team made an instant impact, defeating Toyoshima Normal School by a resounding score of 28–0.[51] The team made news off the field as well, with Gu Maode leading a delegation to meet local news corps by bicycle, demonstrating his recovery from a recent injury.[52] On their initial arrival in Tokyo the players' smart appearance impressed

Japanese observers, who noted that in their neat attire in all-white outfits and hats the young men appeared to be no different from a group of typical Japanese high school students.[53] In their second game the Nōkō players performed well again, drawing 6–6 in a ten-inning game with Waseda High School at the Rikkyō University stadium. Gu Maode, clearly by this point the central attraction of the visiting team, engaged in a conversation with his opposite number on the Waseda team after leading his fellow aboriginal Taiwanese in a spirited performance, matching the Japanese side until the end.[54]

The game proved a harbinger for the remainder of the tour. Nōkō performed admirably, securing a record of four wins, four losses, and a draw.[55] As Andrew Morris points out, the reaction to the Nōkō visit to Japan was colored by an analysis with distinctly racial overtones driven by the question of where to place aboriginal Taiwanese within the imperial imagination.[56] In this regard the 1925 tour mimicked the reaction among colonial Japanese baseball enthusiasts in Taiwan the previous year. The young aboriginal Taiwanese, in their smart all-white attire off the field and with their impressive performances on it, may have impressed Japanese subjects, but coverage of the team continued to be patronizing toward the players' ethnic origins.[57] To be considered indistinguishable from baseball players from other ethnic backgrounds remained the highest compliment paid to the team. One could argue that Nōkō's reception in Japan would have been similar to that afforded any baseball team from the colony, or at least one that could "astonish those looking on" by securing a draw and a narrow loss against capable Japanese high school teams.[58] However, Nōkō was defined by the ethnicity of its athletes. The fact that these young men were aboriginal Taiwanese rather than ethnic Chinese Taiwanese or even Taiwanese-born members of the colonial Japanese community bestowed an added novelty on the team's identity and subsequent adventures west of the Central Mountain Range and across the East China Sea.

After the conclusion of the 1925 tour, four members of the Nōkō team returned to Japan to play baseball for the Heian High School team in Tokyo. One of the four, Luo Daohou, went on to play as a professional.[59] Otherwise Nōkō quickly faded from history, its erstwhile famous mentor, Lin Guixing, moving on to the next stage of his life, cofounding a musical research institute in Hualian.[60] There was no new generation of aboriginal Taiwanese adolescent athletes, and the team did not continue to compete in organized baseball alongside the established baseball teams of the Taiwanese west coast. Nōkō's importance in the history of Taiwanese baseball is clear: the team was the first to reciprocate the tradition of Japanese touring teams visiting the colony, not only visiting the imperial homeland, but also posting respectable results on the field. Lin Guixing's biographer further points out that in so doing, Nōkō was the first all-Taiwanese team to play in Kōshien Stadium, albeit as visitors in an exhibition game and not as competitors in the national high school tournament that made that arena a household name in Japanese baseball.[61] However, contrary to narratives asserting that Nōkō represented an example of aboriginal Taiwanese successfully wearing away at the foundations of racial assumptions central to Japanese imperialism, the 1924 and 1925 tours had more in common with the baseball tours by non-Taiwanese teams in Taiwan in the early 1920s. The *Nichi Nichi Shimpō* subsequently covered the team extensively, affording it equal space on its pages as that of a visit from a prestigious Japanese team such as Waseda University while openly focusing on the novelty of the athletes' ethnicity in a manner reminiscent of the coverage of the visit of the Caucasian Americans led by Herbert Harrison Hunter in 1921. The treatment of the Nōkō players as something alien and foreign to the rest of Taiwan betrayed the overwhelming assumptions of the appropriate place for aboriginal Taiwanese in colonial Taiwanese society. Rather than undermine these assumptions, Nōkō merely offered a chance for their modification. Baseball functioned as a public activity characterized by mass participation in the playing of games, attending of games, and reading and writing about games in colonial Taiwan. The appearance of box scores, articles, and photographs from Nōkō games and public appearances gave aboriginal Taiwanese a space in the public conversation about baseball that existed in the pages of the Japanese-controlled press. This space in the conversation, however, colored by assumptions based on racial difference, introduced an image of aboriginal Taiwanese that countered the caricatured headhunter and tribal savage, an image that would not have existed if not for the prevalence of baseball as a participatory public activity in colonial Taiwan.

Nōkō's time in colonial Japan's media spotlight was short-lived, however, and the success of the team failed to create a long-term presence in Taiwanese baseball similar to that of the Waseda University team from Tokyo or the amateur clubs established in the north of the colony. Yu Junwei describes the team in the context of an independent venture hijacked by Japanese authorities uninterested in voluntary participation in the sport or any other type of public association without official regulation. Rather Japanese aims in showcasing a baseball team composed entirely of aboriginal Taiwanese adolescent athletes fell more in line with the broader imperial goals of advertising the Japanese capacity for civilizing savage communities.[62] Similarly Andrew Morris focuses on the Nōkō trip to Japan in 1925, commenting on the relationship between the Nōkō team's reception in Japan and the impact of "colonial dreams, desires, and fears." Whereas for Yu, Nōkō is evidence of an attempt by local Taiwanese to create something free of colonial control only to be appropriated by that control anyway, Morris sees baseball as "one of the only avenues toward success for members of non-elite socioeconomic classes." The Nōkō team in essence represented a small group of aboriginal Taiwanese boys throwing Japanese colonial prejudices on their head, even if it may not have been so obvious to those expressing such prejudices at the time.[63]

Nōkō stands out as an important step in the process of baseball's transition from a sport that celebrated Japanese colonials' connection to their homeland to a sport that reflected a broader colonial culture within Taiwan. Although the team's historical impact is often overshadowed by the more widely recognized multiethnic Kanō team that emerged a handful of years later, it is important to understand the impact of the Nōkō team as a collection of local Taiwanese (and specifically aboriginal Taiwanese) athletes in a sport commonly presented to the colonial public in terms of Japanese participation. Such participation remained framed specifically within a Japanese context. The Nōkō tour of Japan in 1925 serves as an effective sequel to the travels to the north of Taiwan the previous year in the narrative of Nōkō's history as told up to the present day. Traveling to Japan to play against elite Japanese high school teams, including an exhibition at the famed Kōshien Stadium, elevated the Nōkō team beyond its parochial origins in the eastern city of Hualian. For some this would elevate the team as a united and singularly Taiwanese representative of baseball in the colonial period. Eguchi's and Umeno's stewardship rather compromises such an evaluation. Still, regardless of questions over representations of the team or the possibilities of recasting the young men as avatars of Taiwanese national determinism, it is clear that the Nōkō team succeeded, at the very least, in gaining attention in the pages of the Japanese press both on the imperial periphery and within its core. Such attention may have stressed the uncivilized origins of the players, but it nonetheless included them within the broad baseball community that reached across the East China Sea. Nōkō's success in Japan, and the team's successful capture of Japanese imaginations, signaled a success for Taiwanese baseball: affirmation for Taiwan's demesne secured from the center of the wider imperial baseball realm.

The Nōkō tour was, in many ways, a fascinating expansion of barnstorming beyond the North American continent. The activity was defined in some senses by its existence outside of the rigid organization of a baseball hierarchy that otherwise in theory drove the sport's importance historically. Barnstorming as conceived in the United States was intentionally and willfully free, inhabiting a space beyond official leagues and thus beyond official organizations. Nōkō fit into this tradition extremely well as a force outside of the developing norms of organized baseball in Taiwan and Japan. This was a defining element in its appeal. However, it was quickly incorporated into visions of Japanese empire. Nōkō in a sense proved the success of Japanese colonial assimilation, but it is not a straightforward tale of cultural obliteration; baseball in Taiwan reflected a Japanese-led baseball scene that purported to be catholic in its sense of inclusion, however problematic and contradictory the racial assumptions underlying such motivations might be. Japanese replication of international systems of cultural exchange as experienced in the numerous tours of American cities by Japanese university teams was now complete, the cultural world surrounding Japan's evangelization of baseball beyond its own borders comprehensive and sustained.

The colonial government continued to reach out to the aboriginal Taiwanese community through organized education. However, not only did classes focus strongly on subjects related to agriculture and trade, as in common schools throughout the colony, but also policemen served as instructors in the vast majority of cases. Relations with the aboriginal Taiwanese continued to be characterized by the need for discipline.[64] As late as 1930 popular representations of aboriginal Taiwanese in the Japanese public space focused on their cultural practice of headhunting and descriptions of aboriginal lands as "an alien place" beyond the reaches of Japanese culture, though for the most part pacified. After the 1930 Musha Incident, when on October 27, 1930, over three hundred Atayal aborigines stormed the fields of the annual interscholastic sports meet, massacring 134 Japanese and shocking the colonial government system, colonial officials revived the specter of Go Hō, a legendary Qing translator who had sacrificed his life in attempting to introduce particularly bloodthirsty and savage aboriginal Taiwanese to civilizing aspects of modern society.[65] The legend, reproduced in film, aimed to unite local Han Chinese Taiwanese and Japanese officials as a civilizing force against aboriginal Taiwanese by sharply exaggerating the aboriginal community's supposed savagery and cruelty.[66]

My discussion of ethnic Chinese on Taiwan glosses over the differences among members of the Hakka, Fujian, and Han ethnicities, but these ethnic groups at this point joined together, however loosely, under a common Chinese cultural heritage.[67] Despite the practical obstacles to fully including aboriginal Taiwanese in Taiwanese society—not the least of which was the poor treatment of aboriginal Taiwanese by the colonial government—a sense of collective consciousness developed that was at the very least aware of aboriginal Taiwanese communities in Taiwan. This could take the form, in the case of the Go Hō legend, of negative propaganda. Thanks in part to their demonstrated abilities in the increasingly popular sport of baseball, aboriginal Taiwanese could also present another face to the debate, a possible transition from rank outsiders to stakeholders in the island's common community. To be Taiwanese at this time was not a classification that set ethnic criteria for entry, nor did it specify a hierarchical relationship among ethnicities within membership of this social group. Baseball was important in the process, most saliently with the success of the Nōkō and Kanō teams, but also in the changing of perceptions among ethnic Chinese Taiwanese and Japanese colonials regarding aboriginal Taiwanese involvement in the game. Baseball acted as a uniting force and an entry point for aboriginal Taiwanese into the public realm. By the end of the colonial period Japanese discussion of the aboriginal Taiwanese had progressed from illustrating the geographical distribution of tribes alongside descriptions of the Taiwanese countryside to openly presenting the aboriginal Taiwanese as part of the colonial experience.[68]

Unfortunately this shift in focus belied the continued exclusion of aboriginal Taiwanese from the common colonial experience in practice. Japanese treatment of the aboriginal Taiwanese was nothing new; the Chinese ethnic majority had been heavily involved in the act of dispossessing the aboriginal Taiwanese of their homelands when it had first migrated to the island.[69] Japanese acceptance of aboriginal Taiwanese participation in the colonial experience was based strictly on those aboriginal Taiwanese that the colonial forces considered suitably civilized in the modern Japanese sense. Baseball served as one popular form of displaying acceptably civilized character, even if the Japanese reaction remained patronizing in tone. Colonial solidarity was possible for those willing to accept Japanese criteria, though it was perhaps more easily achievable as a presentable ideal in the pages of the *Nichi Nichi Shimpō* than in the day-to-day realities of colonial life.

For those who could accept the Japanese criteria, baseball became a facilitator for the celebration of civic unity over ethnic difference within the unified colony of Japanese Taiwan. In colonial Taiwan the disparity between the daily lives of aboriginal Taiwanese and the representations of those aboriginal Taiwanese who excelled at baseball served not only to muddle the issue of aboriginal Taiwanese participation in colonial life, but also blurred the distinctions between the Han Chinese Taiwanese identity and colonial Japanese identity. The narratives have changed considerably in the last thirty years in Taiwan, where the nature of a "Taiwanese" claim to this united identity has taken on a different political tint, but regardless of one's interpretations, we are still left with myriad issues. Not least among these is the issue of how to approach the Chinese heritage of the racial groups presumably most heavily invested in the present-day Taiwanese nationalist movement. The aboriginal Taiwanese, ostensibly the social group with legitimate claim to a typical monoethnic nationalist narrative, are either politically ignored or welcomed in as minor partners in the nationalist enterprise.[70] These are not new problems, and solutions, such as moving away from the standard appraisal of aboriginal Taiwanese as one ethnic bloc, emerge slowly. One must be wary when studying the Taiwanese colonial period that one does not mistake the gradual evolution of an independent Taiwanese identity for the sprouts of a modern Taiwanese nationalist movement—that is, a movement with the clear goals of forming a Taiwanese nation-state fit to take its place in the international nation-state system as an equal member beside China and Japan.

When we look at the colonial period in Taiwan, the question is further complicated by the issues surrounding conceptions of race in East Asia at the beginning of the twentieth century. Social Darwinism was popular among East Asian intellectuals and often utilized as a key concept in the formation of ideas seeking to locate China and Japan in a global framework dominated by Western imperial powers.[71] Although Chinese and Japanese intellectuals sought to place their own ethnic groups in a narrative of dominance and subjugation, the classic concept of the savage survived, most clearly applied to groups such as the aboriginal Taiwanese. The ramifications for the study of baseball's role in society are clear: the athletic skills of an aboriginal Taiwanese were reduced to the inevitable advantage of his or her savage heritage, and baseball initially formed another aspect of a system of discrimination within Taiwanese society.[72] This was nothing new: Chinese settlers in Taiwan had relegated the aboriginal Taiwanese to the status of "mountain people" centuries before the arrival of the first Japanese colonists.[73] Furthermore, Japanese attitudes toward the aboriginal Taiwanese were colored by an inherently racist analysis that viewed the native peoples as savage even before the first arrival of colonial Japanese in 1895, a view reinforced by the subsequent violence of aboriginal resistance to Japanese colonial rule.[74] This resistance lasted considerably longer than the initial period of unrest that Governor-General Kodama had been successful in quelling during the initial years of colonization.

However, as the 1920s and 1930s progressed, the popularity of baseball within the aboriginal communities exposed to Japanese colonial life proved comparable to that within the Taiwanese communities that began to take the game up in increasing numbers.[75] By 1931 the presence of aboriginal Taiwanese players on the highly successful Kanō team from Jiayi was given equal merit to the presence of Taiwanese and Japanese players, as the Kanō team received plaudits for representing the colony's multiethnic composition and proving on the field that all races could work together toward a common goal.[76] The Nōkō team had already achieved national notoriety as an unbridled success of colonial athleticism. Aboriginal Taiwanese, who only a couple of decades earlier had regularly been presented as the epitome of the savagery lying beyond the borders of modernized Japan, now participated in a success story for multiethnic, assimilated Taiwan.[77] Aboriginal Taiwanese children were fully a part of the colonization project, no longer outside the margins of a civilizing mission to include ethnic Chinese Taiwanese in a civic imperial identity. Official photographs of the aboriginal Taiwanese community now included more civilized images—for example, children in classrooms learning how to read and write and playing games outside, just as ethnic Chinese and colonial Japanese children did.[78]

It was a notable shift from the aboriginal Taiwanese people's status as either the subject of intense Japanese sociological curiosity or the source of violent opposition in the first twenty years of the twentieth century.[79] In this case baseball formed an integral part of a nascent and vaguely multiracial Taiwanese identity, a circumstance that suited Japanese assimilationist designs for a Taiwanese identity that would not seek to exclude the colonial masters of the island. This development also denied the emergence of a Taiwanese identity analogous to a conception of the modern nationalist ideal centered on the nation-state; even taking aside for a moment the multiracial component of the Chinese community on the island, the inclusion of aboriginal Taiwanese in a collective social consciousness of the island's identity precluded the emergence of a linear nationalist tale of one ethnic group in search of representation in the global system.[80]

The aboriginal Taiwanese, on the other hand, found themselves the subjects of a systematized body of scientific curiosity on behalf of the Japanese colonials in Taiwan after 1895. Japanese curiosity continually approached the aboriginal Taiwanese as another indigenous natural feature of the fascinating colony, just as the subjects of this curiosity continued to defy the military power of Japanese imperialism.[81] Baseball in Taiwan became an unlikely avenue into colonial society for aboriginal Taiwanese, as those who succeeded on baseball fields completed a journey from photographed subject and symbol of racially inevitable savagery to willing teammates and respectable athletes. Baseball thus served to blur the political distinctions among races in Taiwan within the broader umbrella of the sport's clearly Japanese cultural identity. However, baseball in Taiwan tended to reflect the public face of Japan's colonial project rather than the social reality. Nōkō represented a frontier of aboriginal Taiwanese involvement in a game defined by Japanese experience. Aboriginal Taiwanese, so completely alien to both the Chinese settling experience and the Japanese colonial experience, were invited into the common public sphere dominated by Japanese publications, of which baseball proved a prominent part. This occurred thanks to the continued growth of popularity in the game and its spread down the east coast and into the remaining enclaves of aboriginal Taiwanese communities. Although the Japanese recognized the possible merits of teaching the sport to these most uncivilized of native Taiwanese, they were unwilling to appreciate talented aboriginal Taiwanese outside of familiar parameters of enjoyable novelty and apocryphal evidence of savage strength and athleticism.[82]

The role of aboriginal Taiwanese in Taiwanese baseball remains a central component in the narrative of the sport's evolution as a "national game" on the island today. Aboriginal Taiwanese have consistently been prominent in the history of the sport's development through the colonial period, the postwar years of amateur flourishing, the Little League championship years of the 1970s, and the development of a professional league in the 1990s. As of 2012 players of aboriginal origin supplied 41 percent of the Chinese Professional Baseball League (CPBL), a rather significant increase on the 2 percent share of the overall Taiwanese population for which aboriginal Taiwanese account.[83] This has been much remarked upon in Taiwanese history books of varying approaches, from the academic to the popular, with similarly varying degrees of comfort in discussing the superior skills and athleticism the aboriginal Taiwanese apparently possess. The discussion can get awkward rather quickly, and this is nothing new: the aboriginal Taiwanese appetite and capacity for playing baseball has attracted attention among other ethnic groups on the island from the sport's first introduction to aboriginal Taiwanese communities.

This continued externalization of aboriginal Taiwanese permitted Nōkō to assume and benefit from the trappings of a barnstorming team akin to Hunter Herbert Harrison's mercenaries or Abe Isoo's cultural envoys: honored guests to be embraced from a distance. Both within the island of Taiwan and in Japan itself, Nōkō was an identifier of something foreign, unknowable, and unmistakably premodern. In this sense the young men from Hualian truly did achieve a unification of Japanese and Taiwanese society; in truth Nōkō's adventures in Japan were yet another result of the expansion of Japan's baseball community to the southwest, the sporting infrastructure and media coverage indicative of the extent to which Japanese baseball enveloped its Taiwanese counterpart. Nōkō ultimately participated in a baseball community that comfortably spanned the internal borders of the Empire of Japan and increasingly welcomed visitors from across the Pacific Ocean. Those exchanges, between Japanese university teams and counterparts in the United States, linked the core of one cultural power to another. The Nōkō visits were colorful and lively interruptions from a periphery increasingly willing to celebrate its relationship with the imperial center.

4 | The Road to Kōshien

Nōkō's success in achieving notoriety from the colony to the imperial heartland was something vaguely if acceptably transgressive, confirmation of the depth of the sporting culture developed by the Japanese cultural sphere that spread southward with military and political expansion. The aboriginal Taiwanese players confirmed for many Japanese the viability of their colonial project, not just because of the players' success on the field and their comportment off it, but also because of their emergence from a colony with a steadily growing and structurally sound baseball environment of its own. As the 1920s had progressed, local Taiwanese participation in organized baseball had grown across the board; Nōkō proved not only that Japanese modernity could rescue the most savage of the premodern peoples on the edges of the Japanese imperial reach, but also that the civilized administrative hierarchies being created around Japanese baseball could be recreated in the colonies to good ends. The network of local and island-wide tournaments that helped produce the Nōkō phenomenon occurred within a clear context of connections between competition in Taiwan and competition in Japan.

Traveling to Japan to play the empire's finest teams on their home turf came to define the two most well-known Taiwanese teams of the colonial period. Nōkō's success was followed by that of a high school team from Jiayi, halfway down the west coast of the island and just over

150 miles from the colonial capital, Taipei. Composed of players from Chinese, Japanese, and aboriginal Taiwanese ethnic backgrounds, the Kanō team joined Nōkō in becoming a symbol for colonial success and eclipsed the notoriety of the all-aboriginal squad as a widely popular cultural phenomenon. Kanō served as both a signal of the ascension of baseball to a position of unrivaled popularity among Taiwanese sports in the colonial period and a declaration of the arrival of local Taiwanese athletes to organized playing fields, the tri-ethnic composition of the team central to its relevance in Chinese-language historiography in complicating the relationship between Taiwan and Japan during the colonial period. Kanō's success and lasting historical relevance rests strongly on one iconic location: Kōshien.

Kōshien Stadium, in the city of Nishinomiya, just outside of Kobe and Osaka, hosts two tournaments every year: the National High School Baseball Invitational Tournament, held in the spring, and the National High School Baseball Championship, held in the summer. The summer tournament is the older and more prominent, founded in 1915, but the affiliation with Kōshien Stadium began in 1924, when the stadium, purpose-built to host the increasingly prestigious championship, was unveiled alongside the debut of a new spring invitational tournament. The Japanese-language press in Taiwan and Chinese-language accounts afterward all simply refer to the summer tournament as "Kōshien," the location itself and the tournament that it hosts possessing a layer of mystique that has been there from the very start. The original sponsors, the *Asahi Shimbun* and the Hanshin Electric Railroad Company, came together in a joint venture to build the stadium in the early 1920s, a pinnacle achievement to crown decades of urban and industrial development in the swiftly growing metropolis and a clear sign of Japan's ever forward-marching modernism, powered by the vibrant institutions of the national press and Japanese railroad companies. The tournament immediately captured national attention, benefitting from vigorous support from its sponsor newspaper and manifestations of appropriate moral values as part of a national narrative.[1]

This national narrative embraced the regions brought under Japanese jurisdiction with the country's rise as a regional power, with representatives from Korea and Japanese-occupied Dalian joining Taiwanese participants in the tournament throughout the 1920s and 1930s. Regional representatives typically, though not exclusively, fielded all-Japanese teams.[2] Kōshien lay at the center of a baseball network that stretched out across the Empire of Japan. The rapid modernization of interwar Japan and the open, self-conscious reflection by Japanese on the nature of the modernity that such development represented gave the stadium life. Japanese cities became both host and catalyst for the great modernizing activities of the age, hubs of great railroad networks that emulated British success in placing logistical expedience at the center of a successful, commercially driven empire, in no small part influenced by seeing firsthand the importance British financial interests placed on the construction of railway systems across south and eastern China.[3] Following the World War I boom, Nishinomiya, almost equidistant from two of the "big six" Japanese metropolises (Tokyo, Osaka, Yokohama, Kobe, Kyoto, and Nagoya), became part of the hinterland of the new, modern Japan, right off the newly established Tokyo-Osaka railway corridor, the heart of almost four thousand miles of track laid across the country.[4]

The Kōshien Stadium existed not as a receptacle for supplication to the imperial center but as a node for expression of imperial identity outward. The post-1868 modernizing wave within Japan left an important intellectual legacy to join the material products of Japan's modern industrial complex, a centrality of Japanese modern thought to the Asian modernizing experience. This idea, extrapolated in the late 1930s and 1940s into odious and disingenuous propaganda pushing for racial unity under the contradictory umbrella of Japanese-led egalitarianism, had at its roots a specific Japanese interpretation of modernization that swiftly translated into a grasp for singular legitimacy. This was particularly true in the colonies; in Korea, for example, Japanese assimilation channeled intellectual claims to the Japanese state's role as an agent of historical change on the part of Koreans severed from the Joseon Period (1392–1897) with no indigenous modern state to serve as successor to the old or harbinger of the new.[5] In Taiwan this separation was further emphasized by the island's separation from the Qing dynasty just under two decades before its collapse and the arrival of a Chinese nation-state.

The Chinese nation-state owed Japan a certain debt, Tokyo having harbored intellectual leaders and fugitives from Liang Qichao to Sun Yat-sen. Indeed it was while in Japan, following his exile in 1898, that Liang began to argue for a new historiography that focused on harnessing nationalist energies to drive Chinese modernization as a historical agent to counter the cyclical visions of the past. By the 1930s with most of the Republic of China's early years chewed up by warlordism and the continuing debts due Western imperial powers, Jiang Tingfu, historian and cofounder of the political magazine *Duli Pinglun* (Independent Review), broke with both Nationalist and Communist historiographers in looking to domestic Chinese factors in the failure to modernize in the late nineteenth and early twentieth centuries, citing the lack of modern institutions and modern forms of knowledge.[6] Japan acquired Taiwan before more purposeful attempts at modernization took place and, crudely put, Tokyo beat Beijing to the punch. Taiwan experienced modernization on Japanese terms.

The Chinese move toward modernization moved forward in the early twentieth century divorced from Taiwan's progression as a colony of Japan. This created significant divergences between Taiwanese experience and that on the mainland, particularly centered on race. In China after 1911, as intellectual conceptions of national Chinese identity evolved, prominent place was given to the Han ethnicity. The liberal trappings of the early years of the republic, as symbolized by the five-barred flag representing China's five major nationalities, gave way in the 1920s. Sun Yat-sen raised the Guomindang flag for the first time on New Year's Day in 1925. Two political movements now divided Chinese politics, each hoisting distinctive national flags to lay claim to the country's national character and destiny.[7] In practice the Han Chinese majority formed the heart of both of the two major Chinese machines, political and economic, but the development of ethnocentrism had occurred in a context of multiethnic awareness, as recognized by the original flag. Japan, on the other hand, was aggressive in its assertions of a path of glory for the Japanese race, with very little room to accommodate minority points of view in the national interest. In this respect the acquisition of Taiwan as the first imperial colony introduced the concept of a multiethnic Japanese empire.[8] The Japanese colonial government's most pressing responsibilities were initially to suppress armed rebellion, but it quickly moved on to the efficient development of Taiwan as a peaceful colony that functioned as a productive component of the empire.[9]

Local reactions to Japan's modernizing project took different forms: violent resistance, particularly among aboriginal Taiwanese, until 1915; competing movements in the 1920s to develop Mandarin as a common Taiwanese language to preserve the Chinese heritage and to push for home rule in order to preserve the power and privilege of local elites; and finally a movement from the 1930s onward among Taiwanese intellectuals raised within the Japanese education system to push for social justice and equality for local Taiwanese *within* the universal sociocultural subject identity of the Empire of Japan. By the 1940s Taiwan was on the verge of truly turning Japanese, albeit as the result of an incredibly tumultuous five decades.[10] The educational system that had helped shape such late-colonial-period intellectual viewpoints, a central element in Japan's state-driven approach to modernization of both the homeland and the colonies, was vital to the development of enthusiasm for baseball in Taiwan as a delivery system of the game and by extension of a key element in popular and public Japanese modernity. Discussing Little League baseball in the United States, Gary Alan Fine is clear in identifying such regimentation of play as "not merely activity . . . [but] situated activity," arguing that the more organized an activity, the more resources required to successfully execute it.[11] Hosting tournaments for school teams and adult teams on school grounds, procuring uniforms and equipment, and training young children in basic skills all took various human and material resources. The process was ancillary to the education system's main goal—to render the colonial populace more productive—but less likely to cause political trouble. Nevertheless, baseball became an example in popular life of the modernizing and cultural influences of the Japanese colonization of Taiwan.

The Japanese state did not intentionally spread the sport as a tool of assimilation (the promotion of the Japanese language took on much of that strategic burden), but the physical acts required in the hosting and performance of games assisted in the transmission of elements of modern Japanese society to communities throughout Taiwan.[12] Regular events among representative teams from north and south Taiwan, for example, were common at the beginning of the Western calendar new year. Series among these teams featured the now ubiquitous ceremonial qualities of pristine modern uniforms and lining up for photographs before commencement of a game, mirroring countless examples from Japan.[13] The sport clearly reflected goals within Japanese imperialism focused on the spread of Japanese cultural identity, and as the popularity of the game grew, public participation expanded beyond that of a colonial Japanese community maintaining links with its homeland. Taiwanese, both Han Chinese and aboriginal, were exposed to the cultural connotations of Japanese baseball. The game had quickly attained an important role in the cultivation of Japan's youth, evidenced most conspicuously by the influence and popularity of the Kōshien tournament beyond Japan. Educators in both Japan and Taiwan were by no means ignorant of baseball's usefulness in socializing young Taiwanese as part of the production of a diligent and obedient populace.[14] Tying this development to a universal model of Japanese advancement fit the more optimistic visions of Japanese assimilationist thought. By the 1920s the colonial Japanese press supported a growing sporting environment in Taiwan that was motivated by popular participation and dominated by baseball. In addition to the reporting of domestic baseball events in Japan, such as games from the developing rivalry among Japanese universities in Tokyo, a plethora of baseball competitions occupied the pages of the colonial newspaper on a regular basis.[15] In addition to coverage of various amateur and adolescent baseball competitions, the *Nichi Nichi Shimpō* even carried a regular column in 1922 entitled "Baseball Terms," explaining many of the common terms used in the game (often in the form of loan words from English), written in katakana, such as *sutoraiku* (strike) or *hitto* (hit).[16] In general, articles conveying news of a previously held baseball game, an upcoming tournament between amateur sides or another students' athletic meet dominated by baseball became increasingly common as the decade wore on.[17]

Baseball had been present in Taiwanese schools first, before professional men organized teams to represent companies, industries, and private clubs. The first organized game came between staff from the Taiwan Colonial Government High School and the National Language Normal School, an institution created in 1906 for the training of secondary-level teachers. The two teams were joined in a three-way rivalry with East Gate Night School over the next few years.[18] The first record of a contest between students themselves describes the Colonial Government High School's hosting of a game in 1908 between fifth-year students and a team composed of a mixture of third- and fourth-year students.[19] For the next few years organized baseball in early colonial Taiwan was played by adult men, particularly by the employees and students of the three teams mentioned above, as well as by teams formed under the auspices of the "Sports Club" set up by the colonial police department in 1903.[20] Larger numbers of privately run clubs and representative teams for educational institutions had begun to emerge throughout the 1910s, leading to larger baseball tournaments involving more players.[21] This period of prominence for adult amateur baseball soon gave way to an explosion in the popularity of youth baseball.

The term *shōnen* came into prominent use by the colonial press beginning in 1920, with the first use of the term in the pages of the *Nichi Nichi Shimpō* in a brief regional byline on a baseball game featuring a narrow win by Tainan No. 1 Primary School.[22] The game was part of a wider tournament among primary schools held at Tainan Park Ground.[23] A week later the tournament continued with more games featuring more schools in the Tainan area.[24] The references to young people (specifically boys) engaged in baseball activities began to proliferate. In some cases this reflected the increasing popularity of the game in a climate dominated by prominent visiting teams touring the island; interest in the Herbert Harrison Hunter tour drove public announcements promoting pricing for elementary student admission.[25] In other cases the increase in references was due to increased public activity involving boys of varying ages participating in organized games. In April 1921 a "young citizens" game was played at New Park in Taipei, with photographs of a large crowd of onlookers and young boys awaiting pitches under the watchful eye of an older umpire.[26] That year saw the beginning of an increased activity in youth baseball in Taiwan that would persist until the end of colonial rule and beyond.

Previous to 1921 the activity by teachers and other personnel working in Taiwanese high schools established to educate the children of colonial Japanese had spread beyond Taipei. Tainan High School held regular tournaments during the 1910s.[27] However, it was in 1921 that youth baseball gained a significant public island-wide profile. The inaugural Taipei Secondary School Baseball Tournament was the first major tournament in the colony to exclusively feature young athletes of school age. The tournament, held amid a hubbub of summer baseball activity featuring adult teams such as the colorfully named "Diamond Club" and the government-general team, pitted three high schools against each other: Taipei High School, Taipei Commercial School, and Taipei Industrial School.[28] After a significant victory for Taipei Industrial School by a score of 17–7, the team lost to Taipei High School by a similarly large margin of 18–10.[29] Taipei High School went on to defeat Taipei Commercial School and become the first Taipei secondary school baseball champions.[30]

The tournament persisted throughout the 1920s, only to be superseded by the first All-Island Secondary School Baseball Tournament in 1923. What had caused this explosion in interest in youth baseball? Politically Taiwan had been veering away from Gotō Shimpei's gradualist policy of coexistence since 1919, when Governor-General Akashi Motojirō had begun to insist on an expansion of the colonial education system to provide more secondary-level opportunities for the local Taiwanese population.[31] The subsequent educational reforms under Akashi and later Governor-General Den Kenjirō would have ramifications for the influx of local Taiwanese into high school baseball in the late 1920s and early 1930s. In the meantime the change in tone of Taiwan's political atmosphere from one of coexistence to a positive approach to assimilation coincided with an increase in sporting events in public life. Sumo wrestling, tennis, and baseball occupied pride of place in the Japanese conviction to further develop the role of sporting culture in its colony.

The broader popularity of baseball and wider adoption of the game in schools in Taiwan mimicked similar developments in Japan, where the inception of the Kōshien tournament in 1915 had elevated youth baseball to a national event. Such developments were repeated in the colony, where school facilities that had hosted contests among adult teams since the first exhibition games in Taipei now provided excellent infrastructure for a blooming youth baseball scene.[32] The impact of the educational system, and more directly the role of children and young people, were crucial to the rapid rise in popularity of baseball in Taiwan. This rise in popularity remained more or less an exclusively cultural phenomenon with no explicit official or active promotion of baseball as being inherently "Japanese." Rather the benefits to the relationship between colonizer and colonized became apparent in large part thanks to momentum from the bottom of society upward. In only a few years the formation of Kanō, arguably the most famous team in Taiwanese baseball history, came about as the result of a colonial Japanese coach's dream to reach Kōshien, a transplantation of the tournament's desirability into the playing fields of the rural colony through the ambitions of an individual fueled by a Japanese narrative.[33]

Just as the increase in privately run clubs and the formation of baseball teams to represent large companies and government departments in the 1910s reflected the development of the sport in Japan, the increased interest in and promotion of youth baseball in Taiwan owed much to the existing infrastructure in the imperial home country. The success of the main Tokyo universities had spawned a baseball culture containing its own school songs, specifically written to cheer on baseball teams.[34] The culture surrounding Waseda and Keiō Universities in particular had even penetrated basic textbooks written to educate Japanese on how to write letters in English, teaching the reader how to offer "a kind invitation to a baseball match" to a foreign friend or visitor.[35] By the 1920s baseball was a fixture in Japanese popular sporting culture, featuring in collected illustrations such as one by

Yoshioka Torihei showing an account of a baseball game across nine innings, with illustrations of gathered masses of fans, athletic players, and entertainers performing for the amusement of the grandstands and the cameras along the sideline.[36] Such enthusiasm extended to the formal organization of youth baseball. Following the inception of the Kōshien National High School Tournament, the Youth Baseball Association in Japan issued formal guidelines that gave clear examples of the accepted standardized rules of the game, including appropriate dimensions for the playing field, directions for equipment, and the number of innings to be played in a game in various situations.[37] There were clearly stated criteria for the accurate recording of baseball records, including at bats, runs scored, and hits.[38]

Youth baseball in Taiwan in the 1920s was an extension of this enthusiasm for and formalization of the phenomenon in Japan. The Japanese-controlled press regularly featured pictures of young students in immaculate white baseball uniforms and bestowed tournament winners with victory wreaths reminiscent of those awarded at high-profile games in Japan. Taipei No. 1 High School's baseball team had a song of its own to emulate the increasingly popular Japanese practice.[39] Although still in the shadow of the increasing number of matches among adult teams in the early 1920s, references to youth baseball tournaments continued to grow.[40] In 1922, only a few weeks before the beginning of the second annual Taipei Secondary School Baseball Tournament, notice of a smaller youth baseball event even earned a small byline on the *Nichi Nichi Shimpō* front page.[41] In contrast, the Taipei tournament itself received relatively lighter coverage compared to the year before, somewhat lost in the news of a tournament featuring adult athletes under the auspices of the Taiwanese Baseball Association, but public interest and official support were sufficient to establish the first All-Island Secondary School Baseball Tournament a year later.[42] Just prior to the beginning of the tournament that June, the *Nichi Nichi Shimpō* carried articles covering the third annual Taipei tournament and a composite of two photographs showing young students engaged in sumo wrestling and baseball. Both photographs showed large crowds in attendance.[43]

The spread of youth baseball occurred not only in a Japanese context but specifically in a colonial Japanese context featuring schools dominated by colonial Japanese students that fielded teams comprised entirely of colonial Japanese children. One brief article describing the opening of a small youth baseball tournament in Gaoxiong noted a rare exception. The tournament, featuring local schools, included two common schools, the earliest type of primary-level institution established to educate the local population. Both schools in question, No. 2 Common School and No. 3 Common School, were predominantly attended by local Taiwanese.[44] In a minor foreshadowing of one of the biggest stories in baseball to come over the following decade, both common schools won their respective games in the tournament.[45] Both the results and the tournament itself were buried in the depths of the newspaper, earning only cursory mention, though it is difficult to determine if this was owing to some disinclination to give the local Taiwanese children their due or simply owing to the fact that Gaoxiong was still a relative backwater in the colony. The baseball environment in particular remained dominated by teams based in and around Taipei.[46]

The summer of 1923 saw more articles in the colonial press focused on youth baseball than at any time before. The first annual All-Island Secondary School Baseball Tournament failed to cause the enthusiasm that might greet a visit from an established Japanese team like Waseda University, but the press nonetheless tracked the tournament's progress. The first tournament to ostensibly be open to all teams on the island proved essentially to be an expansion of the Taipei tournament, featuring three Taipei teams (Taipei No. 1 High School, Taipei Industrial School, and Taipei Commercial School) and one from Tainan (Tainan No. 1 High School).[47] Over two days all four teams competed in a single elimination tournament, with Taipei No. 1 High School emerging victorious after a victory over Tainan No. 1 High School in the final.[48] Taipei No. 1 High School enjoyed considerable support from fans attending the games, and the winning squad posed in front of the scoreboard with its victory wreath for the press.[49] The *Nichi Nichi Shimpō* also delivered a detailed account of all three of the championship games before reminding readers that the winner of this tournament would go forth to represent Taiwan at the National High School Invitational Tournament at Kōshien.[50]

The Taiwan press initially covered the trip to Kōshien enthusiastically. In early August 1923 the newspaper featured a picture of the young athletes looking excitedly at the cameras from the decks of the boat taking them to Japan.[51] Unfortunately the young men suffered a heavy defeat in their first game, to Ritsumeikan High School, and progressed no further in the competition.[52] Their return to Taipei was noted quietly.[53] Despite their inability to make much of a mark in the national tournament in Japan, Taipei No. 1 High School's invitation to Kōshien signaled the confirmation of youth baseball's role as a cultural bridge between Japan and its first colony. The still developing framework for youth baseball competition in Taiwan now filtered into one representative place at a national tournament covering the entire Empire of Japan. Over the next couple of years the frequency of youth baseball tournaments and exhibitions continued to grow, including the notable visit of the Nōkō team to Taipei with much fanfare. By 1925 the All-Island Secondary School Baseball Tournament had earned a measure of anticipation in the pages of the Taiwanese colonial press; the fact that the winner of the tournament earned a spot at the *Asahi Shimbun*-sponsored national tournament at Kōshien now earned its own headlines in anticipation of the All-Island Tournament kicking off a few days later.[54] In fact the tournament was now explicitly referred to as a preliminary qualification for the national finals themselves. The paper carried detailed stories on the tournament's two days of action, including a photograph of the captain of the winning team, Taipei Industrial School, accepting a winner's pennant and the adolescent players standing to attention for the camera's recording of their auspicious victory.[55] The young men proudly posed for more pictures in Japan, eye-catching photographs of the high schoolers attired in immaculate white baseball uniforms with a large crowd behind them.[56] Coverage of the result, however—another early loss—was again muted.[57]

Over the next few years Taiwanese representatives would be little more than fodder in early rounds of the national-level games. The All-

Island tournament continued to thrive, although it remained dominated by teams located in Taipei for most of the decade. Both of these trends ended memorably in 1931, when the multiethnic Kanō team successfully won the All-Island tournament and proceeded to reach the finals in Kōshien, a performance leagues beyond the achievements of earlier Taiwanese representatives at the national tournament. The Kanō team had been competing in the annual All-Island tournament since 1928, and its success emerged in the context of increased momentum for the sport outside of Taipei and among non-Japanese athletes, built in no small part on the success of the Nōkō team, novelty and all. Schools in the south of the colony with predominantly local Taiwanese lineups began to emerge.[58] As the 1920s ended and the 1930s began, youth baseball was an established cultural practice up and down the island, one that had been dominated by colonial Japanese but was increasingly open to participation by local Taiwanese. The Kanō trip to Kōshien provided the most spectacular example of a wider phenomenon.

Larger tournaments were now becoming more common outside of Taipei, in part fueled by Kanō's success, drawing larger and larger crowds. The Kanō lineup continued to exhibit the multiethnic character that had helped make the team famous, but it no longer provided the only opportunities for local Taiwanese to play at the organized level.[59] Teams began to crop up and grab the attention of the Taipei-based press and baseball community from further down the island in Taizhong, Tainan, and Pingdong. Taizhong No. 1 High School established teams in both baseball and softball composed entirely of local Taiwanese adolescents.[60] In 1930 Taizhong No. 1 High School competed at the All-Island Secondary School Tournament in Taipei, where the school joined Kanō as the only two representatives with local Taiwanese students taking the playing field. The tournament, already established as major news in the press, now ran over four days and included eight teams.[61] The local players of Taizhong No. 1 High School swiftly lost in the first round to Taizhong Commercial School.[62] Taipei No. 1 High School successfully earned its second title in a row before going on to another ignominious early defeat at Kōshien, oblivious of the heroics that would come from the Kanō team's performances a year later.[63]

In fact the hype that surrounded the Taipei team before it carried out yet another ill-fated trip by a Taiwanese team composed entirely of colonial Japanese children to the national tournament now serves to highlight the differences between the 1920s and the 1930s as far as youth baseball in Taiwan is concerned. The 1930s featured considerably more local Taiwanese children competing in the game at a level considered noteworthy by the wider public. Just days before Taipei No. 1 High School set off to represent Taiwan in the 1930 National Secondary School Baseball Tournament, Taipei hosted an All-Island Youth Baseball Tournament for teams from primary-level schools around the colony. The children were welcomed in an evening tea party at the Railroad Hotel in Taipei, and the tournament earned considerable coverage in the *Nichi Nichi Shimpō*, including a full layout of the list of events.[64] Participation by local Taiwanese was more conspicuous in this tournament than it had been in the secondary schools competition, thanks to the participation of Taiwanese common schools. The children from these schools attracted curious coverage from the press, the *Nichi Nichi Shimpō* choosing to display two large photographs of the team from Gaoxiong No. 1 Common School: the upper photograph showed a group of bemused, if not bewildered, local Taiwanese children squatting on the floor with their luggage; the lower photograph showed the same group, now in its official team photo, in sparkling white uniforms and standing to attention beside a championship pennant.[65] The children got to the semifinal of the tournament, itself the subject of heavy newspaper coverage, reflecting the official addition of the "All-Island" prefix to the name of the tournament, which had simply been described as a Taipei-based tournament the year before.[66] Even the *Taiwan Minbao*, a newspaper run by local Taiwanese intellectuals and published in Tokyo to avoid governmental censure, made a rare mention of baseball in a report on the agitation of a mostly colonial Japanese crowd at the Gaoxiong school's success, a somewhat sniffy approach to the game that stood in contrast to the consistently effusive coverage from the Japanese-controlled press that nevertheless reflected baseball's growing public profile.[67]

The emergence of Taizhong No. 1 High School and the increased participation by local Taiwanese children in baseball games at the primary-school level revealed that the Kanō team was not some bolt from the blue that changed Taiwanese baseball forever. Rather the Jiayi team's success was the crest of a slowly gathering wave of local Taiwanese participation that apparently threatened to overcome traditional colonial Japanese dominance of the sport, at least on the field itself. In 1928 Taipei hosted the first meeting of an annual national baseball championship featuring teams from Taipei, Xinzhu, Taizhong, Tainan, and Gaoxiong.[68] The representation from cities all along the western coast of the island displayed the continued popularity of the sport both in the Taiwanese communities and beyond Taipei. The game had long been popular outside the capital, if within the parameters of competition among teams comprised of Japanese athletes, but the spread of the game down the relatively underpopulated east coast infringed on the remaining territory of the aboriginal Taiwanese.[69] Taidong and Hualian, with their significantly higher aboriginal Taiwanese populations, became centers of baseball activity.[70] As the 1930s wore on, the colonial Japanese monopoly of organized baseball became confined to Taipei. Youth baseball was pivotal, both in the high-profile visits to Japan by the Nōkō and Kanō teams and through the increased participation by local Taiwanese primary- and secondary-level students. Tainan No. 2 High School participated in three All-Island Secondary School Baseball Tournament competitions, in 1932, 1934, and 1935. The team lineups on all three occasions were dominated by local Taiwanese athletes, in particular ethnic Chinese.[71]

The gradual incursions of local Taiwanese student athletes into the world of Taiwanese baseball did not preclude the continued dominance of colonial Japanese athletes, however. In the final year that Tainan No. 2 High School participated in the All-Island championships (1935) the Kanō team that season started only two local Taiwanese athletes, one ethnic Chinese, and one aboriginal Taiwanese.[72] Such gradual incursions also did not dilute the firm placement of baseball in Taiwanese culture within a colonial Japanese context. Despite the increased popularity of youth baseball in the colony, organized competitions among formally organized amateur clubs still held much of the press attention. Furthermore, although the success of the All-Island tournament, held to select a Taiwanese participant for Kōshien, had spawned another stand-alone tournament for youth baseball in January of each year, such games were easily overshadowed by a high-profile visit from a Japanese baseball team—for example, a visiting tour by Keiō University.[73] In the final years of Taiwan's status as a Japanese colony, baseball continued in the public eye much as it had grown in the 1920s, with youth baseball providing a major component of the sport's public presence. The increased role of teams in Xinzhu and Pingdong, as well as the infiltration of Taiwanese athletes into the baseball team of the privately run Taipei High School after 1935, did nothing to dispel the overbearing dominance of colonial Japanese athletes.[74]

The continued dominance of colonial Japanese on the field accompanied the unquestionable centrality of connections to Japan in the competitive and ideological structures of Taiwanese baseball. For youth teams in particular the road to Kōshien offered the clearest pathway to demonstrating excellence and superiority over other teams playing throughout the colony. This narrative found its way to the pages of the Japanese-language press in Taiwan during the colonial period and has persisted to this day in historical accounts of Kanō's success, so much so that one might forget that the most successful Kanō team (the 1931 vintage) did not actually win the tournament but reached the finals only to lose in acceptably close and honorable fashion. The Japanese stadium loomed large in the imaginations of colonial Japanese in Taiwan and transitioned smoothly into a legendary site for Taiwanese baseball, the goals and models of the Japanese game replicated in the Taiwanese experience even as local Taiwanese participation in organized games grew steadily in the 1920s. Kanō represents the rise of local Taiwanese participation in the game; its marriage of aboriginal Taiwanese, Han Chinese, and colonial Japanese elements places the team clearly within specific narratives, whether as evidence of Japanese colonial success at the time or as further evidence of complex colonial social structures today. This has made Kanō very popular in studies of Taiwanese baseball, a mechanism for the investigation of the possibilities of a nascent Taiwanese identity present during the colonial period or a window into the comfortable crossings of subtle boundaries among ethnic groups in Taiwan during the colonial period. The team's journey to Kōshien lies at the heart of these narratives, the 1931 trip to the finals in particular an achievement that brought legitimacy to a Taiwanese baseball community that looked to Japan for recognition from the originators of the game, the model of its administrative and ideological structures. This journey originated in Japanese colonial policies that helped transform organized baseball in the colony from the province of the colonial Japanese community to a broader cultural practice participated in and driven by the participation of local Taiwanese on the playing field.

5 | Kanō

The emergence of the Kanō team in the late 1920s confirmed a change
that had been brewing in the practice of the sport in Taiwan during
that decade. This multiethnic team, composed of Japanese, ethnic
Chinese, and aboriginal Taiwanese athletes, projected the public face
of a sport that had gained popularity and crossed community lines
within the colony. Japanese visiting teams had caused excitement in
Taiwan before, and the "savage" Nōkō team had in its own way evoked
similar reactions before moving on to its tour of Japan. Kanō was the
first team treated by the colonial Japanese media as a truly indigenous
colonial side rather than a collection of alien aboriginal schoolboy
athletes or an association of colonial Japanese professionals. Whereas
colonial Japanese teams in Taipei had garnered support and visiting
teams (including Nōkō) were welcomed with enthusiastic curiosity,
Kanō generated local excitement in the colony, and members of various communities identified with the team. The subsequent trip to
Kōshien brought legitimacy through recognition rather than through
victory; even the moral victory of losing in the final game of the tournament vindicated the team by the free transfer of respect from the
hosts rather than the drawing of a costly pyrrhic win. Japanese players,
administrators, and fans were not nemeses of an emerging national-

ist identity; they were partners in the wider baseball community and recognized gatekeepers.

Identifying the nature of Kanō's relevance in relation to participation either inside or outside of Japanese imperial-defined spheres is challenging, though the tri-ethnic composition of the team lends itself well to analyses that stress a departure from a monolithic Japanese norm. Yu Junwei has described the excitement seen across the island as a form of "baseball fever" that gripped the colony, highlighting the depth of feeling among local Taiwanese residents for the sport.[1] Andrew Morris argues that the Kanō team represented an alliance between colonial Japanese and local Taiwanese in a collective Taiwanese identity that lay between one pole absent of Japanese influence and another consumed by it; such an alliance allowed colonial Japanese to embrace a peaceful and exhilarating union with their neighbors in the wake of the Musha Incident, a worrying reminder of the potential for violent backlash against imperial rule.[2] Chinese-language historiography similarly lauds the multiethnic composition of the team, crediting the team's successful visits to Japan for making baseball a component of Taiwanese life and culture going forward.[3] Anyone who writes about Taiwanese baseball simply must mention and discuss Kanō. The multiethnic composition of the squad offers an insight into the cultural roles that baseball occupied in colonial Taiwan and the political potential for both colonial officialdom seeking opportunities for fruitful propaganda and individuals interacting with the colonial superstructure; Kanō's marriage of success on the field and apparent success off it in uniting representatives of various sociopolitical groups makes it a unique and popular phenomenon.

The Kanō team came into being in 1928. The Jiayi Agriculture and Forestry Institute, shortened in Chinese characters to 嘉農 (jianong in Chinese or kanō in Japanese), was founded in 1919. The school's sporting teams achieved little of note until principal Tōguchi Taka heard that a prominent graduate of the Waseda baseball team, Kondō Hyotarō, was traveling to Jiayi. Kondō, after some subtle and not so subtle encouragement, swiftly accepted the invitation to become the coach of the school baseball team.[4] He soon proved himself a strict disciplinarian, presiding over practices that have since proved fertile ground for the legends surrounding the team, making it clear that the athletes would be forced to conform to his training practices, with those who satisfied his requirements becoming eligible for the team regardless of their ethnic background. The young men attended compulsory training sessions during class time; Kondō subjected them to intense practice on their skills in batting, fielding, and base running. The Japanese coach ensured that his players ran two kilometers a day and swung the bat over three hundred times in each practice.[5] This new approach to baseball in Jiayi, which focused on competing and winning rather than providing young men with athletic diversion, so reminiscent of legendary Japanese team practices dating back to the Ichiko school and beyond, produced a team with a mission.

These measures did not pay immediate dividends on the field, however. Kanō's first appearance in the pages of the *Nichi Nichi Shimpō* came in July 1928. The team garnered a brief mention in its uneventful defeat to Taizhong Commercial School, the only evidence of the team's new approach betrayed by a glance at the supplied team lineups featuring ethnic Chinese and aboriginal Taiwanese names amid the more familiar Japanese. This small initial step toward ethnic integration on the field led to an ignominious 13–0 defeat in the July 1928 game.[6] Despite the lopsided defeat, the Kanō squad already represented a marked difference from the predominantly colonial Japanese squads competing in the various island-wide tournaments. The team had arrived on the colonial scene. This appearance was the first in a series of games in which Kanō participated in 1928, as the team continued to compete in tournaments in the Tainan area even if, again, results on the field were not overly positive.[7]

The form of the team matured the following year, when Kanō participated in the inaugural South and Central Taiwan Secondary School Baseball Tournament. It met with its nemesis from the year before, Taizhong Commercial School, this time battling to a 1–1 draw before going on to lose 7–5 to Tainan No. 1 High School.[8] The team received another invitation to the All-Island Secondary School Baseball Tournament but lost again, this time 8–5, to Taipei No.1 High School.[9]

Despite their continuing troubles on the field, the Kanō players were gaining in popularity. The head of the Sports Association, Mr. Hayami, who had been present at the game between Kanō and Taipei No. 1 High School, felt moved to comment on the team's abilities and contribution to a fine game.[10] Over the following two years Kanō made a name for itself as a successful team in baseball competitions organized in southern and central Taiwan, earning its first championship in November 1929 in the inaugural Jiayi Baseball Tournament while never quite succeeding in matching the powerhouse all-Japanese baseball teams of northern Taiwan such as Taipei No.1 High School and Taipei Commercial School.[11]

Up to this point Kanō had failed to materialize as the significant social phenomenon it would become in 1931. Articles in the colonial press listed the Kanō lineup with little or no comment. The presence of ethnic Chinese players and even aboriginal Taiwanese players passed with little discussion. Kanō was very much just another high school baseball team in a colony where high school baseball had become extremely popular. The press did not yet identify the team with any of the curiosity or racially dominated perspectives that had greeted the Nōkō side almost from the very beginning. In this relative absence of special attention from Taipei, Kanō quietly came to dominate the high school baseball landscape beyond the colonial capital, before arriving at the All-Island Secondary School Baseball Tournament in 1931 as a genuine contender. The tournament brought with it qualification for Kōshien, the promise of joining baseball champions from across the Empire of Japan and the prestige such an honor would bring saturating coverage of the tournament. On this occasion the Kanō team performed admirably, winning four games in a row on its way to securing the championship, including an 11–10 victory over Taipei Commercial School.[12] More than fifteen thousand people attended the final game.[13]

The All-Island Secondary School Baseball Tournament had been founded in 1923 with the purpose of selecting a Taiwanese champion to send to the National High School Baseball Championship in Japan after agitation by baseball enthusiasts in the colony following the admission of teams from Hokkaido, Manchuria, and Korea. Until

1931, however, the predominantly Taipei-based representatives at the games in Kōshien Stadium had made little impact.[14] Possibly as a result, coverage of Kanō's participation in the Japanese tournament was initially rather muted in the Taipei-centered press. In this respect at least Kanō received the same treatment as any other Taiwanese representative at the empire-wide tournament, the glory and glamour of participation in the prestigious events at Kōshien somewhat tempered by consistent mediocrity. Kanō's formal submission to the tournament by the Taiwanese Baseball Association received some attention, but there was little of the enthusiasm and excitement usually reserved for touring teams visiting Taipei.[15] Coverage of the high school tournament appeared in the form of brief bylines and match summaries for all games played.[16] This changed after Kanō's first game in the tournament, when the colonial newspaper reported the team's warm reception in Japan.[17] The crowd attending the first game had shown its appreciation for the endeavors of this "unique" team, cheering on successful hits and the Kanō base runners.[18] Kanō's second positive result in the tournament, and the accompanying score of 19-7, signaled an acceleration in attention to the team's progress. The article about it included a full recap of the game typical of baseball games that drew large interest in the colony as Kanō's momentum gripped the public imagination.[19]

Interest continued to build now that the Kanō team had successfully qualified for the tournament's semifinal.[20] The team defeated Kokura Engineering School, 10-2, continuing what had become a dominant display in the tournament, the press in Taipei now confidently describing not just the colony's representative's wins, but also the wide margin of victory.[21] On the same day the paper carried a brief article relaying the expectations of an Osaka-based baseball fan on the upcoming finals between Kanō and Chūkyō Business School, indicating confidence that the Taiwanese team held a strong advantage over its Japanese opponent.[22] Unfortunately for the young men from Jiayi, Chūkyō proved too good for them, and their run was at an end after suffering a 4-1 defeat.[23] The Kanō team had reached the finals at the Kōshien tournament but fallen short of winning it all, despite an aggregate score of 32 runs scored (with 16 runs against) in a run in the sport's most famous and celebrated tournament that utterly outshone all previous showings by Taiwanese teams.[24]

Getting to the finals had been enough to make the Kanō players superstars in Taiwan. Star pitcher Wu Mingjie's home welcomed journalists and photographers on the day of the final game.[25] The Wu family gathered at a public club in Miaoli, Taiwan, as the pitcher's father was joined by forty fans listening to the broadcast of the game's result on the club radio. Though disappointed by the result, the crowd generally agreed that despite the loss, there was not much difference in skill between the two competing teams.[26] The following day, the *Nichi Nichi Shimpō* carried an article focusing on the four aboriginal Taiwanese players who had started the final game at Kōshien Stadium.[27] The article stressed the merits of the young men as indistinguishable from those of the citizens of Japan proper, citing their diligence and quiet, bordering on shy, manner.[28] This effort to present the young athletes as supremely civilized—and therefore only distant relatives of their fellow aboriginal Taiwanese—was the exception rather than the norm in Japanese-language coverage. The newspaper did not present the Kanō team as an "aboriginal" or even "savage" side as it had exclusively presented the Nōkō team only a few years earlier. In fact, despite the gradual increase in the side's fortunes over the previous three years, it took an astonishing run at Kōshien for the team to truly capture the imagination of the *Nichi Nichi Shimpō* editors, earning headlines and coverage to match those of any baseball team on the newspaper's pages. Even on the team's return to Taiwan, occasional headlines offered Kanō joint billing with the return of the Taiwan Transportation Department baseball team from a tour of Manchuria and northern Korea.[29] They at least enjoyed top billing, and returned to Tainan County as heroes.[30] Two weeks later its achievement was formally celebrated at the opening of a baseball tournament at the New Park stadium in Taipei.[31] The Kanō team's place in history was sealed.

What of Kanō's place in history? Where should it lie? Unlike the Nōkō team, "Kanō" survived as a team name celebrated by the public for years to follow, enjoying a more prominent position than Nōkō's in the popular memory of Taiwanese baseball even today. The Jiayi Agriculture and Forestry Institute continued to produce top-level baseball teams, though none were able to emulate the 1931 team's achievements.[32] The 1931 Kanō team became the face of baseball in Taiwan before the international successes of Little League teams in the late 1960s and early 1970s. Its multiethnic character has produced much grist for the mills of historians eager to look for the historical impact of baseball on the relations between Japan and its first colony. Tales of Kanō fans huddled around a common radio for news of the Kōshien games and the Kanō team's heroes' welcome back in Taipei and Tainan would support arguments that the 1931 success belied an underlying groundswell of popularity for the game in Taiwan as part of a singularly Taiwanese experience. However, the Kanō team ultimately reflected a victory for Taiwan in the context of its modern identity as a colony of Japan. Kanō's honorable defeat to a Japanese side, no matter how fine a sporting achievement, was another event in a shared experience between Taiwan and Japan dominated by the imperial power. Kanō had emerged as the crest of a wave of baseball's growth in popularity during the 1920s, but this growth still saw the predominance of colonial Japanese influence in the administration and practice of the game, particularly in northern Taiwan.

The established dominance of Japanese cultural norms and the lack of evidence that Taiwanese baseball players, on either the Kanō team or other teams, actively reacted against them or sought to undermine them points to a sporting community defined by the legitimacy and example of its core, emanating from Japan but enshrined in Kōshien. Furthermore, a convincing argument can be made that the Kanō team's success was another example of Japanese interaction with more civilized "savages" from the imperial fringe; the *Nichi Nichi Shimpō* was quick to adopt Kanō as a team fully representative of Taiwan, with relatively little comment on the ethnic composition of the team, certainly in comparison to the Nōkō team, which was defined entirely by its ethnicity. The multiethnic composition clearly suited Japanese ideals of civilizing Taiwan, and its importance can be reflected by the consistent use of the word "unique" to preface most mentions of the Kanō team in *Nichi Nichi Shimpō* articles, the exceptionalism of the group contributing to narratives of success in colonial policy driven ostensibly to engender communal harmony. However, the Kanō team's importance also derived from its exceptionalism on the field: Kanō remains only one of two non-Japanese teams to reach the final at Kōshien.[33] They had traveled to Olympus and nearly returned with fire.

Ultimately, although the four Kanō aboriginal Taiwanese athletes to start the final game at Kōshien drew attention and somewhat false praise due to their ethnic origins, ethnic Chinese Taiwanese pitcher Wu Mingjie was by far the star of the tour, pitching in all four of the games and maintaining a batting average of .432. He went on to play for Waseda University, further confirmation that his ability merited a place at one of the sport's higher tables.[34] Wu has been joined in celebrity by his coach, who in both Chinese- and Japanese-language accounts of the Kanō participation in the Kōshien tournament enjoys considerable praise for his open approach to team selection and dedication to "spartan" training methods. Kondō even had his players perform running drills on the boat to Japan with luggage in hand for added weight, so concerned was he at almost a week's loss of training time, an approach typical of the idealized Japanese approach to baseball based on teamwork and physical effort.[35] The presence of aboriginal Taiwanese players on the team clearly played into the complicated dynamics of Japanese imperialism, but ultimately Kanō reflected imperial success on a broader level through cooperation under Japanese leadership.

That is not to say that the Kanō team did not inspire young local Taiwanese who wished to reduce the dominance of colonial Japanese teams. Ethnic Chinese participation in Taiwanese baseball grew outside of Taipei in the 1930s. However, the performance at Kōshien was itself no great statement of Taiwanese independence. If anything, the successes enjoyed by the Kanō team en route to qualifying as the Taiwanese representative in the tournament did more to open doors for local Taiwanese in organized baseball. Since 1931 the Kanō team has grown in perceived importance as the years have passed and historians have had opportunities to discuss the ramifications of a group of young men of various ethnicities cooperating on a baseball field. Participation in baseball teams by ethnic Chinese Taiwanese grew in the early 1930s in large part thanks to the efforts of the Kanō team, but the disparity between a Taipei baseball scene dominated by colonial Japanese and the growth of teams in the south of the island featuring mostly ethnic Chinese and aboriginal Taiwanese players persisted. It is fascinating that the Kanō team's influence has been notable for those in Taiwan looking for the roots of baseball's existence as a national game, historians eager to accept the facts of Japanese influence but reluctant to depict the sport as a cultural hand-me-down from a larger and more powerful neighbor. For these historians 1931 remains "a glorious year."[36]

This sentiment is matched in the public sphere. *Kanō: Mogui shunlian* (Kanō: Monster training), the first volume of a three-part graphic novel series accompanying the 2014 film *Kanō* in celebrating the famous 1931 youth baseball team, opens with a handful of pages depicting the city of Jiayi in an art style completely different from the standard manga drawings that follow in the pages of the story itself. The clean, angular lines and effusive typography of the book's pages are preceded by an almost impressionistic collection of images of bucolic colonial Taiwan. A young couple shares a bicycle by a tree under the warm, dim glow of a late spring sun; farmers work in the fields; young men in full baseball uniform trot past their school and through the town itself. The young men are mostly faceless, and the features of the initially indifferent but ultimately rejoicing Jiayi populace are similarly roughly sketched. The unspecific art style adds a sense of myth to it all, focuses the reader's attention not on the young men's identities or even their accomplishments but their determination. Their long, trudging runs through the fields and past the buildings on the outskirts of Jiayi end at the fountain in the center of town, the same place where the players later cavort in front of throngs of locals waving Japanese flags. This introduction, essentially a series of images with headlines and brief descriptions, happily declares that the Jiayi Agriculture and Forestry Institute produced Taiwan's "first baseball miracle."[37]

The graphic novels are a tie-in with the movie, and as such the illustrations provided at the beginning of this initial volume represent storyboarding work. The second and third volumes begin with still images from the film itself. Taken together, the graphic novels and the film constitute an unselfconsciously commercial enterprise, with the first two volumes ending so abruptly as to barely qualify as cliffhangers and neither medium shy in emphasizing melodrama. Still there is something genuine, almost sweet, to the graphic novels' production in particular. Each book ends with a postscript, a sketched comic piece over a couple of pages describing the reactions of a young fan to the release of both the graphic novels and the film. The series also takes seriously its position in the creation of a piece of public history: the first volume ends with a concise but responsible history of the Kanō team and its adventures in Japan; the second, with biographies of each major figure depicted in the film and the actor who played that part; the third, with a brief production diary showing shots behind the scenes of crew working on the film and actors in full costume. This attention to detail and the determination to follow specific historical narratives in the 2014 film and these books are nothing new in the Taiwanese experience of celebrating the Kanō team as part of the evolution of a Taiwanese identity through the period of colonial rule. The team has retroactively become a symbol of universally admired characteristics such as bravery and self-sacrifice that fit neatly within a narrative easily celebrated by everyone in Taiwan.

The narrative neatly fits the complexities of modern Taiwanese nationalism. The movement, though in theory unified within the broader goals of the Democratic People's Party (DPP) and the Pan-Green political faction it leads, reflects the DPP's origins in the *dangwai* movement, a group of activists in the 1970s and 1980s seeking to break down the constraints on democratic representation enshrined by the GMD's continued support of martial law. Despite desires from outside Taiwan to break down the island's status into one or another variation of a "renegade province," domestic political and ideological disputes alike converge and diverge on representations of Taiwan. Taiwanese nationalism is inherently nuanced by necessity, lacking Sun Yat-sen's emulation of ethnocentrism, presented as a Chinese adoption of the original European model. *Kanō* offers an opportunity to celebrate unity, the existence of a Taiwanese experience that is neither Chinese nor Japanese. This nuancing allows the team to serve as a stable touchstone within what Steven Phillips describes as the "shifting mixture of competing values," the amorphous body of Taiwanese nationalist sentiment that seeks to embrace creative interpretations of an ethnic but unified "Taiwanese" identity as much as it looks to Wilsonian-influenced precepts of national character.[38]

The politics of the film and the accompanying comics reflect this multifaceted identity, but the production of the film lies within a Taiwanese public narrative that seeks to celebrate Taiwanese achievement without necessarily driving toward a clear political message that would bring controversy. On day ninety-eight of the film shoot Japanese and Taiwanese members of the crew wore clothing to show their loyalties in advance of a baseball game between Japan and Taiwan that evening, and the rival fans on set had plenty of fun joking about the connections between the contest that night and the content of the film on which they were working.[39] On set, as in the film itself, the potential fault lines among interpretations of Taiwanese loyalty formed by present-day views on the viability of a Taiwanese nation-state were apparently put mostly to the side. This little moment of levity on set also highlights the remarkable comfort with which the Kanō story embraces the role of the Empire of Japan in producing the heroes of the tale. Indeed the entire narrative structure relies heavily on Japanese recognition of Kanō's achievements. The film begins with a group of Japanese World War II soldiers traveling in Taiwan on their way to the Philippines and bantering about the course the war will take, with one of them asking his friend to wake him from his sleep when they reach "Kagi," the town of Jiayi. A third soldier immediately recognizes the name as "that of the baseball team from Kōshien." The film ends with the valiant finalists saluting a crowd roaring its support and a tender moment on the ship home as they play baseball together and hold aloft the Asahi Medal, a trophy created for them in their honor by the *Asahi Shimbun*. An interstitial scene just before this moment informs the audience that the original medal was lost during the war, but second baseman So Seisei returned to Kōshien in 1996 to receive a replacement in celebration of the team's sixty-fifth anniversary.[40]

The film's politics should not be written off too quickly, however. The choice of language in the film's original cut, with Japanese dominant, supplemented by local Taiwanese dialects but with an absence of Mandarin, makes a clear play for historical accuracy. The prominent role ascribed to the Empire of Japan in what is essentially an underdog story, complete with a score hovering somewhere between maudlin and opportunistic, very much supports the portrayal of the profound uniqueness of the team's achievements. *Kanō* does something interesting. It embraces complexity. The film ends with the young men looking across the sea toward Taiwan, joyfully holding aloft their trophy and declaring they are coming home. The film's final lines are given to its avowedly most important and central figure, Japanese coach Kōndo Hyotarō, who is asked by one of his players what awaits the team upon its return, the young man doing the asking unsure if he can expect to be greeted as hero or failure. Kōndo tells him to expect "boundless fields of gold swaying in the wind."[41] The statement, clearly tugging at the audience's heartstrings, places Kanō firmly within the context of its bucolic purity. However, given a framing device featuring Japanese soldiers being sent to war in Southeast Asia, the presentation of Kanō's journey to Kōshien and the importance of Japanese assent to the team's relevance becomes significantly more bittersweet. The Japanese soldiers are young men given only a hint of the danger that awaits them when they travel further south. The individual tragedies likely faced by these men intertwine with Kanō's success thus coming in the bright light of a brief imperial glow. *Kanō* accepts and potentially celebrates the Empire of Japan as a force of change in Taiwanese history but teleologically as a transient environment within which a cohesive Taiwanese identity grew.

This framework may not quite allow Kanō to be all things to all people, but it does allow the team to become a prominent example of how historical representations neatly encapsulate the ambiguity of Taiwanese nationalism and Taiwanese identity. In recent years Kanō has increasingly become representative of Taiwanese ambivalence to Japanese colonial rule. Liu Wan-lai, a noted translator of Japanese works into Chinese during the postwar period, chose to title his 2015 autobiography *Memoirs of an Old Kanō*, despite his having been a child of two at the time of Kanō's great Kōshien moment. Liu chose the title because of an enduring fondness for his time as a student at the Jiayi Agriculture and Forestry Institute and a pride in his origins as a native of Tainan, but the usage is intriguing. His writing offers a detailed look into the life of a Taiwanese person growing up under the Japanese flag and coming into adulthood at the end of World War II. Spending very little time on his years as a translator during the postwar martial law period, Liu instead reflects on his youth with the eyes of a historian. His pride in being an "Old Kanō" may derive mostly from his experiences as a student, but the nod to the exploits of the baseball team is there. As Taiwanese historian Zhou Wanyao notes in her foreword, Liu knew that readers would be aware of Kanō thanks to the popular film, and he wanted to take the opportunity to share with them what the feeling of being a student at the institute was really like. He wrote about the colonial period to help his fellow Taiwanese dig deeper into the complexity of their history.[42] Liu's treatment of that complexity is intriguing, his discussions of colonial Japan focusing on his personal experiences up until his being drafted into the Japanese military during World War II. At that point his narrative shifts to become more familiar to GMD postwar historiography in his indictment of Japanese rule, not just in the details, but also in the broader sense of a Japanese revocation of Taiwan's five-thousand-year legacy of Chinese cultural development, a reminder that *Kanō*'s representations of Taiwanese identity during the colonial period are far from unopposed in Taiwanese discourse.[43]

Indeed the film's representation of colonial Taiwan as a halcyon period that saw the gentle incubation of a Taiwanese cohesiveness that reached beyond the polarities of Japanese and Chinese dominance is convenient, sometimes overly so in light of the realities of the Taiwanese governor-general's oversight of a police state, economic node of empire, and staging ground for further expansion.[44] The popular narrative centered on Taiwanese baseball increasingly invests in the viability of the sport as an incubator for Taiwanese nationalism in its infancy, the coming together of the major ethnic groups on the island both symbolic and representative of an ideological union of communities into a cohesive Taiwanese whole independent of the broader Japanese identity. Such analyses are seductive, particularly in light of the character of Taiwanese democracy since the 1990s, when democratization and Taiwanization came hand in hand, and particularly for Taiwanese baseball fans who can at times succumb to a mild panic at the state of the Taiwanese game. Massive bribery scandals at the very end of the twentieth century severely dented the reputation and popularity of the sport across the country. Baseball now competes with other interests for the attentions of young Taiwanese, suffering from the decline in participation in team sports increasingly typical in rich nations but also losing out most prominently to basketball for the attentions of young Taiwanese; the decline is a testament not to the long-term delayed success of Chiang Kai-shek's followers in promoting the game but to the continued aggression of the National Basketball Association in promoting itself in Asian markets, assisted by the success of ethnic Chinese players Yao Ming and Jeremy Lin, the latter an American-born son of Taiwanese immigrants. Baseball, however, has something Taiwanese basketball does not: signature victories against powerhouses of the sport, a record of success at youth level that rivals any other nation, and a credible claim to the status of "national game."

The Kanō team sits comfortably within such a narrative, routinely included in treatments of Taiwanese baseball's evolution as a clearly and distinctly Taiwanese team that succeeded during the colonial period, emblematic of the sport's inherent redoubtable character and lasting viability in the face of its various obstacles.[45] The team is also cited in more thoughtful and complex analyses. Xie Shiyuan, primary authority on the history of Taiwanese baseball, argues that the Kanō team represented the coming together of various ethnocultural sects of an identifiably Taiwanese society and that victories at Kōshien represented the forging of effort and accommodation across societal boundaries that presented a clear Taiwanese consensus, made possible by the efforts of Japanese colonialism in seeking to transform the face of the aboriginal Taiwanese community but resulting in something other than the casting of new imperial subjects in a uniform Japanese mold.[46] For Xie baseball in the colonial period became a form of communication among communities, a transmitter of ideals, and a unifier of disparate identities. It is tempting to see local Taiwanese participation in the game as a riposte to Japanese imperial dominance and to see Kanō's performances in particular as a retort to the Japanese assumption of Asian leadership.

However, the structure of Taiwanese baseball, including the road to Kōshien, was entirely a Japanese construct, the product of an imperialist modernist project that sought to transform the colony. This it unquestionably did, and Taiwanese baseball clearly lay within the cultural sphere of the Japanese. The various tournaments held across Taiwan building up to the All-Island Secondary School Baseball Tournament, itself a qualifier for the main event in Kōshien, all led to the inexorable and ultimately unachieved prize of a Taiwanese champion of the Empire of Japan. The Kanō team's ethnic composition caused it to stand out amid its fellow teams because of the continued domination of the game by colonial Japanese. Those Japanese naturally viewed representation at Kōshien as the great validation of their community, created in emulation of the Japanese model. This is not a tale of a pusillanimous Taiwanese spirit cowering in abeyance as Han Chinese and aboriginal Taiwanese bowed before imperial masters; the bestowal of national identity to this team is something undertaken in reverse and with the postwar experience in its entirety behind us. That includes recent waves of support for Taiwanese independence (or at least clearer expressions of Taiwanese identity beyond Chinese irredentism), but it also includes the collective memory of victory after victory on American fields in the 1970s as Taiwanese children defeated the world. It is not hard to see why Taiwanese baseball fans would proudly situate Kanō as a precursor to such unlikely dominance of the mighty by the inhabitants of a small and isolated island off the coast of the Asian subcontinent. However, particularly given the lack of animus toward the colonial period more broadly, the Kanō players were hardly raiders from the periphery seeking to strike at the imperial core.

It is exactly the nature of Kanō's participation in the empire-wide Japanese baseball community that provides a useful window into discussions of the imperial period. Despite Kanō's going on to play at Kōshien three more times in the 1930s (1933, 1935, and 1936), reaching the finals in 1931 remains comfortably the high point for both the Kanō team itself and Taiwanese baseball during the colonial period more broadly. When we extrapolate from Taiwanese baseball a vehicle for Taiwanese nationalism, it allows us to skate past, as much as one possibly can, the intensification of propaganda and aggressive assimilation of 1930s Japanese rule, particularly after the outbreak of the Second Sino-Japanese War in 1937. Although major tournaments persisted into the 1940s, baseball joined other elements of colonial public life in fading before the needs and drive of national mobilization in support of Japan's war effort. Perhaps if the demands of war had not converted baseball fields into triage centers and emergency farmland, the increased pressures of Japanese ideological indoctrination may have drawn out clearer lines of opposition for local Taiwanese playing a Japanese game.[47] Instead we are left with a pleasantly complex treatment of the sport's role in forming Taiwanese identities. This elevates Taiwanese baseball beyond a dichotomy of colonizer and colonized competing across discourses on the same playing field, not through the rejection or marginalization of Japanese inputs but through the embrace of the colonial period's role in a historical dynamic that looks to that era as a moment of genesis.

Colonial Taiwan occupied a space during the colonial period between a late imperial identity and a postwar existence fraught with the fundamental sociopolitical changes brought by retrocession to the Republic of China, a Cold War existence characterized by friendship with and reliance upon the United States, and a democratic awakening that both feeds and is fed by a growing Taiwanese consciousness. The colonial period is not a prequel to this current state of Taiwanese mind, nor was it a sequel to the slow and painful collapse of China's last dynasty. The Japanese press in both Japan and Taiwan celebrated Kanō because of the perceived evidence that the colonial project was working, yes; the team's showing at Kōshien also reflected a return on more than two decades of effort by colonial Japanese in developing the game in Taiwan, crafting a sporting community as a cultural outcropping of the game at home. Kanō was a success on Japanese terms, winning games played by Japanese rules. Taiwanese baseball existed as a construction built on Japanese cultural foundations, and by every measure, bar its actually winning the whole thing, Kanō confirmed the legitimization of the sport in Taiwan as a cultural enterprise. The Kanō team achieved its greatest successes on Japanese soil with the assent of Japanese commentators and gatekeepers of cultural legitimacy; the players toiled together, under a Japanese coach, with all the classic austerity and stoicism of Japanese youth baseball, but assertions that Kanō's victories signaled the coming together of different Taiwanese ethno-social groups rather than an echo of deeply set Japanese dominance are essentially correct. This was not lame acceptance of Japanese superiority. It was celebration of a baseball community formed on the edge of empire looking to the imperial center for recognition. Kanō may indeed have fit Japanese visions of imperial harmony that by necessity played a little loose with the realities of the price of conquest and the continued inequity of colonial life, but it also represented a landmark achievement for a sporting community that increasingly dug its roots further beneath those Japanese cultural foundations to the laterite below, implanting a cultural practice born of Japanese experience into the memory of a nascent shared Taiwanese community. The two had fused together and would not easily be separated.

6 | Chiang's China and Taiwanese Baseball

The end of the war was not kind to Japan or its empire. Defeat was at first grinding, prolonged and horrific as Japanese soldiers and civilians held out against MacArthur's inexorable advance north along the western edges of the Pacific, then jarring in its suddenness. The American decision to drop atomic bombs on Japanese soil instantly set parameters for the shape of Japanese postwar identity. Emperor Hirohito's understated admission that the war had not gone according to expectations, broadcast across national radio, punctured the political cult established during the Meiji period and exposed the lofty claims of assured victory by the wartime military elite to the scorn of the Japanese public. Millions of Japanese troops and civilians found themselves stranded across the lands of Japan's now defunct empire, many living in fear of the wrath of liberated Filipinos, Manchurians, and other victims of Japanese war crimes. The colonies of Taiwan and Korea, erstwhile foundations of Japanese imperial reach, quickly assumed new roles in what was soon to become a new postwar order.

Taiwan's importance in the war was not merely symbolic. The island played an important role in Japanese logistics, with the application of the more aggressive assimilation policy *kōminka* following the needs of Japanese conquest, particularly following the Marco Polo Bridge Incident of 1937, which marked the beginning of the Second Sino-

Japanese War and World War II in East Asia, and the Japanese attack on Pearl Harbor in 1941. The colonial government pushed four core cultural practices in Taiwanese life: changing local names to Japanese names, teaching the Japanese language, imposing the Amaterasu sun goddess cult on private life, and abolishing local temples and the idols within. Results were mixed, particularly in the push for all Taiwanese to adopt Japanese names, the weakness of the measure emphasized by a lack of interest among both the colonial government and the Taiwanese population itself. *Kōminka*'s successes at any rate foundered on class divisions, with local Taiwanese elites coming ever closer to the Japanese culturally as those further down the socioeconomic ladder failed to embrace the new and more aggressive assimilation policies. Indeed even the most Japanese-friendly sections of the Taiwanese elite became frustrated at the barriers placed between them and their supposedly equal Japanese imperial siblings by the deeply ethnocentric political ideologies of wartime Japan.[1] Assimilation policies drifted further after 1940 as Taiwan's importance to Japan became ever more centered on the material needs of waging war, the deterioration of Taiwan's public cultural sphere highlighted by the collapse in coverage of baseball in the colonial press, culminating in a paltry two mentions of the sport in 1944.[2]

The Allies had by then made it clear, following the Cairo Conference in November 1943, that Taiwan would be returned to Chinese authority by the end of the war. The GMD established the Taiwan Investigation Committee in April 1944 to prepare for the coming retrocession, with an eye to the decolonization of the Taiwanese population and utilization of the island's industrial base in the coming war against Mao Zedong's Communist forces.[3] In the late 1940s hundreds of thousands of Chinese people retreated to Taiwan as the fortunes of the Communist forces improved in mainland China, leading directly to an increase of population density on the small island by 111.4 persons per square mile.[4] By 1949, with the People's Republic of China formally declared in Beijing, Taipei had become home to a Nationalist regime in exile. Chiang Kai-shek and his fellow Nationalists initially viewed the GMD retreat to Taiwan as a temporary contingency despite this defeat. Taipei was the wartime capital of the entire Chinese nation-state, the ROC the only viable heir to the 1911 revolution that had brought an end to imperial Chinese history. The Legislative Yuan and National Assembly continued to host representatives from all mainland provinces of the ROC, with those elected in 1947, before the Communist victory, essentially guaranteed political positions for life.[5] Chiang Kai-shek was very clear: the ROC held the legal right to govern all of China, and Mao Zedong's government had effectively temporarily usurped power. This point of view, though understandable given the difficult position in which ROC officials found themselves and consistent with Chiang Kai-shek's profound enmity for Mao Zedong and Chinese communism, effectively ignored the reality of the Chinese civil war. The Nationalists had comprehensively lost, their legitimacy on the mainland eroded by a failure to resist Japanese aggression or offer any satisfactory alternative to Communist promises of social justice. Furthermore, Taiwan was far from a willing Chinese province, grateful to return to the national bosom, having been released from the clutches of the villainous Japanese.

Instead the GMD returned to Taiwan to discover a local population that had been thoroughly influenced by Japanese culture, in no small part thanks to the pervasive influence of the Japanese educational system. Japanese-language use was common, as was the prevalence of Japanese loan words in the most popular Chinese language on the island, *minnanhua*.[6] Young Taiwanese played baseball, a team sport with a severely less visible presence in mainland China and clearly introduced by the Japanese authorities. Even the predominant architecture in the section of Taipei that had previously hosted the colonial government bore the mark of Japanese imperialism.[7] The apparent depth of Japanese cultural influence immediately became a point of concern for the GMD government. A robust language policy that aimed to make Mandarin Chinese the vernacular language of the entire island while eradicating all other linguistic choices for the local Taiwanese formed the center of GMD policy to de-Japanize the island. Chinese languages other than Mandarin—which was known in Taiwan according to GMD tastes as *guoyu*, or "national language"—were labeled as dialects: *fangyan*. The instruction of Mandarin, ostensibly to prepare the Taiwanese for the inevitable return of ROC power to the mainland, became a mark of loyalty to the newly arrived GMD and its government reestablished in Taipei. Language teachers arrived from the mainland in the years between retrocession and the end of the civil war as the GMD established an unrelenting system of instruction; the use of non-Mandarin languages was penalized using corporal punishment and public humiliations such as dialect boards, wooden boards hung around a child's neck to show that he or she had spoken incorrectly.[8] The intent was to homogenize the population of Taiwan and to bring those present before the mass immigrations of the late 1940s into line with the newly arrived Chinese. There would be a singular culture for the entire island, embodied by Chiang Kai-shek's conception of appropriate Chinese cultural norms and universal use of Mandarin as the vernacular.

In practice Chiang's decision to promote a rigidly defined concept of Chinese nationalism merely created two sets of ethnic Chinese social groups on Taiwan following retrocession that reinforced the divisions between the existing Chinese population that had endured colonial rule and the newly arrived population fleeing communism. *Benshengren*, literally translated as "people of this province," became a signifier for those Han Chinese and other ethnic groups who had lived on Taiwan prior to 1945. *Waishengren*, literally translated as "people of a foreign province," were those who had arrived after retrocession, particularly those who had arrived as part of the massive influx of people fleeing Communist rule. *Benshengren* soon came to see that a new social and political order approved by the new arrivals would take precedence in postwar Taiwan. The divisions were clear all over Taiwanese society, with fluency in Mandarin being a prerequisite for government jobs or postings in the military, a distinct form of discrimination, beyond the classroom humiliations at the hands of teachers from the mainland, that further sought to dissuade Taiwanese from using "dialects."[9] The GMD government sought to make it clear that there was a defined, acceptable form of Chinese identity and that the local Taiwanese were fully expected to conform. The Japanese influence had been poisonous, and the GMD now sought to right the wrongs. The local Taiwanese in this relationship were very much acted upon with little opportunity for agency of their own; Taiwanese elites had worked with and to a great extent had been formed by colonial Japanese political and economic infrastructures, and by 1948 GMD suspicion dashed local elite hopes of involvement in direct governance of the island.[10]

A cult of personality surrounding Chiang further enshrined the exclusivity of *waishengren* control over Taiwan's postwar political frameworks. GMD inclinations to celebrate leaders at the peak of a Leninist political framework long predated retrocession: during the Nanjing Decade of 1927–37, Chiang sought to position himself simultaneously as the disciple of founding father Sun Yat-sen and a paternal ruler for the Chinese people, his authority rooted in the location of the fusion of modernity and Chinese culture in his own public person. As Jeremy E. Taylor points out, this cult did not simply transfer to Taiwan wholesale but rather shifted to "co-opt both the physical and intellectual residue of Japanese colonialism in Taiwan." The cult further found a role in postwar Taiwan as a method of maintaining connection with the now lost mainland for those who chose to participate in the conflation of Chiang's person with the concept of a modern Republican China that retained legitimate claims on all of China, not just the small island to which Chiang had fled.[11] With GMD claims to the control of all of China both abstracted and foundational to its own political legacy, the constant flagging of Chinese nationalism became part and parcel of public life in postwar Taiwan.[12]

There was, perhaps, an opening for baseball to become a component of this publicly promoted and celebrated government ideology. The question lay over the sport's identity—that is, whether baseball was the sport of the colonizer or whether it was sufficiently indigenized to suit GMD purposes.[13] The answer was apparently neither. Taiwanese baseball continued throughout the late 1940s and early 1950s virtually untouched. Public athletic events encompassing numerous different sports were frequent, with baseball often included among many and on occasion as the only reason for an event. There is very little sign of a decline in enthusiasm for baseball among Taiwanese, nor is there much evidence of a government crackdown to match the stern anti-Japanese tone of other government policies. In fact baseball continued to be a salient factor in everyday life and public celebrations that reinforced the harmonious nature of relations among political groups on the island as envisioned and tacitly enforced by the GMD. In 1951 celebrations in Taizhong to honor the resident military forces as part of the Mid-Autumn Festival included offerings from the public of traditional mooncakes, and musical groups performed as throngs of Taizhong residents gathered to honor the troops. Local city officials expressed their happiness at the establishment of an army barracks in the city and made ceremonial gifts on behalf of the city's community to the barracks of two pieces of baseball equipment and one piece of basketball equipment.[14] Sporting events specifically set up for Taiwanese youth also continued after retrocession. In the same month that Taizhong residents were handing out mooncakes and baseball bats to the local garrison as a sign of their support and appreciation, the city's mayor, Wu Sanlian, attended a three-team baseball tournament among Taiping Pacific School, Yingqiao School, and Zhong Shan School. Taiping School won both of its games to win the tournament, and Mayor Wu handed out medals to participants on all three teams.[15] Six years after retrocession and two years after the final retreat of Chinese Nationalists to Taiwan, baseball, despite self-evident connections to the colonial period and Japanese rule, continued to thrive. In Taizhong, like in many other cities and towns in Taiwan, GMD language policy initiatives were well under way. De-Japanization had been in full swing for several years. Yet baseball was openly an important part of community activities involving local schools and was even represented in ceremonies honoring the GMD troops garrisoned in the city.

The interaction between the families of Taizhong who lined up to cheer on the garrisoned troops and the troops themselves is interesting. GMD policy successfully regulated participation in the armed forces so that advanced fluency in the "standard" use of the language was a prerequisite for career advancement. Many of the troops, particularly so soon after the retreat from the mainland, were *waishengren*. The choice to include both baseball and basketball equipment in the gift (noted above) alluded to the popularity of the latter game among main-landers. However, despite this open tolerance of baseball in the new *waishengren*-dominated Taiwanese society, baseball remained a game heavily influenced by the legacy of its importation to the island. The name of the game changed overnight, one Chinese character replaced to tweak the Japanese word *yakyū* (野球) to the Chinese *bangqiu* (棒球). As for more substantial changes, there was no way to regulate the lan-guage used on the field, as Taiwanese baseball players continued to speak among themselves in *minnanhua*, using Japanese loan words from the original English to describe positions on the field or typical actions. Some players even spoke openly in Japanese, an action other-wise unthinkable in postwar Taiwanese society.[16] The use of common words such as *picchaa* and *kyacchaa*, katakana transliterations of the American words for pitcher and catcher respectively, was strictly for-bidden beyond baseball playing fields.[17]

GMD encouragement of new normative cultural standards in Tai-wanese society was not solely ideological; Chiang Kai-shek had prac-tical political reasons for curbing open discussions of many aspects of Taiwanese society. As late as 1960 Chiang responded to the popular protests in South Korea surrounding Syngman Rhee's resignation by approving the arrest of *Free China Review* publisher Lei Zhen on charges of sedition, despite increased pressure from the United States to avoid actions that limited democratic opportunity in Taiwan. Lei's sin had been in his plans to form a new China Democratic Party to build on the informal opposition group he had started three years earlier. Chiang was fully aware that the GMD would be vulnerable to an embarrassing defeat in any free elections and had no intention of allowing a new party.[18] Political persecution in Taiwan continued unabated, system-atized in a context of coercion and the suppression of civil rights that assumed the correctness and predominance of "Chinese" (that is, mainland Chinese) cultural traits. The GMD was in this regard a curi-ous political beast: a Leninist party focused on selective membership, nationalist ideology, a centralized decision-making structure, and con-trol of the military that saw itself not as an actor in a struggle between progressive and reactionary forces but as an arbiter and guarantor of moral and cultural correctness.[19] That correctness needed to fit Chiang's own view of Chinese culture as well as the needs of a Taiwanese postwar reality defined by the newly installed dominant superpower of the Pacific: the United States.

Chiang's arrival in Taiwan was less the glorious return implied by the language of retrocession but the latest stop in a series of retreats that had taken him from the southern capital of Nanjing to the more isolated, defensible, and arguably less prestigious cities of Chongqing and Chengdu on a helter-skelter route down through southern central China. In the United States much angst was expressed, much ink was spilled, and many hands were wrung over the "loss" of China, but it was Chiang who had lost and lost utterly. Furthermore, Taiwan would now be part of an American cultural domain or at the very least be defined in large part by its role in American foreign policy. Taiwan became an "unsinkable aircraft carrier" in the Cold War, as General Douglas MacArthur so memorably and rather insensitively put it, part of its new role, that of American perimeter defense on the western edge of the Pacific Ocean.[20] With the intensification of the Cold War that followed the Korean War and the subsequent first Taiwan Straits crisis of 1954, the American president, Dwight Eisenhower, and his secretary of state, John Foster Dulles, agreed to Chiang Kai-shek's request for support and entered into a mutual defense treaty between the United States and the ROC.[21]

By the early 1950s baseball often featured as another form of cultural interaction between American military personnel in Taiwan and representatives of the ROC government. Organized exhibitions between Military Assistance Advisory Group Taiwan (MAAG) personnel and Taiwanese teams instantly assumed a certain level of formality; the *Lianhe Bao* (United Daily News) frequently referred to Americans representing MAAG under the personal leadership of General William C. Chase, and the newspaper was not shy in complimenting the Americans' ball-playing skills. Despite the Taiwanese press's attempts at emphasis on sports more popular in the mainland, such as table tennis and basketball, baseball quickly assumed the role of an avenue of cultural diplomacy between MAAG personnel and their hosts.[22] One early example of such interaction came in September 1951, only a few months after the establishment of MAAG in April of that year, with a game between a Taiwanese side and a baseball team from the American military held on the grounds of National Taiwan University. The result gave each side a suitable amount of respectability, a close game that lasted ten innings, giving a narrow victory to the Americans.[23]

Citizens of the ROC were aware of the Americans' affection for the game they referred to as their national pastime. In a slight mistranslation of comments made by President Truman at a press conference in 1952, the *Lianhe Bao* reported the American president stated that politics was "no different from baseball or football; it is a game that Americans like to play."[24] The actual quote, in relation to whether Truman would run for the Senate after completing the term of his presidency, described politics as "the great American game," defeating sports such as baseball and football.[25] The *Lianhe Bao* article failed to distinguish between American football and Association Football, the latter of which was a popular sport with the ROC authorities. In any case the exclusive role of baseball in sporting cultural exchanges between American military personnel stationed in Taiwan and local athletes, as opposed to other sports enjoyed by the Taiwanese such as basketball or tennis, made the American affection for the game clear. In 1953 MAAG personnel competed with the Taiwanese provincial champions, the Banks Association team, in a game the Taiwan Baseball Association titled a "Celebration of Chinese and American Cooperation."[26] The game, organized to celebrate the second anniversary of MAAG's presence in Taiwan, also served as an opening event to an upcoming international "soft ball" baseball tournament to be held in Taipei.[27] General Chase was again invited to attend, with the promise of receiving both the honor of the first pitch and a bouquet of flowers for his troubles.[28] Unfortunately the game was postponed three times due to inclement weather, finally seemingly going ahead almost two weeks later than planned and somewhat in the shadow of the upcoming international tournament.[29] However, the game was postponed yet again. Undeterred, the plan for the game proceeded over a month later, with General Chase still fully expected to throw out the first pitch and politely receive his bouquet from the delegates of the Young Women's Association.[30] This the general finally did, in front of thousands of spectators in New Park in Taipei who watched the Taiwanese champions narrowly defeat the MAAG athletes, 3–2.[31]

Taiwan's place within the emerging postwar international order now became tied to its relationship with the United States. The state-supported (and censored) press regularly featured articles on international competitions featuring the Chinese national baseball team and exhibitions among various representative teams of Chinese athletes and teams composed of Americans from MAAG. The games between Taiwanese teams and MAAG personnel reflected another utilization of the game by the ROC government: a tool for international exchange. The GMD willfully refused to acknowledge Taiwanese baseball's colonial roots, both as a muted tribute to its American allies and as part of a concerted push for Chinese nationalists on Taiwan to treat baseball as a modern, international game rather than an importation from a regional neighbor and former imperial power.[32] When we consider the games between American military personnel in Taiwan and local athletes, baseball becomes another tool to maintain Taiwan's Cold War relationship with the United States. Chiang Kai-shek was well aware that American support for Taiwan was by no means guaranteed, and he had experience in courting public opinion to put pressure on American leaders.[33] Indeed, if one is to support the assertion that the ROC government's aggressive promotion of Chinese culture in postwar Taiwan was a strategic choice, then the willing support of the American pastime should also be seen in the light of active efforts on behalf of the GMD to maintain positive relations with the United States.[34]

Baseball fit within the developing Cold War model of international diplomacy via cultural exchange, allowing Taiwan to identify with the American side of a global cultural dichotomy frequently characterized in the sporting realm by conflict between two distinct civilizations.[35] Although the government-supported press did not attempt to present baseball as a sport invested with some type of innately cultural element borne of distinct Chinese incidence, the colonial (and thus Japanese) origins of Taiwanese baseball were not dwelled upon at length.

Instead the press frequently promoted the activities of the national baseball team, often as a priority when compared to domestic adult amateur baseball. In 1951, for example, the *Lianhe Bao* presented a brief announcement of the sixth annual Provincial Men's Baseball Tournament principally to convey the news that several of the nineteen teams in attendance would feature players who had participated in the national team's tour to the Philippines earlier that year.[36] In 1952 the Provincial Physical Education Association created the Free Chinese Amateur Baseball Association, ostensibly to promote the sport among Chinese both at home and abroad. The formation of the association was a prerequisite for membership in the International Baseball Federation and thus entry into organized play against other national amateur teams such as those of the United States and Japan.[37] A few weeks after its formation, the newspaper announced the terms for qualification from Asia for a global amateur baseball tournament in 1954. A tournament the following year would feature the ROC, Japan, the Philippines, South Korea, and Thailand. The article somewhat redundantly pointed out that the ROC and Japanese teams should be the strongest of the five.[38]

In April 1953 a representative ROC team traveled to Manila to compete against similarly organized teams representing the Philippines and Japan.[39] The Taiwanese players sported red uniforms with the initials IWBT emblazoned on their shirts, the final letter referencing the fact that this team was officially named the Taiwan Representative Team, as apart from the "Free China" team that participated on Taiwan's behalf in sanctioned World Amateur Baseball competitions.[40] However, the actual identity of the team is confusing despite the explicit use of the word "Taiwan." Upon its return to Taipei the team was described in full as the "Free China Taiwan Baseball Team." The following year, in a trip to South Korea, there was no ambiguity about the identity of the team, with the title "Taiwan" dropped in favor of the exclusive use of the adjective "Chinese."[41] The tour itself was considered a success, with a loss to a Japanese semiprofessional side tempered by two victories against American teams, including a victory over an American Navy team at Subic Air Force Base in Olangapo, Philippines.[42] Still confusion reigned, and such confusion was not incidental: the naming of Taiwanese sporting teams would remain controversial until well after 1972, when the People's Republic of China's admission to the United Nations resulted in years of fraught negotiations mediated by the International Olympic Committee, which saw the formulation of the "Chinese Taipei" moniker for Taiwanese teams going forward.[43]

Later in 1954 the ROC again sent a baseball team to the Philippines, this time to represent the country in the inaugural Asian Baseball Championship alongside the hosts, Japan and South Korea. On this occasion there was even less ambiguity than before, with the Taiwanese team described simply as the Republic of China team.[44] This official identity did not help the athletes much on the field, as the ROC players finished dead last as the host nation won out.[45] The team lost all three of its games, betraying a glaring difference in ability between the Taiwanese players and their foreign rivals. A disapproving *Lianhe Bao* reporter recommended four measures to improve national performances going forward, including the need to improve defensive skills and to hit breaking balls rather than relying on an ability to hit the more straightforward fastball pitches; the reporter directly tied the perceived weaknesses of the Taiwanese athletes on the field to the ROC's international reputation.[46]

The second Asian Baseball Championships were held in Manila again in December 1955. The ROC team fared slightly better this time, defeating the hosts in its first game and going on to finish second behind a dominant Japan team. Future Asian Championships were confirmed for 1957, 1959, and 1961 featuring the same four teams.[47] It was no coincidence that the Philippines, an Asian nation with close ties to the United States, should feature so heavily in the beginning of the Asian Baseball Championships, serving as host for the first two years. Nor is it a coincidence that Taiwanese teams, such as that in 1953, made additional trips to Manila for exhibition games. The GMD refusal to admit the colonial legacy of Taiwanese baseball fit neatly with American expectations of why Asians might play the American pastime, both stances fitting neatly with the new postwar and Cold War order in the South China Sea. Taipei, Manila, Seoul, and Tokyo all now acted as partners with the United States in defiance against the Asian communism emanating from Beijing, with its deep and insidious roots in Moscow.

The question of to what extent baseball became a state-sponsored sport in the decades immediately following 1945 is tricky. Public GMD acceptance of the sport, particularly in connection with Cold War alliances, created what Andrew Morris describes as a "safe" realm for a form of Taiwanese consciousness that enjoyed continuity through the otherwise traumatic historical break of retrocession.[48] The absence of state interference, as opposed to any active efforts at construction, helped ensure that realm's existence. Apart from its relationship with the United States, the GMD's interest in promoting baseball was half-hearted at best. Youth baseball, which had flourished under colonial rule, and adult amateur baseball received limited media coverage until the late 1960s though games continued to be carried on radio and television. There was no overt censorship or media blackout of the game but the *Lianhe Bao*, in loyal operation as a government-friendly publication, assiduously sidestepped any acknowledgement of the game's roots in colonial times.

This silence stood in stark contrast with GMD support for Chinese citizens who celebrated cultural homogeneity as part of the state's active promotion of itself, with Chiang at its head, as the true guardian of Chinese culture in the face of Communist iconoclasm and Mao's own predilection for social conflict. Take, for example, the highly publicized travels of a fifty-member troupe of Taiwan-based Beijing opera performers on a tour of Europe between September 1957 and February 1958, performing on 105 occasions in seven countries from Ireland to Portugal. GMD officials saw the London performances in particular as a huge political success, particularly in light of the British decision to extend official recognition to the People's Republic of China in 1950.[49] The decision of the London *Times* to label the Taiwanese troupe as practitioners of the "original" Beijing opera particularly infuriated the apparatchiks in Beijing. In Taiwan itself Beijing opera was given a central role in the formation of the national culture, which was a euphemism for cultural norms that Chiang and his advisers considered typical of their preferred path for modern China. In other words, Chinese culture in line with that seen to be correct by Chiang and his contemporaries was promoted, while cultural forms indicative of a distinctive Taiwanese quality were actively suppressed. In 1960s Taiwan the opera troupes that regularly performed for the military began to schedule more regular public appearances, as the medium was labeled "national opera," promoted at the expense of the more local Taiwanese variants where performers sang in *minnanhua*.[50] As far as European audiences were concerned, the opera performances reflected an appropriate reflection of Chinese high culture. The visit of the Taiwanese Beijing opera performers was likely "to make us revise some of our definitions," the *Irish Independent* wrote, noting that by contrast the "Italians would not know what the [visitors] meant" when speaking of opera.[51] The newspaper reported with great interest the long career path of the typical Chinese performer from a young age and repeated the ROC officials' accounts of the cultural form's popularity in China. Chiang Kai-shek would have been happy to see the Irish publication inform its readership that this was indeed "the Chinese Classical Theatre as it has been preserved" by the company as it fled from mainland China only a few years before.[52]

The refusal of the GMD to coopt baseball can be only partly explained by a preference among most of the mainlanders for basketball as their team sport of choice. The early 1950s offered the ideal opportunity for the state to recognize baseball as an indigenous sport, but this did not happen outside of clearly demarcated frameworks surrounding Taiwan's relationship with the United States and other Cold War allies. If anything, this diversion of the sport's ideological trappings at the international level successfully headed off the possibility of baseball's becoming a field of contestation among conflicting versions of Taiwanese identity. Taiwanese identity was a vague concept before retrocession, but when the Taiwanese populace was faced with an aggressive definition of its supposed Chinese identity, imposed by the GMD government, many began to reexamine what it meant to be "Taiwanese." The GMD found it difficult to understand baseball in Taiwan, a social phenomenon that could be traced back to Japanese colonial rule, a time before massacres such as the February 28 Incident of 1947, a violent moment in the history of the island that has since taken on intense symbolism for Taiwanese nationalists.[53] The didactic nature of GMD pronouncements on local politics and national identity had been present during colonial times, particularly after the militarization of politics in Japan, but the GMD was more aggressive in demanding Taiwanese loyalty as an inherent principle of each individual's identity and heritage. The reclamation demanded by the GMD surpassed Japanese efforts at assimilation prior to the late 1930s. It was all the more surprising perhaps that Taiwanese baseball could survive between the extremes of a more fully throated public sponsorship and outright prohibition.

This place for baseball in a large ideological gray area, when not cited specifically as part of the ROC's Cold War obligations, also skirted around a more traditional postcolonial form for the sport. The GMD's distaste for baseball's Japanese roots prevented it from successfully celebrating the sport as a tool to fight the colonizer, a dynamic further hamstrung by the awkward friendship necessitated by the realities of East Asian postwar geopolitics. The years immediately following retrocession provided a window for the Taiwanese baseball community to assert itself as the guardian of a Taiwanese identity in opposition to colonial dominance, but this didn't happen. The realities of Chiang's police state and the GMD's confrontational approach to Taiwanese languages truncated opportunities to stoke possible anti-colonial sentiment. In fairness, such opportunities were hard to come by to begin with; the failure of baseball to emerge as a postcolonial sport defined in opposition to Japan rested only in part on the refusal of the GMD to take it on more vigorously, owing a far greater debt to the importance of the wider Japanese cultural sphere in the foundations of the game in Taiwan.

This reality would be difficult for Chiang and his peers to stomach. The Japanese had contributed to Chiang's greatest failure. By the end of 1949, with the ROC government ensconced in Taipei and Mao Zedong the declared leader of the People's Republic of China in Beijing, Chiang found himself defenestrated by one enemy and living among the cultural and political infrastructure provided over five decades of colonial rule by the other. In fifty years the Japanese authorities had succeeded in introducing a sophisticated educational system to Taiwan, in improving the infrastructure of the island to support continued sugar production, and in implementing Japanese as the official language of the colony.[54] The Japanese also left the Taiwanese people with an appreciation for baseball. The popularity of the sport represented the impact of Japanese colonial rule and the extent to which the Japanese government had left a profound cultural mark on the colony, alongside the prevalence of the Japanese language and the established practice of Taiwanese parents to send their academically talented children to Japan for secondary- and third-level studies.[55] The introduction of baseball to Taiwan alongside all types of physical exercise, from tennis to soccer to general calisthenics, had been a crucial element in shifting Taiwanese culture away from its predominant Chinese cultural heritage toward something more in line with Meiji Japan's modernizing aspirations.[56] Mainland China itself had also undergone serious cultural transformations since the fall of the Qing Empire in 1911, but the GMD retreated to an island in the late 1940s that had lain separate from the massive cultural and intellectual tides of the nationalist period in China, from the May Fourth Movement of 1919 to the New Culture Movement of the 1930s to, finally, the popular support for land reform and redistribution of wealth that resulted in the Chinese Communist Party's resounding victory in the Chinese civil war.[57] GMD policies seeking to root out Japanese influences in Taiwan defied these historical divisions.

Taiwanese baseball failed to fall into a postcolonial dichotomy of oppressors and oppressed because there were three positions of identity emerging on the island throughout the twentieth century, with GMD postwar efforts severely muddying a more traditional view of the recently departed Japanese imperialists as nemesis to emerging concepts of Taiwanese nationalism. If one takes the view that baseball was a unifying force in Taiwanese society before retrocession, one of the elements that brought disparate social groups on the island together, the context of social relations had now completely changed, with the entrenchment of a culture of opposition well under way. Children in Taipei and Gaoxiong who picked up a bat and ran the bases began to become involved in decisions more politically confrontational than ever before. However, the process was gradual; the bifurcation of Taiwanese identity, thanks to the influx of an entirely new social and political class, was far from immediate. Postwar Taiwanese baseball existed as the product of two competing identities, the only recently departed Japanese colonial mindset and a highly prescriptive Chineseness adopted and promoted by the newly arrived GMD government. In practice the sporting infrastructure of the colonial period persisted with little change other than the departure of the colonial Japanese community that had so dominated baseball's organization, particularly in the adult amateur game. Public discussion of the sport became focused on Taiwan's relationship with the United States at the behest of the GMD, so we can see early support for representative baseball teams at the international level with a rather more muted tone of support for the infrastructure beneath that fed and sustained it. The late 1940s present a clear dividing moment in Taiwanese history as colonial Japanese power gave way to a retreating Chinese Nationalist state, but baseball's development in Taiwanese society spanned both the colonial and postwar periods. Japanese rule on the island had been integral in such development and could not simply fade away, or at least it *would not* fade away, thanks in large part to the sustained echoes of the game's imperial past that would prove difficult for the GMD to credibly ignore.

7 | Echoes of Empire

In 1967 the *Lianhe Bao* carried an article remarking on a fascinating oddity from a professional Go match in Sapporo City in Hokkaido, Japan, between two of the world's most famous players. ROC citizen and professional Go player Rin Kaiho (Lian Haifeng) had moved to Japan in 1952 at the age of ten to be trained by the legendary Go Seiho (Wu Qingyuan), another Chinese-born master of the game. In 1965 he had challenged the legendary Japanese player Sakato Eio, twenty-two years Rin's senior and the first man to hold Honinbō and Meijin chess titles simultaneously. Rin's daring, in challenging such a distinguished player when he himself had not yet reached the age of thirty, paid off: this match was the second of their third series in three years, a rivalry that burnished the younger man's growing reputation. As the morning progressed, each player took his time pondering each move and the moves to come until finally it came time to break for lunch. Then, in the middle of a vital match at the highest level of this ancient and prestigious game, the older man suggested they extend the lunch break by half an hour to watch the beginning of the Kōshien Championship game between Kōryō High School of Hiroshima and Narashino High School. Rin, an avid baseball fan, happily agreed. The newspaper, eager to provide much needed context for a Taiwanese public that surely lacked any frame of reference for such intense interest in the sport, helpfully pointed out that the tournament was one of the most popular baseball events in Japan.[1]

Coverage of Rin's career, in addition to the newsworthiness of such a young man's taking on one of the best Go players in the world and winning, played into ROC constructions of postwar Taiwanese identity. Born in Shanghai, Rin had never lived in Taiwan yet remained a Chinese citizen and was therefore fair game for the GMD's appropriation of his successes and presentation of his achievements as those typical of modern Chinese determination and skill. Such determination and skill proved to be a common theme in postwar Taiwanese presentations of sporting achievement, particularly in the realm of baseball. Given the choice, the GMD leadership much preferred that the local population of Han Chinese living in Taiwan prior to 1945 take to basketball and soccer alongside their recently returned fellow citizens. However, the popularity of baseball continued, dominating much of the public imagination. The GMD's interactions with baseball lacked a clear unifying form, mostly coming into focus when it could "reify mythologies of Chinese-ness in Nationalist Taiwan." Such opportunities came almost exclusively when Taiwanese baseball teams participated in international competition, an environment where public perception could clearly affect Taiwan's legal rights as a member of the international community. The challenge remained domestically, where the local sporting population remained one of Japanese systems of organization and a history of play defined by Japanese experience. Into the breach stepped one of the most intriguing characters in Asian baseball and certainly one of its biggest stars: Oh Sadaharu, whose visits to Taiwan in the 1960s offered the GMD a very public play for legitimacy in political arenas both global and domestic.[2]

Like Rin Kaiho's, Oh Sadaharu's ethnicity and citizenship brought ready-made connections for exploitation by the Taiwanese press. He dealt his entire life with the reality of his ethnicity: a perceived distinct lack of Japaneseness reinforced by the presence of his Chineseness according to the Japanese among whom he grew up. His Chinese heritage was in turn controversial in postwar Japan, with his loyalties to the ROC and its government in Taipei ostensibly clear and free of vacillation. The child of a Zhejiang native who emigrated to Japan before the Chinese Civil War, Oh became a prominent celebrity who publicly ignored his rights to be a citizen of the PRC or Japan, instead holding an ROC passport. This apparent openness to celebrating a close relationship with Taiwan was itself rather vague, considering that the ROC had controlled all of mainland China when Oh's father was born, but such facts were never going to deter the GMD from celebrating the connection. If anything, the continued persistence of prominent figures such as Rin and Oh in maintaining their ROC citizenship buttressed GMD claims that the loss of the mainland was a temporary tragedy, a jurisdictional problem awaiting the rightful solution. Oh's own interactions with identity were complex; here was a man who forthrightly spoke of his troubles aligning with Japanese teammates and neighbors as a teenager on account of his Chinese parentage but later in his career symbolizing the most Japanese of inscrutable baseball practices. American hitters in the 1980s within spitting distance of Oh's numerous records found themselves flinging bats at pitches thrown in the vague vicinity of the plate but nowhere near any recognizable strike zone; a young Japanese pitcher willing to risk being known as the man who gave up one of the game's records to a foreigner proved hard to find. For his own part Oh was not shy about his fame, deftly navigating propriety while taking credit for his achievements. He has long given credit for his success to his legendary high school (and later professional) coach and mentor, Arakawa Hiroshi, and his parents, while being sure to point out that the pinnacle of those successes came in surpassing Hank Aaron's home run record. Oh is a man who studiously models social expectations of reserve and modesty while happily leaving his audience to reflect on the enormity of his achievements, an avatar fused of appropriate fulfillment of social expectations and the ego required to survive as a superstar in the burgeoning era of postwar celebrity.[3]

Oh's celebrity offered opportunities for the GMD to secure propaganda victories, to make hay with Taiwan's rich baseball past while mentioning it as obliquely as possible. The sport presented the GMD with a genuine conundrum. On the one hand, the decision not to attempt to excise baseball from Taiwanese public life was adroit. On the other, the somewhat ambivalent support of the game, prominent when Taiwanese representative teams played Cold War allies but otherwise lacking, had limited efficacy in shoring up the broader postwar cultural goal of establishing the Taipei government's primacy over Beijing in the representation of Chinese culture to the world. The degree to which baseball could be considered Chinese provided the rub. It is certainly true that the GMD recognized the benefits of physical activity among young citizens, its appeal having spread to mainland China with other modernizing cultural waves of the early twentieth century.[4] Baseball was popular and immediately available to be utilized by a refugee government exiled to the periphery in improving the health, physically and figuratively, of the national populace. However, basketball was gaining popularity. Association football and tennis, though not as popular as baseball, also enjoyed participation from the Taiwanese. With the growth of these sports, why would baseball continue to emerge as a clear tool for GMD management of interactions between Taiwan and the rest of the world and as a potential tool for the continued cultural rectification of the island community despite the sport's origins in the very culture supposedly outlined for eradication? Why not simply adopt basketball or tennis as a national sport, buttressed by state support in the form of money and propaganda?[5]

The obvious answer is that baseball remained considerably more popular in Taiwan than any of these other sports, administered by sophisticated formal organizations in both private competitions and those organized and competed in by Taiwanese schools and individuals. Any attempt to introduce overt symbols of statehood into games of tennis would have had little to no effect compared to doing the same in the regular baseball competitions throughout the island. Furthermore, baseball and basketball came to represent two different communities within postwar Taiwan, the former a sport celebrated by a community that remembered Japanese rule and the latter practiced by a community that strove to ignore all remaining evidence of colonialism.[6] Basketball was so popular with GMD officials that Taipei hosted an international basketball tournament among overseas Chinese teams from across Asia every October on Chiang Kai-shek's birthday, an endorsement of the sport that could hardly pass as subtle. In 1951 the ROC government constructed the twelve-thousand-seat Chinese Sports Hall, a state-of-the-art stadium for the purpose of playing high-profile basketball games. Unlike in baseball, basketball coaches and players were predominantly mainlanders, and Mandarin Chinese was the chosen language both on and off the court. This state of affairs changed slowly, with *waishengren* composing more than half of the ROC national basketball team as late as 1970.[7]

Despite such overt attempts at producing officially sanctioned sporting avenues, baseball continued to hold much of the public imagination in Taiwan. This was in no small part thanks to the continued success of the game in postwar Japan. Professional baseball began in Japan during the 1930s, following the sponsorship of teams by major businesses, led by the *Yomiuri* newspaper company. Competition switched from tournament to league format in 1938 and resumed in 1947, in part thanks to General Douglas MacArthur's belief that the game would encourage pro-American feelings in occupied Japan. MacArthur also believed that a two-league structure was more democratic than the single-league structure employed before the war.[8] The Nippon Professional Baseball League, founded in 1960, culminated in the Japan Series, a best-of-seven analog to the World Series of American Major League baseball, and offered a high-profile professional game unmatched in Taiwan, where the networks of amateur adult baseball did not coalesce into a professional league until 1990.[9] Oh's fame as a professional ballplayer in Japan was swiftly growing by 1965, when he visited Taiwan to receive the Outstanding Overseas Chinese Youth Award from the ROC government.[10] Having joined the Yomiuri Giants in 1959, Oh established himself third in the batting lineup by the early 1960s. He was still a young man at twenty-five and already the star of the most famous baseball team in Asia, playing alongside fellow future legend Nagashima Shigeo, who followed him in the batting order. Together the two men formed the "Oh-Nagashima Cannon," a formidable duo that helped propel Oh to numerous batting awards by the end of his career: five-time batting average champion, fifteen-time home run champion, thirteen-time player with most hits in a season, and twelve-time player with most bases. He was the Most Valuable Player nine times, his first award coming in 1964. That same year he set the record for most home runs in a season (fifty-five), most home runs in a single game (four), and most consecutive games in a row featuring home runs (four). He was entering the prime of what is now recognized as one of the great careers in Japanese baseball, surrounded by some of Japanese baseball's already legendary names.[11]

In his role as a major celebrity in the pages of the Taiwanese press, Oh in many ways replicated the phenomenon of Waseda University's and other Japanese baseball teams' visits before retrocession: a singular personification of a quality long since brought in by university teams and touring professionals since the late 1910s, the legitimacy of recognition from the center of the sporting world. The political implications of Oh's choices (or lack thereof) regarding his citizenship were clearly favorable to ROC politicians, but media coverage of his visits to Taiwan frequently betrayed a public enthusiasm for Oh's celebrity, a status based completely on his professional baseball career in Japan. After one early newspaper report describing Oh's life as a prominent Chinese person in Japan, the government-friendly Taiwan press quickly took ownership of Oh's nationality, openly describing him as a "Chinese baseball star."[12] In one article in early 1965 Oh shared the spotlight with other prominent Chinese nationals abroad in the fields of photography and medicine.[13] By the beginning of a visit by Oh to Taiwan in late 1965, the young baseball player had become a full-blown celebrity. The December 5 edition of the *Lianhe Bao*, the day after Oh's arrival from Japan, displayed seven separate articles on the athlete's visit.

The man himself was comfortable with the attention, stepping out onto the tarmac at Songshan Airport in Taipei on his arrival, clutching the ROC flag in his left hand, before thousands of onlookers welcoming him "back" to Taiwan. Local reporters, in keeping with a keen interest in Oh's private life, made note of more than a few attractive young women in attendance.[14] Oh's presence in advertisements in Japanese magazines and the athlete's enthusiasm both in speaking his mind at a press conference at Songshan Airport and in his upcoming public performances in Taipei presented a clear confidence popular with the Taiwanese press, whose interest refused to waver from what was quickly becoming a fevered pitch.[15] Oh was moved to refute suggestions, fueled by visiting Japanese media conversing with local reporters, that his true objective in visiting Taiwan was to find a Chinese sweetheart. The Tokyo media seemed unconvinced by his five-year relationship with Japanese girlfriend Oyae Kyōko, their neglect in failing to announce an engagement allowing Oh's bachelor status to persist.[16]

Oh announced his intentions to put on a hitting display the following evening, to present the famed "Waseda hitting style" (more popularly known as his "flamingo" or "scarecrow" stance) to the Taiwanese public in person. The style was in fact of Oh's own creation and had become a trademark of what we would today call an athlete's brand, whereby he placed most of his body weight on one leg.[17] Oh himself was a graduate of Waseda Jitsugyo High School rather than the famous university, but the name clearly still carried merit in Taiwan.[18] The batting stance itself received some press, with a high-profile meeting between Oh and National Baseball Association official Xie Dongmin. After an exchange of souvenirs, the older Xie called on Oh to give him a lesson in the "Waseda hitting style." After several failed attempts to position himself on only one leg, the older man admitted defeat with a smile and a cry of, "I'm old! I'm old!," much to the amusement of those gathered.[19] Oh was graceful in his attempts to hide his embarrassment.[20] Coverage of Oh's visit, while always taking for granted his national status as a returning Chinese national, focused completely on his celebrity, a fusion of his high-profile career as an athlete, his good looks, and his comfort in speaking to the press and in front of large crowds. The media covered with detail his public appearances and baseball demonstrations and continued to question him on his personal life. Oh, somewhat light-heartedly, informed reporter Zhao Musong that he would pick a wedding date once he had successfully obtained his third championship.[21] The ROC journalistic community was perhaps disappointed when Oh returned a year later with his Japanese wife, having married Ms. Oyae, although he had chosen to return to his "homeland" for the honeymoon.[22]

Oh was hardly the native son returned, as presented in the pro-GMD Taiwanese press, though nor could he claim to be inseparable from the Japanese among whom he lived and worked. He encountered the edges between his identities in a manner that first engaged with his Chinese identity as a young man, when he was informed by his high school principal that he would not be permitted to participate in the Kokutai, or National Amateur Athletic Competition, because he was not considered Japanese. The incident shattered a young Oh's assumptions of full participation in Japanese society, causing him to consider himself differently from his Japanese teammates for the first time.[23] This is how Oh interacts with his identity, at least publicly, to this day: as a conflict between his status as an icon of Japan's most popular sport and his non-Japanese ethnicity, in direct contrast to his public role as a favorite son of modern Japan. In his various autobiographies in English and Japanese (and in Chinese translation for the Taiwanese audience), Oh makes little to no mention of his visits to Taiwan or his relationship with the ROC. He instead focuses on the dilemmas of his identity centered on his relationship with his parents and the impact on his development as a young man growing up in the years following World War II, when during the American postwar occupation of Japan his "Chinese" family received favorable treatment from American authorities, a clear contrast to his father's need to field calls from the police during the war itself as a result of that same affiliation.[24] Oh's discussion of his parents dwells on his father's wishes that his two sons, fresh from degrees in medicine and electrical engineering, might return to his homeland to improve the terrible living conditions, borne of decades of warlordism and the vagaries of war. The Oh children were sent to Chinese-language schools for very brief spells. A precocious young Sadaharu's tenure was cut short almost immediately by a robust reaction to a female Chinese-language teacher's use of corporal punishment.[25] Oh's allegiance to China was tied up in his allegiance and gratitude to his parents, in turn a vital component in his public performance as an ethically upstanding member of the Japanese community. In any case, the China to which Oh felt he owed allegiance and the China that the ROC claimed to safeguard in temporary exile were equally the work of human imagination but by no means the same conception. Oh's father dreamed of his sons returning to his homeland to help his family and neighbors rebuild while the GMD dreamed of a return in the glory of military victory.

Taiwanese media coverage gladly overlooked such nuances, however. The outlines of the story proved too attractive. Oh's mother had met his father when the latter worked at a Chinese noodle restaurant in Tokyo, the couple enduring discrimination in Japanese society against both Chinese nationals and the Japanese who married them to raise one of the country's biggest sporting stars.[26] The young man's willingness to return to Taipei and perform for the crowds was a welcome boost to ROC propaganda. Nevertheless, the fact could not be escaped that Oh Sadaharu's fame relied on his ability to play baseball. It was this that elevated him to such a universally popular figure in Taiwan. Oh symbolized another cultural marker in exchange between Taiwan and Japan, following the same route as Waseda and other touring teams before him. As he visited various sites across Taiwan, joked with reporters, and posed with political figures, he personified the echoes of a Japanese baseball world ricocheting around a Taiwanese society under significant pressure to conform to specific ideals of Chinese identity. The baseball infrastructure on the island owed its origins completely to Japanese endeavor, regardless of how the GMD may or may not have felt about such a fact. Oh, carrying with him the first few of what would turn out to be an astonishing number of batting titles, was an emerging star on a team of stars in the best professional baseball league in the world beyond American shores. His celebrity was meaningless without Japanese connections. Regardless of how much the Taiwanese press may have downplayed or ignored Japanese influence in the Taiwanese appreciation of baseball, the most popular events related to the sport, both before and after retrocession, occurred in the context of comparison with Japan. The increased role of baseball in the ROC relationship with the United States and the official encouragement of national teams to engage in international competition proved that the sport was moving beyond the mere status of a colonial cultural remnant. However, recognition among Taiwanese baseball fans that Japan represented the highest standard on the continent remained.

Still times were now changing; the GMD achieved a certain level of success in claiming Oh as a Chinese hero, and the colonial period was quickly fading into the past. Oh's visits in the mid-1960s in many ways presage the success of the Hongye team in 1968 and the advent of baseball as an avatar of Taiwanese nationalism born of government attempts to channel it into a Chinese nationalism distinctly attuned to unification but celebrated by all Taiwanese. The GMD succeeded in creating new ideological constructs for the sport, though in the long term the idea has backfired somewhat, as shown by the more recent Chinese-language historiography celebrating the origins of Taiwanese baseball in the colonial period as a distinctly Taiwanese experience. The celebration of Oh Sadaharu, intended to Sinicize the Japanese game, only played into and enhanced popular participation in and perceived ownership of the sport. That ownership predated the return of Chiang Kai-shek and his fellow mainland Chinese. Still Oh's easy grip of the public imagination in Taiwan and the willingness of the GMD to celebrate his Chinese status opened the door to efforts at creating cohesive senses of Chinese nationalism among the broader Taiwanese population. The message was clear: Oh plays in Japan, but he belongs to us. The question remained of who constituted the "us."

Warm welcomes for Oh Sadaharu offered the ROC state and the press that it controlled an opportunity to capitalize on baseball's popularity in Taiwan while pushing a specific pro-Chinese agenda, offering the ballplayer to the public as an avatar of Chinese achievement internationally, playing upon thousands of years of Chinese heritage and assumptions of importance while embracing the underdog status developing as a result of the ROC's diminishing geopolitical relevance. The problem lay in how such presentations were received. Postwar Taiwan's relationship with Japan was complicated in a broader political sense, but the connections between Taiwanese baseball and Japanese baseball remained strong throughout the 1950s and early 1960s. Visitors from Japan with clear connections to the baseball world, although no longer under the auspices of colonial rulers, brought with them a clear sense of legitimacy, a bright light in which Taiwanese ballplayers and administrators could share. Oh personified this dynamic, but it also held true in echoes from the colonial period with the continuation of touring visits by Japanese teams to Taiwan, including prominent visits by Japanese university teams. Waseda University returned in the postwar period as an important influence in Taiwanese baseball despite the removal of the Japanese colonial infrastructure that had generated this relationship in the first place, one going back to the 1917 tour. Unlike Oh's personal connections to the ROC, Waseda's institutional relationship with the local game lay beyond semantic frameworks that made appropriation by the GMD remotely plausible beyond welcoming guests from a fellow American ally.

The Waseda University baseball team made its first postwar visit to Taiwan in 1953 with little in the way of press coverage compared to the fevered welcome of the colonial Japanese press over thirty-five years earlier. The *Lianhe Bao* presented postwar Taiwan as a society where the exploits of Waseda University's finest student athletes became relevant only within the context of their visit. A month in advance of the traveling team's arrival, the *Lianhe Bao* released Waseda's schedule: the familiar baseball venues of Taipei, Taizhong, and Gaoxiong would again welcome Waseda, now as guests in *youyisai*, "friendship games" between citizens of neighboring sovereign states. The Japanese student-athletes would also visit Jiayi, a city acknowledged by the Taiwanese press, though with a nod to Taiwan's peripheral importance within the increasingly ephemeral "one China" under GMD rule, as the "birthplace of baseball in this province."[27] The paper similarly nodded toward the Japanese visitors' status as Big Six champions, skirting around Taiwanese baseball fans' obvious familiarity with the prestigious intercollegiate tournament. Waseda's schedule, as it had been during the colonial period, was comprised of games against various representative teams, the first of eleven planned against a northern Taiwan team in Taipei.[28] Articles briefly previewing the team's arrival continued to appear much as they had in the colonial press, spelling out in detail specific game dates in each Taiwanese city, as well as dates on which the team would rest from competition.[29]

The *Lianhe Bao* even listed the entire Waseda roster, including squad numbers, and the personnel comprising the all-Taiwan team to face Waseda in its first game, almost two weeks in advance.[30] The Waseda team brought a complement of twenty personnel, including university officials, former players, and the playing squad to Taiwan in a sizeable delegation befitting the political implications of the tour. The newspaper dutifully reported brief biographies of each and every member, courtesy of translations supplied by the Taiwanese Athletics Association. Individual achievements among the players in the Big Six tournament and the Kōshien high school competition in Japan were reported with no further elaboration or explanation for the Taiwanese audience, the articles again falling awkwardly between identifying the tournaments as something irrelevantly foreign and acknowledging a typical Taiwanese baseball fan's familiarity with the most prestigious tournaments in Asian amateur baseball.[31] A full breakdown of prices for the games was published in the newspaper just over a week before the team's arrival; these ranged from NT$50 for the most expensive ticket to a significantly more modest NT$3 for students and members of the armed forces seeking seats in the outfield.[32] As much as the conditions in Taiwan had changed since the last Waseda tour in 1934, some things had remained the same, the Taiwanese press becoming rather breathless in its coverage of the upcoming games. The *Lianhe Bao* published a brief article on December 16 confirming yet again that the Waseda baseball team would arrive the next day.[33] The December 17 edition confirmed that, yes, this had in fact happened, although the 1953 Waseda squad enjoyed traveling to Taiwan via a Northwest Airlines flight, a world apart from the voyages by ship endured by its predecessors.[34]

The opening game of the tour, on December 19, was an auspicious event. Hosts greeted the Japanese players with bouquets, and representatives of National Taiwan University held a banner that read *wenwu shuangquan*, the four-character idiom encouraging both sides to show appropriate competitiveness and sportsmanship. Taipei mayor Wu San-lian led the opening celebration. Unfortunately the amateur players of the ROC did not fare well against the visitors on the field. Waseda won the first game against the northern Taiwan team, 4–1. The *Lianhe Bao* detailed the events of the game, but not before devoting a paragraph to the visiting team's numerous advantages over the local amateurs, chief among them the strength and vitality of the young university students and a depth in players that allowed them to switch pitchers every three innings.[35] The following day Waseda defeated the Banks Association team, 7–1, in the presence of a significantly larger crowd than had attended the first game. The Lianhe Bao, though continuing to note the Japanese players' youth and physical gifts, was considerably less forgiving of the local players' display, commenting that it seemed the local team was gripped with fear in the face of the visitors' pitching prowess and batting power.[36]

Results only got worse, both for Taiwanese baseball fans hoping for an upset and for officials dreaming of something to bolster Chinese propaganda, the balance between recognizing Japan as a Cold War ally and memories of Chiang Kai-shek's humiliations at the hands of the Empire of Japan still fresh. A team from the ROC Navy went down, 15–2.[37] The Waseda visit to Jiayi provided an occasion to honor the home of Taiwanese baseball, though the result was not what the locals had hoped: thirty thousand fans filled Zhongshan Park to watch the students defeat a United Taiwan team by 12–3 after receiving gifts from the Jiayi Athletics Association and Waseda Alumni Society in the pregame formalities.[38] Waseda won again against the same team the following day in Taizhong, 6–3.[39] The United Taiwan side finally handed Waseda its lone loss of the tour on December 29, 1953. The propaganda event had finally delivered something positive to say about Chinese relations with Japan on the field as well as off. The Lianhe Bao reported with no little satisfaction that after the "surprise attack, . . . a first win, the lowest score yet, and an occasion never before seen, only this: two runs to one."[40]

The Waseda tour captured the public imagination, as shown by the large crowds (such as in Jiayi), and though the Lianhe Bao consistently supported such a clearly popular and politically important event, the newspaper's coverage did not completely give itself over to pro-baseball propaganda. One brief opinion piece took a dim view of the Japanese players' reception at Songshan Airport, in particular the unreserved enthusiasm of ROC citizens who identified themselves as members of the Waseda Alumni Society. The newspaper accepted that on such "major diplomatic occasions" it may not hurt to show open friendliness to foreign guests, but it warned against behavior when lost in the moment as a "brother or sister fan" that may give a negative impression of Taiwanese society.[41] Overall, however, the propaganda aims of the "China-Japan" games were clear, and although the Waseda team returned to Japan with nine wins out of ten against its Taiwanese hosts, that lone United Taiwan victory gave the ROC officials some saving of face. It is fascinating that the visit ended in a manner again reminiscent of Waseda visits during the colonial period, with a game between teams identified only as "Red" and "White," composed of both Waseda students and United Taiwan athletes. This final friendship game conveniently ended in a tie, 5–5.[42]

The 1953 visit marked the first of several. Waseda baseball teams returned to Taiwan in 1957, 1963, and 1964. The *Lianhe Bao*'s awkward balance between the obvious fluency in Japanese baseball matters and history among the local Taiwanese audience present in Taiwan before 1945 and the need to treat Waseda University baseball teams as a novelty mildly more familiar than visitors from outer space continued. In 1963 Waseda and Keiō Universities imported their famous Sōkeisen rivalry to Taiwan, playing the games outside of Japan for the first time; the newspaper drew rather clumsy allusions to the Oxford-Cambridge boat races and Harvard-Yale football contests.[43] Though easily interpreted as patronizing to its readership or perhaps even insulting to the intelligence of Taiwanese baseball fans, it is more fruitful perhaps to see the *Lianhe Bao*'s struggles with this balance as a studied ignorance regarding the longer-term legacy of Waseda baseball in Taiwan, rigid and unyielding in the face of the obvious. As far as the GMD-approved writers of the paper were concerned, the 1953 tour served as the first of several sporting events created to engender continued good will between the ROC and Japanese governments. Coverage of the sporting events operated under this assumption and this assumption alone. The rampant popularity of the Waseda visits among the wider Taiwanese public reflected the interest of a local community introduced to the sport itself under imperial rule; the *Lianhe Bao* coverage reflected the postwar realities of the relationship between a defeated Japan and the ROC, a member of the successful Allied powers, a close ally to the United States, and a permanent member of the UN Security Council. The contrasts between these divergent experiences of a cultural visit by a university baseball team are fascinating.

The opportunity of a Waseda visit was itself the product of the colonial period, a welcome if unacknowledged windfall for an ROC government eager to continue promoting the island's image as the rightful home of Chinese culture and political representation. However, Waseda provided the one true household name remaining in the world of Taiwanese baseball amid the collection of representative teams such as the northern Taiwan team, the United Taiwan team, or the Banks Association team that otherwise represented a high tide of local Taiwanese appropriation of a formerly Japanese-controlled sport.[44] Whether or not the ROC government chose to acknowledge the fact, the postwar Waseda visits occurred in the context of a long-term relationship between Waseda baseball and Taiwanese public life. Waseda players had featured on the pages of Taiwanese newspapers since 1906 and played on Taiwanese fields since 1917, the university team representing a central focus of the sport's history on the island, a history that spanned across retrocession and fundamentally different political regimes.

Waseda University players had served as ambassadors to American campuses, representing a new and modern Japan that sought confirmation of its equality with the Western powers that had sought to subdue it only decades earlier. The players performed a different function for Taiwan, performing as envoys of cultural legitimacy emanating directly from the cultural sphere's hub: Tokyo, the metropole at the center of Asian empire and home to the physical sites and organized tournaments that composed the ideological foundations of Japanese baseball as a cultural enterprise that stretched out to ethnic Japanese populations on the edges of its empire and beyond. These connections proved hardy enough to survive the end of that empire and the plunging of both Japan and Taiwan into a markedly different postwar order on the western perimeter of the Pacific Ocean. Taiwanese baseball relied on a vocabulary provided by its Japanese antecedence, and until the 1960s Waseda University continued to represent that language at its most eloquent. All of this would change, culminating in the rise of Taiwanese Little League baseball in the late 1960s as a force worthy at last of a Taiwanese baseball identity that transcended the sport's existence within the Japanese cultural sphere. Success at Williamsport, Pennsylvania, would soon render GMD propaganda significantly more believable, though it would also soon transition into a new political debate that truly left the Japanese genetics of the Taiwanese baseball community in the past.

The clear American interest in the game and the ROC regime's recognition of that interest partly explain why baseball continued to grow in popularity as the GMD sought to eradicate other traces of Japanese colonial rule. The leniency that accompanied GMD endorsement of Taiwanese participation in international baseball competitions and the embrace of baseball games as a form of cultural exchange with Americans in Taiwan in turn allowed the drastic growth of amateur adult baseball teams on the island. Japanese colonials had dominated the game at adult level before retrocession. Now local Taiwanese were free to form their own teams and compete in island-wide tournaments. Yu Junwei describes the first two decades after retrocession as a "Golden Era" of Taiwanese baseball, even proposing that Chiang Kai-shek may have seen the continued popularity of the sport as a boon to his attempts to reclaim the mainland, such was baseball's effect on local morale.[45] There is no question that in the years between 1945 and 1968 baseball continued to grow in popularity.

The nature of that popularity changed, however. The postwar Taiwanese baseball world was shifting. The inheritance of the Japanese-organized amateur infrastructure by local Taiwanese came alongside a lack of interest in regulation or proscription from an otherwise rapaciously ideological government. Starting in the late 1940s a newly arrived minority pushed an ideological agenda with a clear definition of Chinese identity that it imposed on the island's majority, for whom the concept of Chinese identity as Chiang Kai-shek understood it had perhaps never before existed; certainly it was at the very least rudely interrupted by Japanese colonialism, a fact the GMD studiously ignored. The imperial heritage of Chinese culture had been obfuscated by colonial rule built on specific visions of modernity. It would be an overstatement to argue that colonial Taiwan had proceeded completely unaware of the cultural outcroppings of the Nanjing Decade and Chiang's own feelings on the path of modern Chinese culture, but local Taiwanese were beyond the reach of GMD attempts to reshape modern Chinese identity until after World War II. By the 1960s this government's interest in utilizing the popular sport as part of the national project had begun to intensify. On the one hand, this played into the need to maintain positive relations with the United States, as well as with other resident nodes of the Pacific defense perimeter in Seoul, Tokyo, and Manila. On the other, the healthy and growing organized baseball infrastructure left behind from the colonial period offered enormous potential to create public narratives of success. The GMD landed on one in particular, a Chinese hero plying his trade in Tokyo.

Chiang Kai-shek conspired to live in an imaginary Taiwan where Oh Sadaharu's popularity reflected the greatness of the Chinese experience abroad, where participation in baseball tournaments featuring other allies of the United States reflected Taiwan's Cold War realities with little or no debt to the colonial period. Taipei was the capital of a government in exile supported by Chinese citizens released from Japanese oppression, unfortunately temporarily contaminated by colonial influence. Retrocession served as a cataclysmic shift in the political history of Taiwan but did not immediately signal a shift in the social role of baseball on the island. That came later, as the detritus of the Japanese cultural domain over the former colony gradually eroded in the face of consistent pressure from the GMD. The Waseda University baseball team visits of the 1950s and 1960s referred back to the regular bestowals of legitimacy upon Taiwanese baseball from Japan during the colonial period. Oh Sadaharu's visits to Taiwan rested on the same legitimacy but the GMD leaped on important differences. His was a Chinese success story written in Japan, at least according to the pages of the Taiwanese press. In the years that followed, young

Taiwanese ball players would write their own stories, which linked back to the youth baseball successes of Taiwan's past but could more readily still be taken as grist for the mill of GMD Chinese nationalism. Taiwanese baseball was soon to move away from the Japanese cultural domain within which it had flourished into contested ground between Chiang Kai-shek's vision of Chinese culture and a nascent ideological movement that would in time become a strain of Taiwanese nationalism that called for independence from the mainland and a departure from the cross-straits relationship that dominated the island's postwar existence.

Waseda's visits and Oh's achievements evoked for local Taiwanese the memories of Kōshien and the connections between baseball in Taiwan and baseball in Japan, but for all the GMD's efforts to assiduously ignore the realities of the sport's development in colonial Taiwan, its drive to recognize Japanese baseball specifically within the framework of Cold War alliances reflected the reality of Japan's postwar connections to Taiwan and its importance in the world. The end of Japanese rule over Taiwan was abrupt, with its southward cultural demesne withering more slowly. In the realm of Japanese-language literature, where GMD language policy was unapologetically aggressive, Taiwanese writers faced a choice among immediate acceptance of the new order, a push for compromise in delaying the transition to *guoyu*, or a need to consign themselves to silence. The door, for them, was all but closed. The realization that the pro-Chinese agenda of the GMD would treat Taiwan as a periphery within an imagined Greater China, just as Japanese imperialists had ultimately refused to accept Taiwanese elites as equals, generated a profound sense of betrayal among those old enough to remember life before retrocession.[46] Their concerns echoed throughout Taiwanese society. GMD attempts to channel baseball's popularity into a shared sense of Chinese patriotism struggled not merely from a muddled sense of how to mobilize these energies, but also from the clear problem of against whom to direct them. If the former imperial power would not play the role of antagonist and other for the development of Taiwanese baseball as an agent for Chinese nationalism, then who would?

8 | Hongye

In 1971 the Tainan Giants won the Little League World Series in Williamsport, Pennsylvania. The *New York Times* reported the victory as a "badly needed lift in morale" for the ROC, as the steady encroachment of PRC foreign policy gains could for one sweet moment be pushed to one side, if not forgotten.[1] The newspaper also reported a "brief fistfight" between two factions of Chinese fans, one composed of Chinese born in Taiwan and the other of Chinese born on the mainland. There were no injuries reported, and the Taiwanese boys went on to win the game 12–3.[2] The skirmish did not merit a mention in the *Washington Post*.[3] The report itself proved not entirely accurate: the groups were not rivals from both Chinese states on either side of the Taiwan Strait but were in fact Taiwan-based Chinese nationals positing opposing views of Taiwanese identity and statehood. Protestors in favor of a Taiwanese identity distinct from the continuation of Chinese cultural universalism mandated by the GMD clashed with sponsored thugs from the American East Coast. The interruption mentioned in the New York paper was actually a sortie by one such group across the field to rip down a banner stating, in both English and Chinese, "Team of Taiwan, Go Taiwan."[4]

The question of how Taiwanese baseball's political energies might finally be directed appeared to be answered. In the early 1970s baseball games formed a political frontier for the Taiwanese. Williamsport lay beyond the control of the GMD's secret police and state-controlled media, but thanks to the intense interest in the Little League World Series games in Taiwan, attendees of the games knew that banners and chants in support of a distinct Taiwanese identity had a chance of being seen or heard at home. In 1968 the Hongye Primary School baseball team had defeated a visiting team from Wakayama, Japan, home to the Little League World Series champions of that same year. The win opened the door for Taiwanese Little League baseball, with the Taizhong Gold Dragons entering the Little League World Series the following year as Taiwan's first representatives at the competition. They won the championship. As if from nowhere, youth baseball was a major event in Taiwanese public life once more.[5] Between 1969 and 1981 Taiwanese teams won ten Little League world titles. Officially approved media coverage of baseball had ignored the growing scene in domestic baseball for years, preferring to focus on ROC participation in international tournaments as diplomatic events and ignoring youth baseball entirely. After the success of Hongye, these two strands intersected. Youth baseball became a potent source of propaganda for Taiwan's image internationally and its official participation in international events as a sovereign nation. Government sponsorship and enthusiastic promotion of Taiwanese Little League baseball quickly followed.[6] The elevation of Little League teams marked the latest and most successful GMD attempts to capitalize on baseball's popularity. The popularity now came into full force with the elevation of a group of boys from southeast Taiwan who would form the most famous team in Taiwanese baseball history.

The victory of the Hongye Primary School baseball team in 1968 over the Japanese players and purported Little League World Series champions began a period of Taiwanese dominance in global youth baseball that the ROC happily adopted as a vehicle for its own brand of Chinese nationalism. However, as events such as those mentioned above would soon show, the debate would become colored by the emerging forces of a separate strain of Taiwanese nationalism that concerned itself far less with the GMD's long-term goal of reunification with mainland China and more with the domestic reform of a Taiwanese state, possibly leading to eventual independence. The 1968 victory and the years of success at Williamsport that followed bring an endpoint in the clear identification of Taiwanese baseball as a component of a broader Japanese cultural sphere, the detritus of colonial Japanese influence finally swept away by international success. For the GMD government the benefits of these victories were clear: a team of young Chinese hopefuls had shocked the world. From 1968 onward the definition of Taiwanese and Chinese identities became a point of contestation as baseball teams played on television. For many watching from home youth baseball became emblematic of a *Taiwanese* ability to compete globally.

Taiwanese success in the Little League World Series from the late 1960s onward cemented the importance of youth baseball in Taiwan's sporting history. Today narratives of Taiwanese success can draw on a lineage going back through Hongye to Kanō and Nōkō, providing invaluable continuity for arguments that seek to sow the legacies of the colonial period and the emergence of independent Taiwanese identity together. In particular youth baseball offers a narrative centered on Taiwan-based accomplishments independent of any postwar encouragement from Chiang Kai-shek's regime. The GMD did not initially openly support youth baseball to the extent that the colonial Japanese government had before retrocession, but youth baseball persisted. In 1952 residents of Xinzhu County took part in the third annual youth baseball tournament in the northern county.[7] The East Gate Primary School team emerged victorious from a field of five teams competing over two days.[8] In the same year the Taizhong city government hosted the fourth annual citywide children's baseball tournament. All primary schools in the city were represented, with preliminary matches to decide participants in the four-day competition.[9] Only two months later another major competition was held further south, in Yunlin County. The *Lianhe Bao* carried details of the competition's rules for admission and grand prize a month in advance.[10]

Media coverage of youth baseball centered on students at the primary-school level in the years immediately following retrocession. This differed from the portrayal of youth baseball in the colonial period. Before 1945 youth baseball in Taiwan reflected the high profile of high-school-level competition in Japan. By the early 1950s, when the domestic political situation had become relatively calm, *Lianhe Bao* reports on youth baseball betrayed a large network of inter-school tournaments across the island. Furthermore, baseball at the primary level enjoyed a significant grip on intramural competition, as high school baseball athletes found themselves frequently sharing the limelight with basketball.[11] Overall, however, youth baseball in the early 1950s received considerably less recognition from the official media than it had during the colonial period. The *Lianhe Bao*'s pages contained a significant number of articles on the subject of the sport in May 1953, but the majority of these focused on games among adults. Performances by the national baseball team earned the headlines, as did the donation of a gold trophy for the winners of the upcoming all-island adult baseball tournament in July by the head of MAAG, General William C. Chase.[12]

If anything, mention of youth baseball in the *Lianhe Bao* declined as the 1950s progressed. In addition to the scant coverage of local baseball activity, the occasional editorial delivered a rather frank view of the sport's importance in ROC society. One such article, discussing the author's recent visit to Tokyo to compare life there after the war with his previous visit in 1940, described streets filled with people gathered to watch baseball games on television, the gathered Japanese with smiles on their faces or emitting sounds of enthusiasm or frustration to match the events portrayed on television, at once "expressing passion and also expressing lunacy." The author pondered what the reader might make of all this as a traveling Chinese person on the streets of Tokyo, concluding that the typical reaction would be one of boredom and incomprehension.[13] Mention of the sport's existence beyond the continued activity of a national team in international competition was restricted to occasional references to the sporting infrastructure left behind by the Japanese. New Park remained, although it was as likely to be referenced as the site for celebrations showcasing students' science projects as the host of an organized youth baseball game.[14]

Despite the reluctance of the postwar press to report on the game, youth baseball survived. Competitions reminiscent of the heyday of youth baseball during the colonial period persisted, although the sport suffered from the GMD's preference for sports imported from the mainland after retrocession. By the end of the 1950s reports of sporting activities among Taiwanese youth were no longer dominated by baseball and included references to basketball and table tennis. There were also signs that baseball's position in the popular culture were broadening slightly: female student athletes now played in competitions of their own, as evidenced by the existence of an all-female tournament receiving top billing with the traditional all-male tournament in the Taipei Mayor's Cup.[15] In general, however, baseball, and particularly youth baseball, had been subsumed into a postwar Taiwanese culture that celebrated sporting activity among young people as a collected set of vague activities resulting ultimately in the increased physical health and well-being of young Chinese citizens. This had been nominally true during the colonial period, but in practice baseball had risen to the forefront of colonial Taiwan's sporting culture. In postwar Taiwan baseball deserved mention only when factoring into the international reputation and interactions of the ROC—for example, in international competitions with other Asian nations and in interactions between the ROC and American armed forces on the island, such as a friendly game between an American team and a team representing the ROC Air Force.[16]

Youth baseball tournaments, such as the Chairman's Cup, did persist but received the minimum of coverage with none of the detailed accounts of colonial times.[17] If one were to go solely by the evidence presented in the pages of the *Lianhe Bao*, one would believe that baseball had simply been joined by other sports as one of many pursuits utilized by the state to motivate and energize the young citizens of the republic. Baseball featured among these sports and in state-sponsored events that could draw upon more than thirty organized events to include over four thousand young students. The baseball games that had enjoyed central coverage in similar events under Japanese rule were lost in the crowd of officially sanctioned sporting activities promoted to keep the children active during their summer vacation.[18]

In 1952 Jiayi hosted the second annual Provincial High School Sports Championships. The games were, despite the tournament's name, open to teams representing universities, high schools, and elementary schools in both all-male and all-female competition. Such tournaments, previously holding baseball as the centerpiece, now included a wide number of sports. The Jiayi Agriculture and Forestry Institute, which had once hosted the Kanō baseball teams, now provided champions in the 100-meter sprints and 110-meter hurdles.[19] Even in the south of the island, home to emerging local Taiwanese student athletes towards the end of the colonial period, the game was lost amid a governmental commitment to blanket all sports as part of a drive to promote appropriate feelings of nationalist loyalty among the Taiwanese youth. Events such as those hosted by the Liu Dui Nationalist Friendship Organization, a group that came into being shortly after retrocession to celebrate Hakka culture in the Gaoxiong and Pingdong area, included a wide variety of sports with no special mention of baseball.[20] The country's most popular game received no special treatment from the state.

It was in this context that the Hongye team originated in a small village of the same name in Taidong in the early 1960s. The village, named after the autumn colors of its scenic surroundings, was home to several households of the Bunun aboriginal Taiwanese tribe. In September 1963 Lin Zhupeng became principal of the village's small elementary school. The school was having trouble attracting the Bunun children to attend regularly. Noting the enthusiasm among the children for outdoor pursuits, Lin formed a baseball team with the hopes of attracting consistently truant students to attend class.[21] The principal's faith in the ability of the children quickly paid dividends, as the new team that formed secured first place in the Taidong County Head Cup only a year later.[22] In 1965 the team made its first appearance in the pages of the *Lianhe Bao*. The article was a form of soft news, a popular-interest story recounting the efforts required to raise enough money for the young athletes to attend the seventeenth annual Students' Baseball Tournament in Taipei. The ten children on the team seemed to have no chance of attending the tournament as there was already a team representing Taidong County, and there were no more public funds available for another team. The article described the passion among the children for baseball that drove them to endeavor to travel to Taipei for the tournament regardless, first reaching Hualian from Taidong by foot and then by negotiating a lift by car on to Yilan, where their trip finally seemed at an end, with the children pacing the streets without a place to stay or any finances to proceed further. The story had a happy ending: Huang Xunzuo, a local policeman, discovered the children and was so moved and saddened by their plight and determination to travel to Taipei on a meager diet of soy milk and mantou bread buns that he provided a roof over their heads and motivated local Yilan residents to donate to the cause. The Hongye team reached Taipei, where it finished fourth and earned a place in the hearts of many in attendance.[23]

The article clearly offered plenty of propaganda opportunities, stressing the admirable tenacity of these young children from the most rural section of Taiwan and the generosity of business owners and other members of the growing middle class in Yilan such as the purveyors of the Mainland Restaurant, who fed the children during the tournament. Of course the kindness and generosity of the friendly and sympathetic Officer Huang did not reflect badly on the government either. Despite the role of the Hongye team at the center of this tale of generosity—a generosity befitting traditional Chinese cultural values surviving the island's steady economic growth—the children were little more than a justification for the article's real message. The Students' Cup itself did not merit the attention of the newspaper. The steadfast refusal of the *Lianhe Bao* to treat baseball in Taiwan as anything other than an avenue for participation in international cultural exchanges resulted in a continued absence for anything resembling in-depth coverage of youth baseball in the newspaper's pages. This was soon to change radically.

The Hongye team earned its next mention in the *Lianhe Bao* with a similar capacity to provide the subject matter for a heartwarming tale. Financial difficulties loomed once more in 1968 in the boys' attempts to travel to Taipei to represent their county at the Students' Baseball Tournament. Helpful Taiwanese attached to the school pitched in once more, and the children were praised for their attitude, coming from a school that lacked a second- or fourth grade-class and required only five people to teach classes and run the school.[24] This time, however, the Hongye team also made headlines for its performances on the field. A sterling performance against Yongle Elementary School in Taipei, featuring three home runs in the sixth inning, earned plaudits for this team with "strengths in abundance."[25] The pro-government press now spoke of the twentieth annual Students' Baseball Tournament in glowing terms after years of giving youth baseball short shrift. "Since the tournament began six days ago," the *Lianhe Bao* gushed, "there has not been a single cold day in the stadium." The standard of the teams and children at the tournament led the newspaper to conclude that the nation's baseball potential had the best possible beginning. The performances had been such that a shining opportunity existed for a significant rise in the fortunes of the national team in the future. Hongye was pointed out as the exceptional representative of an exceptional Taiwanese county, Taidong, in the production of baseball talent.[26] The article noticeably ignored the roots of the sport in colonial times, instead stressing the exceptional nature of Taidong's ability to produce baseball talent and the celebration of the physical capabilities and achievements of the Chinese youths while openly praising government efforts the year before in hosting an aboriginal Taiwanese sports tournament to develop talent in eastern Taiwan. There was no mention of either the Nōkō or Kanō teams, despite the clear historical connections and the possibility of another angle pushing for the inclusion of aboriginal Taiwanese. Most distinctly the coverage clearly celebrated the performances as evidence of a bright future for adult Taiwanese players in adult competition and congratulated the GMD for its success in facilitating the passion for the game of those Chinese citizens living outside of Taipei.

The shift in tone and increase in number of articles in the *Lianhe Bao* covering youth baseball in 1968 is startling. There had been a gradual upturn in attention toward youth baseball in the years immediately previous. Taipei held its first Private Schools Baseball Tournament in 1967, and scattered reports betrayed the continued proliferation of various youth baseball tournaments, such as the hosting of the second annual All-County Youth Baseball Cup in Yilan in 1966, despite a lack of coverage beyond announcements of schedules.[27] The Students' Baseball Tournament in 1967, for example, barely earned a mention, with a cursory announcement of teams involved, no editorial comment, and no articles following up on the winners of the tournament. One could argue that the hosting of the tournament in Pingdong might explain some of the lack of attention—compared to the following year, when Hongye received so much attention for performances in Taipei—but the differences in media coverage are remarkable.[28] The Hongye victory at the Students' Baseball Tournament in 1968, topped off with a "beautiful" home run to win the game, was lauded for the children's diligence in training and for their emergence from difficult economic conditions thanks to the support of the entire county of Taidong.[29] The boys now symbolized the power of hard work and the availability of opportunity in the steadily strengthening Taiwanese economy.[30]

Clearly many factors fed into the team's popularity and the willingness of the pro-government press to publicize sporting activities it had largely demoted from a position of central attention to the periphery of its sports coverage for almost twenty years. Yet again a team of aboriginal Taiwanese boys captured the imagination of the political heartland of Taipei. The team's record over three years in an island-wide competition also spoke to the children's skill and hard work. Finally, the Hongye achievements fit neatly into a heartwarming success story, proof that even in economically depressed Taidong, the advances of Chinese society and the economy in Taiwan offered opportunities to those willing to work hard to take them.[31] The *Lianhe Bao* repeatedly harped on the economic difficulties facing the team in contrast with its success on the field, with articles focused on the team's available fields on which to practice and the difficulties of securing the necessary equipment.[32] The team's attitude regularly came to the fore, with the children's background in a small provincial school with only 120 students a constant reference and the spectacular winning of two championships in three years made possible by a determination expressed in the team's motto that "If there is a way, we will do it!"[33]

The media attention is fascinating as it came months before Hongye's exhibition game against the Little League team from Kansai that has since established the Taidong children's place in history, the increased coverage supporting Yu Junwei's contention that far from being a pioneer in the Taiwanese game, Hongye merely represented the latest and most successful step forward for youth baseball.[34] The progress of youth baseball in Taiwan under the GMD, though not as heavily publicized as during the colonial era, had continued in the proliferation of teams and tournaments throughout the island. As a highly successful team on the field with a media-friendly background, Hongye became genuinely popular. Andrew Morris points out that the tone of the coverage reveals a GMD government quick to leap at the chance to promote such a popular example of "capitalist spirit," unique to the growing economy of the ROC.[35] It was a happy marriage of GMD propaganda aims and a genuine historical tradition of youth baseball on the island that contributed to the summer games against Kansai becoming a transformative event that made the Hongye team legendary in Taiwan and in particular among Taiwanese baseball fans. The Hongye victory became a mass shared social experience thanks to a combination of the cultivation of a baseball tradition over decades and the impact of television coverage, the political aims of a government seeking a propaganda victory over a fellow sovereign state, and the legacy of Taiwanese moral victories against Japanese teams that predated retrocession.[36] However, the intense coverage of the Hongye victories earlier in the year show that these boys had already created a space in the GMD-controlled public realm for youth baseball that had previously been denied.

In fact media coverage was so cozy that the Hongye players visited the *Lianhe Bao* offices, the occasion and accompanying speeches happily reported in the newspaper's pages, with the publisher, Wang Yiwu, donating baseball gloves to each of the children.[37] Only a few weeks later Xie Guocheng, the head of the Taiwan Sporting Association, announced that an invitation had been extended to a Japanese team in Kansai and had been accepted. The visitors would play five games in Taiwan, including two against Hongye and another against an all-Taiwan side with Hongye ballplayers at its core. The visitors would bring fifteen players, and the games would adhere to strict rules as enforced in Taiwanese baseball competitions. All players were to be under the age of twelve. The newspaper named the visiting team as the 1967 Little League World Series champions.[38] The hype overlooked the fact that this wasn't strictly true; the 1967 team had hailed from Wakayama in Kansai but could not accurately be equated with the visiting Kansai team. The two squads had only one player in common. Nevertheless, the arrival of such an accomplished youth baseball team drove public anticipation.[39]

The games were a major media event, particularly the eagerly awaited showdown between Hongye and the visiting Japanese team. Physical examinations for the boys from Taidong were photographed by attending reporters, and a reserve roster in case of injury was announced.[40] The team played a lengthy series of warmup games up and down the country.[41] A summer visit by the baseball team from Aichi University in Japan was completely overshadowed by coverage of Hongye's preparation, with even the announcement of the university team's arrival and schedule supplemented with another reminder of the impending visit of the Japanese little league team and confirmation of the submission of the local teams' rosters.[42] The hype did not let up throughout the summer, with Hongye piling win upon win.[43] The children duly delivered, solidly defeating the Japanese visitors by a score of 7–0 in front of more than twenty thousand spectators in Taipei. "Chasing the clouds, Hongye Takes Flight" crowed the pages of the *Lianhe Bao* before journalist Zhao Gongsong gleefully lost any pretense of objectivity in describing the crushing victory. The children took a victory lap of the stadium to express their thanks to the fans in attendance as Zhao made a play on words using the Chinese characters of the team name to describe the immediately legendary scene: "the [children] appeared in their red-colored uniforms as falling maple leaves in the dazzling sunlight."[44] On the same day the newspaper openly asserted that Hongye had proven it was ready to travel to Japan itself and to enter the world of international Little League baseball competition.[45]

The Hongye victory did just that, opening the door not just for itself, but also for all Taiwanese elementary school teams. In 1969 the Taizhong Gold Dragon team became the first Taiwanese team to play at the Little League World Series in Williamsport, Pennsylvania. In 1971, as noted, the Tainan Giants became champions, kick-starting a four-year run of Taiwanese titles and confirming the beginning of over a decade of Taiwanese dominance in international youth baseball.[46] The Tainan Giants were particularly feted as the Taiwanese media began to feast in earnest on the international successes of the country's youth teams. One headline read, "Japanese Youth Baseball Standards Already Five Years behind Taiwan," a direct quote from head Japanese youth baseball coach Suzuki Hidetoshi.[47] The article barely concealed the pleasure Taiwanese baseball fans were expected to derive from the admission. The comparison with Japan painted the former imperial power as a foreign nation with an established history in organized baseball, while Taiwanese youngsters were the products of Chinese innovation and hard work. There was no mention of the sport's roots in the colonial period. Competition in the Little League World Series was an exciting foray for the increasingly isolated Taiwan into international exchanges with other nations and a chance for those Chinese residing in America and loyal to the ROC to show their support for Chiang Kai-shek's regime.[48] The Tainan players were welcomed home by a victory parade with over ten thousand onlookers, each player photographed in suit and victory sash.[49]

It would not always be so perfect. Yu Junwei has highlighted the dark side to the Taiwanese success in Little League World Series competition: a willingness to flaunt the rules of eligibility for players that dates back as far as Hongye's domestic success before its landmark victory over the Japanese visiting team in 1968.[50] It is important not to ignore such issues when discussing sporting events that the government-supported media willfully promoted to great effect. For our purposes the importance lies in the fact that baseball had come to occupy such an important role in ROC propaganda both within and outside of Taiwan. The Hongye victory symbolizes a central point in narratives about Taiwanese political identities. For the GMD-controlled media that sought to publicize Hongye's success, Little League baseball offered an avenue into high-profile events centered on international cultural exchange, notably in the heartland of Taiwan's erstwhile Cold War ally, the United States. The signature Hongye victory over its Japanese opponent in 1968 marked the beginning of a story that justified GMD political ideals and furthered the country's international interactions. In more recent years, as the political climate in Taiwan has allowed interpretations of its baseball history that can accept the Japanese legacy in bringing the sport to the island, the Hongye victory comfortably takes its place on a narrative line joining the team's successes with those of the Nōkō team in the 1920s and the various Kanō teams in the 1930s.

A place for Hongye on a third narrative line places the team at the terminal point: as much as Hongye's 1968 victory was a beginning for baseball's role in the promulgation of a Chinese identity and subsequently an arena for dispute regarding the composition of that identity as it related to Taiwan, it was the end of Taiwanese baseball's participation in a singularly Japanese cultural enterprise dating back to the first recorded game on Taiwanese soil in 1906. Japanese authorities had been happy to see Taiwanese children embrace a sport so popular in Japan, to take part in a community that spanned imperial core and colonial satellite alike. Youth baseball had persisted as the gateway for local Taiwanese into an appreciation of the sport and as the greatest opportunity for Taiwanese athletes to excel beyond the island's boundaries, all defined by Japanese expectations and expectations modeled on Japanese examples. Even the achievements of the Nōkō and Kanō teams existed in a context separate from an expression of Taiwanese independence, with the former treated as an exotic novelty and the latter the subject of the transposed hopes and dreams of colonial Japanese organizers of youth baseball in Taipei. More and more local Taiwanese filtered into the playing of the game through the framework offered by organized youth baseball, so much so that after retrocession these traditions continued. Though ignored or only briefly mentioned by the official media, the emergence of Hongye and the team's victory in established organized competitions show that baseball had indeed persisted as a popular sport in postwar Taiwan as a direct evolution of the sporting administrative and competitive infrastructures created under Japanese rule. After 1968 there was no ambiguity about the political implications of each Taiwanese victory in Williamsport. Success on the field had become an important tool of political propaganda, and the political system had finally turned its attention to manipulating the popularity of youth baseball in Taiwan. The center of Taiwanese baseball attention now rested on Taiwan itself and its emerging complex ideological battles. The sport's days as a cultural practice on the periphery of Japanese experience were over.

In the late 1960s the function of baseball in Taiwanese society changed. Baseball became the domain of a purely Taiwanese conversation, separated from any Japanese influence for the first time. For decades baseball in Taiwan had been imbued with various political meanings and implications. In the colonial period Japanese officials looked on as local Taiwanese youths put on the same uniforms and took to the field to play the same game as their Japanese counterparts. However, the sport's role in enveloping Taiwan in a Japanese cultural sphere was less the product of specific policy aimed at using baseball as a Japanizing tool and more the result of a cultural practice cherished and pursued by multiple individuals, that spread out from Tokyo to the edges of its young empire. The ROC government was happy to support adult amateur teams in international competition after retrocession—or at least to refrain from persecuting baseball players in the manner it chose to persecute speakers of non-Mandarin dialects—but the Hongye victory in 1968 created the perfect intersection of public support, official interest, and political opportunity. As Taiwanese supporters clashed on baseball fields in Pennsylvania and Little League teams returned to Taipei to heroes' welcomes in the years that followed, it became clear that baseball was a more central part of specifically Taiwanese political questions than ever before.

The transition of baseball in Taiwan from an amorphous body of cultural and political elements to a highly publicized vehicle of national solidarity resulted in a handful of protests at baseball games in Pennsylvania with far-reaching consequences. It is reasonable to deduce that pro-Taiwan sentiments there were shared by many living under the GMD regime who were unable to similarly express their political beliefs.[51] The political connotations of Taiwanese baseball in the early 1970s were mixed, with pro-independence sentiment foreshadowing greater social and political upheavals to come later in the decade with the rise of the *dangwai* movement and the limits of ROC propaganda surrounding Little League teams revealed by the Taiwanese public's deeper interests in the increase in both the ROC's economic fortunes and political isolation.[52] Whatever the limits of ROC propaganda, the government's motives in promoting Taiwanese Little League teams in the early 1970s were clear: to finally sever the popular sport from its colonial past and to assist in improving the ROC's ever-declining international profile. Baseball became appropriated as a tool in the attempted continued integration of an international system. GMD support for Taiwanese Little League teams, despite the continued popularity of the game after retrocession, came to life only once there was a political opportunity attached to baseball competitions. After 1968, as the political manifestations of a gradually evolving Taiwanese identity began to emerge, a new stage of baseball's role in society began.

Big changes lay ahead. The United States formally recognized the PRC in 1979, cementing a process that saw Taiwan's international standing tumble still further as more and more nations throughout the world entered into exclusive full diplomatic relations with the Beijing government. The late 1980s saw a number of political developments that radically changed the nature of Taiwanese cultural and political society. New GMD policies terminated martial law and permitted the formation of new political parties. Lee Teng-hui consolidated his own political power at the head of the ROC government, supported further Taiwanization of that government, and in 1996 comfortably won the first direct election for the head of government in the history of the ROC.[53] *Minnanhua* was no longer confined to the privacy of the family home or baseball field but instead became a new tool for politicians eager to gain popularity.[54] More recently the end of DPP politician Chen Shui-bian's presidency and his fall from grace seemingly brought the curtain down on an era when rhetoric in support of Taiwanese independence was at its highest ebb, only for subsequent president Ma Ying-jeou to see his policy of more open and friendly relations with the PRC crumble in the face of his decline in popularity and the increased frustration of democratic activism in Taiwan and Hong Kong. The DPP's Tsai Ing-wen assumed the ROC presidency in early 2016 with a broad mandate following a thoroughly convincing victory at the polls. The Taiwanese now live in a society slowly moving beyond the previous dichotomies of colonial legacy and retrocession, of pro-unification and pro-independence.

The days when Taiwanese children dominated the world of youth baseball are over. Taiwan's Little League representatives in Williamsport still perform admirably, but the last of the country's sixteen Little League World Series titles came in 1996. In Taiwan itself the popularity of baseball took a spectacular hit when Little League Baseball (LLB) decided to suspend the admittance of foreign entrants to the Little League World Series in 1975, mainly due to rumors of cheating and concerns at the rampant success of the Taiwanese teams.[55] Although LLB subsequently rescinded the ban only a year later, the swift return of Taiwanese teams to prominence—they won five titles in a row—did little to reverse the sport's decline in popularity. By the end of the 1970s baseball was no longer the credible venue for the expression of political sentiment that it had been ten years earlier.[56] By the end of the twentieth century baseball's prominence in Taiwanese society was at its lowest point since the 1920s after a succession of issues, most notably the country's first professional baseball league's embroilment in a sordid gambling scandal.[57]

What does it all mean? History didn't end in 1968 after all. It is clear that sports do not automatically serve as vessels for political expression or incubators for political sentiment, regardless of the broader sociopolitical environment. Baseball in Taiwan, though still popular, has declined as the premier sport in the country, damaged by scandal and its political efficacy reduced by the political liberalization of Taiwanese society. Heterogeneity in social groups has ultimately played against expectations for Taiwan's transition into a nation-state mimicking developments in larger countries, though not for reasons that may have been first suspected. Economic concerns played into an abandonment of semantic contests over the fate of China and Taiwan and the steps taken on a linear path to national salvation, only for Hong Kong's visions of a future within a reunified China to revive the political debates at the heart of Taiwanese democracy. These arguments continue of course. However, such arguments have mostly been shuffled to the margins of each society, and with them have gone the more salient features of the overtly political role for baseball in Taiwan. Although 1968 may have been the end of one process of baseball's involvement in Taiwanese political society and the beginning of another, the latter process was short-lived.

As with any discussion involving concepts of nationalism, we are drawn to the narrative created by those looking to legitimize their respective national stories. Today both Chinese- and English-language works on the history of baseball in Taiwan accept a narrative in which the Hongye team forms a crucial part, confirming the survival of the sport after retrocession and launching Taiwanese baseball into a brave new era. However, in many ways the Hongye team signals the end of one narrative and the beginning of another. In defeating the Kansai visiting team in Taipei, the Hongye team finally achieved a victory that had proved beyond the reach of the Nōkō team in the 1920s or even the Kanō team in 1931. The victory, and subsequent Taiwanese dominance of the Little League World Series in the 1970s, obliterated the cultural bridge created between baseball communities in Taiwan and Japan during the colonial period, a relationship defined in part by Japanese dominance. All of the excitement surrounding visits from Waseda University, the outpourings of support for Oh Sadaharu, and the previous exploits of Taiwanese teams in Japan fed into a baseball culture that viewed Japan as the center of the game in Asia. The team provided a transformative moment for the sport, despite the darker side of the youngsters' success.[58]

The Hongye team was not just an important milestone in the emergence of Taiwanese baseball as an international sport transformed into an indigenous cultural form imbued with political implications for Taiwanese independence. The team was also the terminal point of sixty years of Japanese-led development of the game in Taiwan. The

Japanese creation of the baseball infrastructure on the island and the development of youth baseball led to the Hongye moment, the definitive defeat of a Japanese champion. Taiwanese baseball in some ways provides an anti-narrative: the gradual development of baseball in Taiwan as an enterprise among individuals in both Japan and Taiwan refuses to conform to narratives seeking to develop the Taiwanese (as distinct from Chinese) roots of a popular cultural form. There is no model for such an idealized political journey, as the idea itself is compromised by a certain assumption of linear historical narrative. The long process of extricating a distinct and individual Taiwanese identity from the web of intersections between the island's traditional Chinese inheritance and the best modernizing efforts of the Japanese colonial authorities came to a head and began to hurtle toward an uncertain conclusion. In 1968 the last vestiges of Taiwanese baseball's participation in a broader Japanese world disintegrated in the face of emerging inherently local political concerns.

This transition from a sport within a broader Japanese cultural sphere to an arena of specific Chinese disputes eclipses baseball's ostensible potential for elucidating a more traditional postcolonial narrative. Who are the bad guys in the Taiwanese sporting world, the nemeses to an emerging Taiwanese state? The frustration of that emergence and the wide-ranging ideological conundrums facing those Taiwanese who wish to illustrate a Taiwanese pathway to modernity and statehood completely separate from that of mainland China complicate the potential for baseball to fill that role. Reluctance by the GMD to embrace the sport's colonial roots limited any such narrative around the 1968 Hongye victory, instead casting the Japanese as the avatars of high-level play in East Asia. The transition of Taiwanese baseball into a field of conflict within a broader political and ideological debate, featuring sides who either embrace or reject the terms of that debate as being a domestic affair, has, regardless of which side of the argument holds the upper hand at any one time, seen the sport become representative of an internalized conversation.

For those arguing in favor of a single China awaiting reunification, not just in the abstract but within the context of Taipei's role as a champion of a benevolent Chinese modernity, Hongye functions as a symbol of a vibrant postwar Chinese generation come to life. When the Hongye Little League team succeeded in 1968, its victory was celebrated as a political victory, akin to the reception awarded the traveling Beijing opera performers in London in 1957, with the added bonuses of broad public support and celebration that embraced the Taiwanese working classes and a lack of reliance on contiguous cultural territory with the ancient historical sites of mainland China. By that time compulsory education was more effective in Taiwan that at any time during the colonial period, with over 97 percent of school-aged children enrolled in primary schools. A further 58 percent of those who graduated from primary education went on to attend junior high.[59] A higher proportion of Taiwanese children than ever before now attended school on a regular basis, and in addition to the clear advantages for the state in regulating the population and producing more efficient citizens, more Taiwanese children were regularly exposed to a competitive, formally administrated system for team sport competitions. The Hongye team represented a victory for the Taiwanese educational system as it finally sought to reclaim the ground won by the thoroughness of the Japanese educational system before it. It was a victory for the GMD's vision for a modern China.

Hongye's connections to Kanō and Nōkō hold greater importance for those who wish to tell a Taiwanese history in which retrocession features as the stifling of a potential Taiwanese society ready to emerge from Japan's and China's shadow. In this telling continuity among the three teams reveals a Taiwanese story that both survives the colonial period and refutes the GMD's insistence on its monopoly on definitions of Chinese identity and experience. Baseball thus becomes a vessel for Taiwanese identity, an avenue for expression by the colonized against the colonizer, but only if one accepts the validity of *benshengren* and *waishengren* in those roles, and still then only after 1968. It's a funny thing to celebrate a colonial game without much antipathy toward the imperialists. Conflicts between the GMD and local Taiwanese in the years following retrocession helped in creating a Taiwanese narrative that chose to counter GMD accusations of Japanese colonial enslavement with an embrace of Japan's role in modernizing Taiwanese political society.[60] Baseball offers a clear example of Taiwanese social experience before and after 1945 in Taiwanese life, supporting arguments for a broader view of Taiwanese identity as an indigenous, organic emergence across many decades rather than simply a reaction to the overreach of postwar martial law.[61] For those seeking to fully illuminate baseball's importance in Taiwanese history the game offers not disruption, but continuity. Taiwanese baseball failed to follow a familiar colonial and postcolonial pattern, to present itself as a medium for engagement with, if not protest against, a dominating power both during and after the period of colonial dominance. This failure derived from the realities of the sport's emergence and flourishing within a clearly defined Japanese sphere, as Taiwanese teams participated in a Japan-centric baseball world; it also owed much to the reluctance of the postwar ROC regime to embrace baseball's potential as part of a broader policy of ignoring Taiwan's colonial past in an effort to deny it legitimacy.

Conclusion | BASEBALL'S LONG GOODBYE

Is the Taiwanese celebration of the colonial origins of Taiwanese baseball another iteration of the American fretting over the increased median ages of people going to games, the knowledge that in truth the game resides in the past, the source of its power and the limit of its reach? Taiwanese baseball has had a tough few decades since its heyday of the 1970s; the adults have never reached the heights of the Little Leaguers in terms of global success, and corruption scandals and concerns over commercial viability have rocked professional baseball on the island. Discussing the game's past and the political implications of its origins in Taiwanese society is often more comforting than pondering its future. It's a different set of concerns from those of aging American baseball fans looking over their shoulders at basketball, American football, and social media, but it leaves Taiwanese baseball fans in a similar state of isolated pessimism. When Americans look at the history of baseball, they increasingly view it with skepticism but with confidence natural to the creators and unassailable custodians of the national pastime. John Thorn, maven of Major League Baseball's history, opens his loving but very knowing history of the game, *Baseball in the Garden of Eden*, by stating outright that the sport's "whole history is a lie from beginning to end," from the confused origins of the Doubleday myth to the present day's illusions of fair play and commercial egalitarianism.[1] Taiwanese who look to belatedly create the concept of a "national game" cannot afford Thorn's witty confidence, the viability of Taiwanese baseball itself seemingly under threat and the opportunity to discuss its development in the colonial period relatively recent.

History writing is a creative enterprise, and histories often bear the intent of their writers, whether by conscious intent or otherwise. It is not surprising then that historians are increasingly casting the colonial history of Taiwanese baseball as evidence of a singular Taiwanese identity, existing, even in rough sketches, prior to 1945. These narratives fit neatly into complex and vigorous discussions in Taiwan that center on the meaning of being Taiwanese and how that intersects with Taiwan's Han Chinese citizens' ethnic and cultural heritage. Such approaches also open conversations to more cosmopolitan territory rather than to checkered dichotomies of those in power and those dispossessed. The Japanese become expediters of a Taiwanese consciousness, though not its originators. Taiwanese nationalism seems unlikely to fall into the problems raised by the Irish "building a not-England, but now . . . playing at being not-Irish," as Declan Kiberd put it, albeit thanks in large part to a lack of interest or perceived need in defending culturally Chinese aspects of Taiwanese identity from lingering contaminants of colonial rule.[2] The old GMD mandate in disseminating an unrivaled history of the nation-state's role in Taiwan's history slowly dissipates in the face of such inroads, the insecurities of those predisposed to support some variation of Taiwanese independence somewhat allayed by another example of a Taiwanese community existing outside of definitions derived from the mainland. The transition to democracy in Taiwan, elevated by the direct presidential elections of 1992 and 1996, brought an effective regime change that made such analyses and subsequent conversations possible. The need to create a clear Taiwanese story evolves from a narrative of Taiwanese nationalism that relies heavily on the recent history of opposition to Chiang Kai-shek's authoritarian government and accompanying cultural priorities.[3] The notion of an incipient nationalist communal impulse, flexible in both its treatment of ethnic diversity among Han Chinese and aboriginal

Taiwanese and its ability to gently and slowly flourish under Japanese colonial rule, is an appealing one.

Still it requires a certain amount of moving things around. Japanese colonial control of Taiwan may have been relatively benign, life in Taipei overall considerably less fraught with the potential for violence than that in Seoul, but the Japanese controlled the press and had free reign to enforce their own ideas about colonial identity as a part of the imperial whole. This impulse did not reach its zenith until *kōminka* arrived in Taiwan in 1937, but it was always there. Such willingness to overlook the undoubted hardships of Japanese colonial rule are relatively common, a potent mixture of nostalgia among some Taiwanese and the compounded influence of bitterness over the GMD's overzealous and unyielding re-Sinicization of the decades following World War II.[4] Taiwanese baseball benefits from this, having arrived to Taiwanese shores as a Japanese game, remaining American only in an abstract sense, the same sport played by children in New York but carefully interpreted by Japanese players and administrators for their own use in terms of organization on and off the field. The Japanese heritage passed on to Taiwan lay in the formal frameworks of organized competitive team play, eventually culminating in the possibility of a trip to Kōshien. For some this provides evidence of the sport's utility in ideological conversion of local Taiwanese, as Joseph A. Reaves sees when describing baseball as "a helpful part of the 'Japanization' formula" in the promotion of the sport in high schools and colleges by colonial forces.[5] However, the spread of the sport was far from that of systematic promotion by the colonial government with specific ideological intentions. If anything, the persistent exclusion of local Taiwanese from organized baseball in the 1910s lends credence to Yu Junwei's argument that the colonial Japanese initially actively maintained the sport as a pursuit for Japanese people out of a mixture of racially motivated disdain for local Taiwanese and concern at the possibilities of an awakened Taiwanese youth.[6]

The late 1910s saw a convergence of factors that contributed to the spread of baseball's popularity among local Taiwanese in the 1920s: a commitment from a new governor-general to switch from gradualism and coexistence to assimilation, legislation designed to apply these principles to the colonial education system, and the continued integration of Taiwan into a popular culture dominated by Japan. In this last regard the steadily growing appeal of the Tokyo baseball scene, dominated by collegiate powerhouses such as Waseda University, continued in Taiwan, spreading beyond colonial Japanese support to the local Taiwanese community as the appeal of baseball steadily increased. Regular arrangements among representative teams from north and south Taiwan were common at the beginning of the Western calendar new year. Series among these teams featured the now ubiquitous ceremonial qualities of pristine modern uniforms and lining up for photographs before commencement of the game.[7] The sport became more popular as more people were exposed to it and as the infrastructure throughout Taiwan improved.[8] This process, clearly impossible without the frameworks and machinery of Japanese imperialism and colonialism, nevertheless adopted an organic veneer that translated neatly into an accepted legitimacy.

There is little evidence of the colonial government's utilizing the sport to overtly "Japanize" the local Taiwanese, any more than the government used tennis or sumo. In addition, there is no parallel in Taiwanese colonial history to the coalition of intellectual and cultural forces behind the resurgence of Gaelic Games in late nineteenth-century and early twentieth-century Ireland, for example, where sporting culture became an integral part of newly minted conceptualizations of the modern ethnically centered nation-state.[9] The popularity of baseball in Taiwan owes much to the development of the colonial education system and the willing support of the colonial Japanese press, particularly from the early 1920s onward. The game ultimately thrived thanks to the enthusiasm of young Japanese professionals moving to a new colony in the 1900s, the enthusiasm of colonial Japanese and local Taiwanese children in the 1920s and 1930s, and the persistent numbers of adults attending games. As George Gmelch puts it, "Deliberately attempting to introduce the game is quite different from being an inadvertent catalyst for its growth."[10] Popular appeal, that ethereal concept so frustrating to historical investigation, is the main culprit in the sport's development in Taiwan. For Taiwanese baseball that popular appeal grew within Japanese parameters, fleshed out and sustained by Japanese examples and definitions, driven by colonial Japanese and a government-controlled press but not by specific government policy akin to the imposition of the Japanese language on children in Taiwanese and Korean classrooms.

In the latter half of the colonial period, the increased popularity of the game among local Taiwanese accompanied the continued domination of Japanese colonials in the organization and administration of baseball as competitions became more sophisticated and popular. Japanese influence persisted in the popularity of baseball after the 1945 retrocession, as high-profile visits from Waseda University baseball teams and the flurry of media activity surrounding visits by baseball star Oh Sadaharu attest. Taiwanese baseball was part of a broader Japanese cultural complex from its inception. The growth of the sport on the island as an aspect of a Japanese cultural sphere developed steadily under Japanese control but proved successful enough to last for at least two decades after the removal of the Japanese imperialist government from Taiwan's shores. This process goes beyond the dichotomy of assimilation and resistance played out on so many sports fields across the world. Taiwanese baseball successes prior to 1945 came as the result of active and enthusiastic participation in a regional baseball community centered on Tokyo, successes after 1945 measured against that Japanese standard until the Hongye victory in 1968 opened the door to a new era. From 1968 on baseball was unquestionably a "national game" in Taiwan. Indeed it was a particularly complicated one, the success of Little Leaguers in bringing international attention to Taiwan raising questions Chiang and his fellow GMD leaders had for years refused to countenance. The reality of the postwar games was, as Andrew Morris puts it, that the game in Taiwan "never thoroughly shed its Japanese heritage."[11]

Today Taiwanese scholars point to the postwar cultural clashes between baseball and sports more favorable to ROC officialdom, such as basketball, and the use of language on Taiwanese baseball fields to highlight the relationship between baseball and a *benshengren* identity.[12]

The sport has, since the early 1970s, rested at the center of a conflict among competing views for Taiwan that increasingly incorporate a specific form of identity politics.[13] This makes baseball a quintessentially domestic affair, insofar as Taiwanese politics can remain domestic beyond a determination to frame Taiwanese issues as part of a broader China question on both sides of the strait. The Chinese-language historiography surrounding Taiwanese baseball reflects a concerted effort to locate the sport's development in a narrative of Taiwanese progress that neither denies nor is consumed by either Japanese or mainland Chinese influence. Awkward references to aboriginal Taiwanese taking to the game naturally because of their daily habits of swinging sticks and throwing stones remain in some of the more popular works, as do sparkling reviews of the Hongye team's heroic efforts, despite Yu Junwei's recent work in uncovering some decidedly unsavory gray areas in the players' eligibility to play for the Little League side.[14] Throughout there is a decided effort to pronounce the initiative of local Taiwanese and the progress of the game in representing something unique to the island, something culturally distinct from either Taiwan's Chinese cultural inheritance or colonial Japanese cultural influence. Today's representations of the history of Taiwanese baseball continue in a process of defining Taiwanese identity and presenting cultural evidence of such.

The colonial period is vital to that conversation, with baseball assured an important role thanks to its survival of the postwar GMD anti-Japanese cultural purge and its continued popularity among the Taiwanese. Japanese imperial control of Taiwan now serves as backdrop and context to conversations more preoccupied with diverse political positions within Taiwan and the continued lumbering presence of the PRC. Indeed the Sunflower Movement in Taiwan and the Umbrella Movement in Hong Kong in 2014 hint at a new regionalist chapter in the history of Taiwanese conversations on independence and identity. Is this perhaps the beginning of a new cultural sphere shared between Taipei and Hong Kong, one that would actively sustain and encourage further agitation toward Taiwanese independence? It is rather early to tell, but it is instructive; participation in a transnational cultural sphere hardly precludes the nationalist impulse.

Active participation in cultural practice defined by Japanese parameters does not automatically imply a paucity of nationalist potential or reveal a weakness in the emerging Taiwanese nationalist narrative. Nor, in Taiwan's case, does it tie into a neat narrative of eager Japanese cultural obliteration of its neighbors. The history of Taiwanese baseball rather reveals the depth of shared experience under imperial rule, a window into the possibilities of regional identity emerging in East Asia prior to World War II. Those possibilities were thwarted in large part by the overextension of Japanese ideological claims in terms of that Asian identity and profoundly undermined by the horrors wrought by the Japanese military throughout the region. Still colonial Japanese and local Taiwanese played together with a clear eye toward the playing fields of Tokyo and Kōshien, and baseball thrived because of its popularity with people introduced to the joys of participation through organized play or attending games with others.

Japan utterly failed to emerge in postwar Taiwan as an "other" to Taiwanese group identities formed around the surviving baseball community, largely due to this shared heritage. The GMD's muddled approach to public engagement with Japan did not help, struggling as the party did in playing the part of Cold War ally with Tokyo against the background of political and social programs that emphasized specific views of Chinese identity and modernity in direct contrast with Taiwan's colonial legacies. During and after Hongye's run of popularity the GMD was only too happy to promote the Little League successes of Taiwanese teams in Pennsylvania as a victory for the legitimate government of China. The Japanese opposition played into the dynamic as representative of the highest standard of opposition, not as a former conqueror laid low. The rhetoric now fed into an internationally focused narrative. GMD officials utilized baseball to define the ingroup, proud citizens of the rightful government of China. The Little League World Series swiftly became "a crusade in which the duty of Taiwanese children was to bring home a victory."[15] The pressure on the boys was immense: success in Williamsport brought international attention, a valuable resource becoming increasingly scarce for the ROC as the 1970s went on. Postwar fears for Taiwan's future and recognition of its past were evident, whether on the part of those who dreamed of an independent country or those who supported varying methods of embracing a common Chinese future, the focus not on Tokyo but on Beijing.

The ever-evolving complexity and uncertainty of Taiwan's fate, whether as future independent nation, reconciled province of China, or something in between, renders Taiwan somewhat unique and, from a nationalist point of view, tragic. Hopes for Taiwanese autonomy have been stifled not by the institutions laid down by Japanese imperialists but by the political goals of a constituency that arrived to Taiwan viewing the island as a fallback position for prolonged irredentism. The return of mainland China to the status of a major global power, with Beijing's continued stated intent of reincorporating Taiwan into its own state structure, renders the immediate likelihood of a Taiwanese nation-state remote. Taiwanese baseball as a result has functioned not as a postcolonial hangover but as a symptom of the enduring influence of Japan on Taiwanese society in the decades following retrocession, despite the GMD's best efforts, before transitioning into a mechanism for intra-Taiwanese debates on cultural identity. Memory of Japanese influence today portrays the former imperialists as the cultivators and gatekeepers to a sport that soon became a national game without a nation (or at least without a nation-state). Life would perhaps be easier for Taiwanese nationalists if there were a clearly defined opponent that united the varying factions within Taiwanese politics and breathed life into a grand narrative of defiance. Then again, maybe that's the trick: Taiwanese baseball offers a glimpse at alternatives to sport's providing more battlefields for the same arguments, though admittedly due more to the swallowing up of one society-defining political question by another. It is not a model easily repeated but certainly one that opens the doors to exciting new interpretations of sport's interactions with national identity.

Notes

Introduction

1. Guttmann, *Games and Empires*, 179–80.
2. Guha, *A Corner of a Foreign Field*, 323–25, 343–46.
3. Norman Fox, "8 ft Fence for Hooligans at Wembley," *Times* (London), June 6, 1977, 3.
4. Andrew Hussey, "zz Top," *The Observer*, April 3, 2004. https://www .theguardian.com/football/2004/apr/04/sport.features.
5. Bairner, *Sport, Nationalism, and Globalization*, 163–177.
6. Guha, *A Corner of a Foreign Field*, 3–11.
7. James, *Beyond a Boundary*, 49–65.
8. See, for example, Jiang Mingshan, *Nizhuansheng*, 61–66.
9. Xie, *"Guoqiu" dansheng qianji*, 420–31.
10. Gold, "Civil Society and Taiwan's Quest for Identity," 48.
11. Hopkins, "Introduction: Interactions between the Universal and the Local," in Hopkins, *Global History*, 11.
12. Tanaka, *Japan's Orient*, 3–7, 191–99.
13. Kleeman, *Under an Imperial Sun*, 228–30.
14. Zarrow, *After Empire*, 212–41.
15. Yu, *Playing in Isolation*, 8–11.

1. A Japanese Sport in the Colony

1. Roy, *Taiwan*, 32–33.
2. Peattie, "Japanese Attitudes towards Colonialism," 80–83.
3. Kodama and Gotō held office in the Japanese colonial administration in Taiwan from 1898 to 1906, but policies they put in motion were adhered to and replicated until Den Kenjirō's arrival in Taiwan in 1919.

4. Tsurumi, *Japanese Colonial Education in Taiwan*, 41–42.

5. Gotō Shimpei, preface Yosaburo Takekoshi, *Japanese Rule in Formosa*, v–vi.

6. Duus, *The Abacus and the Sword: The Japanese Penetration of Korea*, 23.

7. Kleeman, *Under an Imperial Sun*, 130–45.

8. Tsurumi, "Education and Assimilation in Taiwan under Japanese Rule," 618–19.

9. Gluck, *Japan's Modern Myths*, 102–11, 146–56.

10. Tsurumi, *Japanese Colonial Education in Taiwan*, 18.

11. It is worth pointing out that Qing attitudes to the island had varied considerably between its recovery from Ming loyalists in 1683 and its ceding to Japan in 1895, from a "ball of mud," according to the Kangxi emperor, to an island wilderness beyond the imperial frontier to an important and integral part of that frontier. See Teng, *Taiwan's Imagined Geography*, 34–59.

12. The *shufang* schools translate into Japanese as *shōbo*, a term used extensively by E. Patricia Tsurumi. Although either term is acceptable when discussing the colonial period, I have chosen to use the Chinese-language transliteration.

13. Tsurumi, *Japanese Colonial Education in Taiwan*, 19.

14. Tsurumi, *Japanese Colonial Education in Taiwan*, 60

15. Brownell, *Training the Body for China*, 35.

16. This approach was part of a wider Japanese commitment to the cultivation of individual physical health as part of a broader interpretation of public health that sought to introduce various forms of physical exercise to the daily habits of the Taiwanese. See Lin Ting-kuo, "Cong (guanyuan xiansheng riji) kan linxiantang de tiyu huodong," 796–97.

17. Tsurumi, *Japanese Colonial Education in Taiwan*, 68–71.

18. Tsurumi, *Japanese Colonial Education in Taiwan*, 81–91.

19. Tsurumi, *Japanese Colonial Education in Taiwan*, 84–86.

20. Shimahara, *Adaptation and Education in Japan*, 56–58.

21. Duke, *The History of Modern Japanese Education*, 249–53.

22. Hirose Kenzo, *Nihon no yakyūshi*, 1–4.

23. Reaves, *Taking in a Game*, 49–52.

24. Tobita, *Waseda Daigaku yakyūbu hyakunenshi*, 83.

25. Tobita, *Waseda Daigaku yakyūbu hyakunenshi*, 255–58.

26. Yu, *Taiwan bangqiu bainianshi*, 13–14.

27. Tsurumi, *Japanese Colonial Education in Taiwan*, 74–76.

28. See Xie, *"Guoqiu" dansheng qianji*, 50–51, where middle-school teachers from across the colony discussed their fears that baseball had fundamentally detrimental impacts on their students.

29. Yu, *Taiwan bangqiu bainianshi*, 15.

30. "Minami kita yakyū sai" [Baseball world north and south], *Nichi Nichi Shimpō*, July 4, 1914, 7. An article describing the growing popularity of base-

ball in the Tainan area recounts the positive effect on the participants of Waseda graduates turning out to play for local teams.

31. The Military Ethics Association branches served as early hosts for Western sports in Taiwan, including baseball. See "Kyō no Yakyū to Tenisu" [Today's baseball and tennis] *Nichi Nichi Shimpō*, September 6, 1908.

32. Yu, *Taiwan bangqiu bainianshi*, 12.

33. "Shimo tai N Yakyū Kai" [Frost vs. N Baseball Association], *Nichi Nichi Shimpō*, April 26, 1908, 5.

34. "Kaku gakkō kishukusha no kinkyō" [The present state of college dormitories], *Nichi Nichi Shimpō*, April 23, 1908, 2. All 347 of the dormitory residents mentioned in the article participated in baseball, as well as table tennis, for entertainment.

35. This focus on Japan's civilizing capacity and responsibility was particularly prevalent in the first twenty years of colonial rule in Taiwan as part of a vision of Japanese imperialism focused on the European standard. See Peattie, "Japanese Attitudes towards Colonialism," 80–127.

36. "Rengō yakyū sai" [Organized baseball game] *Nichi Nichi Shimpō*, June 15, 1914, 5.

37. "Kyō no yakyū sen" [Today's baseball game], *Nichi Nichi Shimpō*, November 23, 1914, 5.

38. Xie and Xie, *Taiwan bangqiu yibainian*, 27.

39. Yu, *Taiwan bangqiu bainianshi*, 15–16.

40. "Yakyū shiai" [Baseball game], *Nichi Nichi Shimpō*, February 11, 1911.

41. "Taihoku no yakyū sen" [Taipei baseball games], *Nichi Nichi Shimpō*, September 27, 1910.

42. "Tainan yakyū shiai" [Tainan baseball game], *Nichi Nichi Shimpō*, January 29, 1911; "Jippa hito karage" [Sweeping generalizations], *Nichi Nichi Shimpō*, December 11, 1913.

43. "Rengō yakyū daikai" [United baseball tournament], *Nichi Nichi Shimpō*, April 1, 1911.

44. Yu, *Taiwan bangqiu bainianshi*, 15; "Hokubu Yakyū Kyōkai" [Northern Baseball Association], *Nichi Nichi Shimpō*, January 15, 1915, 3.

45. Xie, *"Guoqiu" dansheng qianji*, 54.

46. Guttmann and Thompson, *Japanese Sports*, 131.

47. Guttmann and Thompson, *Japanese Sports*, 83.

48. "Yakyū macchi" [Baseball match], *Nichi Nichi Shimpō*, February 1, 1908, 5.

49. "Kinen yakyū daikai" [Anniversary baseball tournament], *Nichi Nichi Shimpō*, June 9, 1915.

50. The CB club, for example, became quite prominent in the late 1910s. See "Kinō no yakyū sen: CB jyū ten zaibu go ten" [Yesterday's baseball game: CB ten runs, Financial, five runs], *Nichi Nichi Shimpō*, January 23, 1916.

51. "Gakujidan katsu" [University graduate team wins], *Nichi Nichi Shimpō*, October 29, 1916.

52. "Tainan yakyū sōha sen" [Tainan competitive game], *Nichi Nichi Shimpō*, October 22, 1917.

53. "Duanting yeqiu jinjian" [Recent baseball events in Duanting], *Nichi Nichi Shimpō*, October 9, 1914.

54. Xie, *Rizhi shiqi Taiwan bangqiu koushu fangtan*, 44–46.

55. The "New Park" in Taipei quickly became the venue for all major baseball events in the colonial capital, as in 1915, when it hosted a baseball tournament convened to honor the anniversary of Japan's acquisition of Taiwan. See, for example, "Kinen yakyū daikai" [Anniversary baseball grand tournament], *Nichi Nichi Shimpō*, June 19, 1915, 3.

56. Peattie, "Japanese Attitudes toward Colonialism," 84–85.

57. It should be noted that the *shufang* schools continued to exist in name at least until 1940. The schools had long since been forced to implement changes to their curriculum at the behest of Japanese authorities, and there were not more than ten thousand *shufang* students at one time at any point after 1919. See Tsurumi, *Japanese Colonial Education in Taiwan*, Appendix C, 246.

58. Tsurumi, *Japanese Colonial Education in Taiwan*, 91–93.

59. Kleeman, *Under an Imperial Sun*, 121–30.

60. Despite the lofty goals of the rescript, Denny Roy accurately describes colonial education as "less openly discriminatory" after 1922. See Roy, *Taiwan*, 42.

61. Tsurumi, *Japanese Colonial Education in Taiwan*, 94–99. It is interesting that a government study published in 1923 showed that Taiwanese common school students were regularly outperforming their Japanese primary school counterparts at various academic levels. The publication of the study was limited, and the more commonly accepted concern that integration would hold back Japanese students remained popular.

62. Tsurumi, *Japanese Colonial Education in Taiwan*, 113.

63. "Shōnen yakyū to gakusei sumō" [Boys' baseball and student sumo], *Nichi Nichi Shimpō*, May 14, 1923, 7. A photograph in the article formed part of broad coverage of student athletic activities happening that week, featuring a variety of sports, including tennis. Although the ideological aims of supporting children's athletics in this way are clear, the coverage features no specific ideological language regarding loyalty to the empire.

64. It is important here to distinguish between a social identity based on residence in Taiwan, separate from participation in either Japanese or Chinese national identities, and the specific phenomenon of the "Taiwanese" identity often discussed as emerging in the 1990s. In addition to being liable to misperception and confusion, the issue of using "Taiwanese identity" as any kind of label at all is itself an exercise in the "performative powers" of language. See Harrison, *Legitimacy, Meaning and Knowledge in the Making of Taiwanese Identity*, 51–63.

65. Despite Gotō's decision to adopt a gradualist approach stressing coexistence, there was no question that the modernization so successful in Japan would be applied in Taiwan. The Japanese felt something akin to a moral obligation derived from Social Darwinist influence. See Duus, *The Abacus and the Sword*, 432.

66. Japanese colonial educational policy in Taiwan was established by the end of Gotō Shimpei's tenure as chief administrator in 1906. The focus was firmly set on preparing a stratum of Taiwanese with the necessary skills to serve the administrative apparatus of colonial government, educating Japanese nationals in Taiwan, and making the colony's education system as financially self-sufficient as possible. See Tsurumi, *Japanese Colonial Education in Taiwan*, 17–18.

67. Peattie, introduction to Myers and Peattie, *The Japanese Colonial Empire*, 13.

68. Thomas, "Naturalizing Nationhood," 126–27. Thomas provides much insight into the various aspects of the "natural" Japanese state as instituted in practice, from education to the Shinto state religion.

69. Yu, *Taiwan bangqiu bainianshi*, 13.

70. Mentions of secondary school involvement in baseball competitions in early colonial Japan were limited to competitions between school staff, such as a match between the National Language Middle Schools Department and the Private Schools Association, featured in "Chūgaku tai kō yakyū kai" [Middle school versus college baseball meet], *Nichi Nichi Shimpō*, March 10, 1907, 5.

71. Izawa Shuji, head of colonial educational policy until his plans to fund education completely through the state became unpopular, had long insisted that Japanese educators focus on language instruction but not at the expense of classical Chinese philosophical virtues, albeit with an added ingredient of the Japanese concept of imperial virtue. See Tsurumi, *Japanese Colonial Education in Taiwan*, 21.

72. The Japanese national language is a "given," with less of the sociolinguistic fragmentation common in China. See Ping Chen and Gottlieb, *Language Planning and Language Policy*, 22–23.

73. The issue of Chinese dialects, or *fangyan*, has encouraged much debate among sociolinguists as to what extent Chinese "dialects" are dialects at all rather than separate languages under a larger Chinese family of languages. See Norman, *Chinese*, 181–83, 249–53, and Ping Chen, *Modern Chinese*, 50–64. GMD language policy assigned a negative connotation to Chinese "dialects" other than standard Mandarin.

74. Tsurumi, *Japanese Colonial Education in Taiwan*, 168–69. See also Yu, *Taiwan bangqiu bainianshi*, 12.

75. See Suzuki Shogo, "Learning the Competence and Skill to Be a 'Civilized' State," 114–39, for a discussion of the depth of Japanese emulation of European modernization.

76. Gluck, *Japan's Modern Myths*, 9–41, 104–5.
77. Tanaka, *Japan's Orient*, 130–52, 163–87.
78. "Minami kita yakyū sai" [Baseball world north and south], *Nichi Nichi Shimpō*, July 4, 1914.

2. Waseda Baseball and Japan's Place in the World

1. Amos Alonzo Stagg Papers.
2. Tobita, *Waseda Daigaku yakyūbu hyakunenshi*, 106.
3. Guthrie-Shimizu, *Transpacific Field of Dreams*, 87.
4. Guthrie-Shimizu, *Transpacific Field of Dreams*, 3–7.
5. Gems, "Anthropology Days."
6. See Zeiler, *Ambassadors in Pinstripes*.
7. Duus, *Party Rivalry and Political Change in Taisho Japan*, 12–24.
8. Ambaras, "Social Knowledge, Cultural Capital, and the New Middle Class in Japan."
9. Guthrie-Shimizu, *Transpacific Field of Dreams*, 88–90. Guthrie-Shimizu highlights Abe's pioneering example in this regard; soon taking a cut from ticket sales became commonplace for Japanese collegiate team administrators.
10. Tobita, *Waseda Daigaku yakyūbu hyakunenshi*, 45–46.
11. Tobita, *Waseda Daigaku yakyūbu hyakunenshi*, 90.
12. Tobita, *Waseda Daigaku yakyūbu hyakunenshi*, 90–91.
13. Guthrie-Shimizu, *Transpacific Field of Dreams*, 90–92.
14. Niese, "Voyage to the Land of the Rising Sun."
15. Amos Alonzo Stagg to Alfred W. Place, July 12, 1910, Amos Alonzo Stagg Papers.
16. Tobita, *Waseda Daigaku yakyūbu hyakunenshi*, 114.
17. Amos Alonzo Stagg to Abe Isoo, June 20, 1910, Amos Alonzo Stagg Papers.
18. Takasugi Takizō to Amos Alonzo Stagg, July 20, 1910, Amos Alonzo Stagg Papers.
19. The "C" indicates that Place played varsity at the University of Chicago. Professor Gilbert Bliss, who took the Maroons to Tokyo in place of Stagg, was himself a "C" man, qualification enough to escort the team, despite the fact that his own achievements were in cycling. Amos Alonzo Stagg to Place, July 12, 1910, Amos Alonzo Stagg Papers.
20. Hugh S. Fullerton, "Maroons Repel Jap Invaders; Desperate Charge by Waseda in Ninth All but Grabs Game," *Chicago Examiner*, May 7, 1911. In Amos Alonzo Stagg Papers.
21. "Maroons to Greet Waseda Team with Oriental Airs," *Chicago Examiner*, May 3, 1911. In Amos Alonzo Stagg Papers.
22. "Chicago Varsity Prepares for the Japanese Nine," May 4, 1911. In Amos Alonzo Stagg Papers.
23. Ralph Wilder, "Banzai! See Who's Here!" *Chicago Record-Herald*, May 6, 1911. In Amos Alonzo Stagg Papers.

24. "Just a Peep at Our Oriental Visitors," *Chicago Record-Herald*, May 6, 1911. In Amos Alonzo Stagg.

25. S. Matsuda, "Captain of Waseda Tells What Team Has Learned," June 20, 1911. In Amos Alonzo Stagg Papers.

26. Gotō Chinpei, *Hawai hojin yakyūshi*, vol. 9.

27. Tobita, *Waseda Daigaku yakyūbu hyakunenshi*, 405.

28. "Beidaigaku tai sōdai yakyū shiai" [Baseball game between American University and Waseda], *Nichi Nichi Shimpō*, December 22, 1906, 1.

29. "Zenbei Yakyū dan no te no uchi" [In the hands of the all-American baseball team], *Nichi Nichi Shimpō*, November 28, 1908, 5.

30. "Tokyo yakyū tayori" [Tokyo baseball news], *Nichi Nichi Shimpō*, October 15, 1910, 4.

31. "Tokyo zoshin" [Tokyo miscellany], *Nichi Nichi Shimpō*, February 7, 1911, 3. The article stated that the professional Americans and university students of Keiō together made "a fine group of individuals with both character and personality."

32. "Waseda yakyū dan" [Waseda baseball team], *Nichi Nichi Shimpō*, April 16, 1911, 3. This brief article notes the Waseda team's safe arrival in San Francisco, the trip undertaken at the invitation of the previously hosted University of Chicago.

33. "Jippa hito karage" [Sweeping generalizations], *Nichi Nichi Shimpō*, April 16, 1912, 7. This particular article queried the exclusion of female middle-school students from baseball and boating activities at school.

34. Yu, *Taiwan bangqiu bainianshi*, 23.

35. "Sōdai raishū" [Waseda attacks], *Nichi Nichi Shimpō*, December 29, 1917, 4.

36. "Sōdai chiimu kiru" [Waseda team arrives], *Nichi Nichi Shimpō*, December 29, 1917, 5.

37. "Abe Isoo shi dan" [Interview with the honorable Abe Isoo], *Nichi Nichi Shimpō*, December 30, 1917, 2.

38. "Yakyū daini kaisen: Shichi tai san Sōdai no shō" [Second baseball game: 7–3 Waseda victory], *Nichi Nichi Shimpō*, December 31, 1917, 3.

39. "Zentai sōdai yakyū shiai" [All-Taiwan Waseda baseball contest], *Nichi Nichi Shimpō*, January 13, 1918, 7; "Waseda to nanbu" [Waseda and the south], *Nichi Nichi Shimpō*, January 13, 1918, 7.

40. "Sōbetsu yakyū shiai: Sōdai dan reibu no shutsujyō" [Send-off baseball game: Leading Waseda players appear], *Nichi Nichi Shimpō*, January 19, 1918, 7.

41. "Waseda yakyū chiimu ensei: Shikago Daigaku chiimu raichō," [Waseda baseball team expedition: University of Chicago team will come to Japan], *Nichi Nichi Shimpō*, March 24, 1925. In 1925 the *Nichi Nichi Shimpō* reported the invitation by the University of Washington for the Waseda team to play there the following spring, with arrangements with the University of Chicago in Japan in the autumn of 1926 already made.

42. "Roku Daigaku Riigu yakyū sen" [Big Six League baseball match], *Nichi Nichi Shimpō*, September 27, 1926.

43. "Roku Daigaku Riigu yakyū sen" [Big Six League baseball match], *Nichi Nichi Shimpō*, September 28, 1926.

44. "Roku Daigaku Riigu yakyū sen: Sōdai tai Hōsei, dorono geemu" [Big Six League baseball match: Waseda vs. Hōsei, drawn game], *Nichi Nichi Shimpō*, October 11, 1926.

45. "Roku Daigaku Riigu yakyū sen: Sōdai san Teida nichi" [Big Six League baseball match: Waseda, three, Imperial University, two], *Nichi Nichi Shimpō*, October 24, 1926.

46. "Roku Daigaku Riigu yakyū sen no gekkeikan" [Big Six League baseball match's victory wreath], *Nichi Nichi Shimpō*, November 20, 1926.

47. "Shikago daigaku no yakyūdan raichō" [University of Chicago baseball team arrives in Japan], *Nichi Nichi Shimpō*, August 31, 1930.

48. See, for example, "Bunka Sanpyakunenkai wo kishi" [Looking forward to the Cultural Three Hundred Years Association], *Nichi Nichi Shimpō*, September 1, 1930, 5.

49. "Kisei no Waseda yakyūbu: Menbaa ketteisu" [Incoming Waseda baseball club: Members decided], *Nichi Nichi Shimpō*, December 13, 1930.

50. "Sōdai yakyū shiai kettei kimaru" [Waseda baseball game schedule decided], *Nichi Nichi Shimpō*, December 20, 1930, 7.

51. "Sōdai yakyū senshu: Kangei kōyō kai" [Waseda baseball athletes, welcoming alumni event], *Nichi Nichi Shimpō*, December 20, 1930, 7.

52. "Sōdai o mukahete: Sokojikara aru" [Welcoming Waseda: The potential is there], *Nichi Nichi Shimpō*, December 27, 1930.

53. "Sōdai tai CB yakyū: Kefu iyoiyo daiichi kaisen" [Waseda vs. CB baseball: Finally the first game], *Nichi Nichi Shimpō*, January 1, 1931, 7; "Sōdai tai Kuroganedan Yakyūsen Gahō [Waseda vs. Railroad Team pictorial], *Nichi Nichi Shimpō*, January 3, 1931, 2.

54. "Kuroganedan dōdō katsu" [Railroad team wins magnificently], *Nichi Nichi Shimpō*, January 3, 1931, 9.

55. "Saigo no tsuigeki: Migoto seijō shita Sōdai" [The final pursuit: Splendid performance Waseda], *Nichi Nichi Shimpō*, January 5, 1931.

56. "CB sekihaisu: Ikizumaru sessen" [CB narrowly defeated: Breathtakingly close contest], *Nichi Nichi Shimpō*, January 4, 1931, 7.

57. For example, see "Takao Taikyō Shibu Shusai: Sōdai senshu kangei kai" [Gaoxiong Branch Sports Association sponsors: Waseda athlete welcoming event], *Nichi Nichi Shimpō*, January 7, 1931, 5.

58. "Jyōi dasha no mōda ni: Ryōgun dageki wo tenkai" [Superior batting is ferocious: Both teams deploy batting], *Nichi Nichi Shimpō*, January 5, 1935. The CB team lost by a single run in the tenth inning.

3. Barnstormers or Emissaries of Empire?

1. Cole, "Ersatz Octobers."
2. Eifers, *The Tour to End All Tours*, 108–21.
3. Yu, *Playing in Isolation*, 21.
4. "Trials and Tribulations of Gene Doyle's Orient Touring Baseball Demons," *Los Angeles Times*, January 28, 1921; "Doyle Held up by "Solid Ten": Baseball Legion Returns from Trip in Orient," *Los Angeles Times*, February 18, 1921.
5. "Yakyū azukaru no mangakan" [Taking part in baseball cartoon], *Nichi Nichi Shimpō*, January 12, 1921.
6. "Yakyū sukecchi" [Baseball sketch], *Nichi Nichi Shimpō*, January 10, 1921.
7. "Migi Hyūbaa no buri" [Right: Huber acting the fool], *Nichi Nichi Shimpō*, January 10, 1921.
8. Xie and Xie, *Taiwan bangqiu yibainian*, 35–36.
9. "Sōdai yakyūdan ikkō: Taihoku Yakyū Kyōkai no kangei" [Taipei Baseball Association welcomes Waseda baseball team squad], *Nichi Nichi Shimpō*, December 29, 1917; "Kinō titaishitaru Hōsei daigaku yakyūdan" [Hōsei University baseball team arrived in Taiwan yesterday], *Nichi Nichi Shimpō*, December 18, 1918.
10. "Daimai yakyūdan no raitai wa ensei" [Osaka Mainichi baseball team's Taiwan expedition], *Nichi Nichi Shimpō*, January 30, 1922.
11. "Daimai yakyūdan: Shiai hiyotei" [Mainichi baseball team: Match schedule], *Nichi Nichi Shimpō*, February 25, 1922.
12. "Daimai yakyūdan no senyakana shuwan" [Mainichi baseball team's bright skills], *Nichi Nichi Shimpō*, February 26, 1922.
13. "Kinō no *Amerika* maru de raitai shita: Daimai yakyūdan ikkō" [Mainichi baseball team squad, arrived to Taiwan yesterday on the ship *America*], *Nichi Nichi Shimpō*, February 26, 1922.
14. "Damei yinghua richeng" [Mainichi picture schedule], *Nichi Nichi Shimpō*, February 26, 1922.
15. "Keiō chiimu hatsu shiai" [Keiō team's first game], *Nichi Nichi Shimpō*, December 28, 1922; "Hōsei yakyūdan no Takemitsu kantoku" [Hōsei baseball team's coach Takemitsu], *Nichi Nichi Shimpō*, December 24, 1922.
16. Gordon, "Japan's Abortive Colonial Venture in Taiwan."
17. Eskildsen, "Of Civilization and Savages," 399–402.
18. Kleeman, *Under an Imperial Sun*, 19–22.
19. Teng, *Taiwan's Imagined Geography*, 122–40. The Japanese also added another category: "transformed." See Morris, *Colonial Project, National Game*, 18–19.
20. Early Tokugawa Confucian Ito Jinsai, for example, asserted "Japan's moral excellence" and considered late seventeenth-century China to have fallen short of its own normative standards. See Wakabayashi, *Anti-Foreignism and Western Learning in Early-Modern Japan*, 22–40.

21. As Robert Tierney writes, the use of the term "savage" reflects the existence of aboriginal Taiwanese in Japanese experience as "fictional creatures" that populated Japan's colonial spaces rather than its empire. Tierney, *Tropics of Savagery*, 7–8.

22. Kabayama Zongdu Zhaojian Yuanzhumin, "Governor General Kabayama Receives Aboriginal Taiwanese," *Taiwan Memory*, ID no. 0000359160, May 1896. http://memory.ncl.edu.tw/tm_cgi/hypage.cgi?HYPAGE=image_taipei_detail.hpg&project_id=tpphoto&dtd_id=10&xml_id=0000359160&subject_name=%e5%8f%b0%e5%8c%97%e5%b8%82%e8%80%81%e7%85%a7%e7%89%87.

23. Taidong Malanshe Yuanzhumin de Fengnianji Wudao, "Savages of Formosa," *Taiwan Memory*, ID no. 002414241, circa 1910. http://memory.ncl.edu.tw/tm_cgi/hypage.cgi?HYPAGE=image_photo_detail.hpg&project_id=twpt&dtd_id=10&xml_id=0000361482&subject_name=%e6%97%a5%e6%b2%bb%e6%99%82%e6%9c%9f%e8%87%ba%e7%81%a3%e5%9c%96%e5%83%8f%e5%af%ab%e7%9c%9f.

24. Hiromatsu, *Saikin Taiwan shi*, 4–5.

25. *The Formosan Native Tribes*, vol. 1.

26. In his study of Taiwanese alpine butterflies Kano places English transliterations of species such as the *Papilio horishanus* alongside the Japanese text in a manner similar to the presence of both languages in the extensive diagramming of aboriginal Taiwanese tribal relations found in *The Formosan Native Tribes*. Kano, *Taiwan san kōzan kochō*, 145.

27. Tsurumi, *Japanese Colonial Education in Taiwan*, 231–35, Appendix A.

28. The popularity of baseball in Taiwan among non-Japanese exploded. In addition to the emergence of the Nōkō and Kanō teams, coverage in the *Nichi Nichi Shimpō* increased dramatically. See, for example, "Yakyū yōgo" [Baseball terms], *Nichi Nichi Shimpō*, July 20, 1922. The regular "Yakyū yōgo" article featured on a page that also displayed an article on the practice of physical exercise in schools in Taiwan. Such coverage had been rare only a few years earlier.

29. Ye Boqiang, *Lin Guixing yu tade shidai*, 8.

30. Yu, *Taiwan bangqiu bainianshi*, 26.

31. Morris, *Colonial Project, National Game*, 18–19.

32. Yu, *Taiwan bangqiu bainianshi*, 26.

33. "Taiwan yakyū shi o kagaru: Jūroku kai no seisen, tetsuwan tōshu Sauma kun" [Taiwan baseball history adorned: Sixteen-inning close game, strong-arm pitcher Sauma], *Nichi Nichi Shimpō*, June 28, 1923.

34. Xie and Xie, *Taiwan bangqiu yibainian*, 41.

35. Xie and Xie, *Taiwan bangqiu yibainian*, 41.

36. "Fanren nenggao jun yuanzheng: Hualiangang yōming zhi fanren" [Aboriginal Nōkō team's expedition: Hualian's famous aborigines], *Nichi Nichi Shimpō*, September 16, 1924.

37. "Banjin chiimu Nōkōdan no ensei: Ōru karenkō tomoni" [Aboriginal Nōkō team's expedition: All of Hualian is together], *Nichi Nichi Shimpō*, September 16, 1924.

38. "Nijūichi nichi raihoku suru banjin chiimu Nōkōdan" [Aboriginal Nōkō team arriving in Taipei on the twenty-first], *Nichi Nichi Shimpō*, September 18, 1924.

39. "Banjin shiku karenkō Nōkōdan no taihoku shiai nittei kettei" [Aboriginal/Hualian Nōkō team's Taipei match schedule decided], *Nichi Nichi Shimpō*, September 18, 1924.

40. "Shikyuu o zu ni kutsute mo heiki na banjin senshu" [The composed savage player headhunts the ball], *Nichi Nichi Shimpō*, September 20, 1924.

41. "Shōhai wa ganchō ni nai: Sono kunren to yuumōshin wo to jyuunibun hakki sureba yoito" [The outcome is not a consideration: That the training and intrepid spirit be displayed is more than enough], *Nichi Nichi Shimpō*, September 18, 1924.

42. "Chinkaku Nōkōdan o mukahete" [Welcome guests Nōkō team are received], *Nichi Nichi Shimpō*, September 22, 1924.

43. "Chinkaku Nōkōdan shōgyō to kaisen su" [Welcome guests Nōkō team and Commercial School team do battle], *Nichi Nichi Shimpō*, September 22, 1924.

44. "Ensei no Nōkōdan futatabi yabaru" [Touring Nōkō team defeated again], *Nichi Nichi Shimpō*, September 23, 1924; "Nōkō sanpai entō kenbō" [Nōkō crushed, Ensuiko good batting], *Nichi Nichi Shimpō*, September 26, 1924; "Nōkōdan taichu de shōtsu" [Nenggaa team victorious in Taizhong], *Nichi Nichi Shimpō*, September 25, 1924.

45. "Nōkōdan tai shintakedan no shiai wa nana a tai ichi" [Nōkō team versus Xinzhu team game result 7A–1], *Nichi Nichi Shimpō*, October 1, 1924; "Nōkōdan mata katsu" [Nōkō team wins again], *Nichi Nichi Shimpō*, October 3, 1924.

46. Xie and Xie, *Taiwan bangqiu yibainian*, 41. Also see Yu, *Taiwan bangqiu bainianshi*, 28. Yu prefers to state that the Nōkō team finished its tour "with roughly as many wins as losses."

47. "Zen karenkōdan no atari wa monozugoku" [All-Hualian team's monumental victory], *Nichi Nichi Shimpō*, September 22, 1924.

48. "Nōkōdan tai Taihoku Shōgyō Yakyū sukecchi" [Nōkō team versus Taipei Commercial School baseball sketch], *Nichi Nichi Shimpō*, September 23, 1924.

49. "Banjin yakyū chiimu toshiteno gōken to junshin sa wa tokoshieni hozonsase doi do" [Aboriginal baseball team's virility and innocence will be maintained forever], *Nichi Nichi Shimpō*, October 18, 1924.

50. "Nōkō zensen" [Nōkō put up a good fight], *Nichi Nichi Shimpō*, June 22, 1925.

51. Yu, *Taiwan Bangqiu Bainianshi*, 28.

52. "Nōkōdan no ikkō, godai no jitensha o retsuwate" [Nōkō team's lineup, five bicycles in a line], *Nichi Nichi Shimpō*, July 11, 1925.

53. Suzuki Akira, *Takasagozoku ni sasageru*, 183.

54. "Waseda Chūgaku Yakyū chiimu to dai sessen o enji" ([Waseda High School baseball team and display of major confrontation]), *Nichi Nichi Shimpō*, July 13, 1925.

55. Yu, *Taiwan bangqiu bainianshi*, 28.

56. Morris, *Colonial Project, National Game*, 22–24.

57. "Kokonoka Tokyo eki mae no Nōkōdan yakyū chiimu" [Nōkō baseball team in front of Tokyo station on the ninth of this month], *Nichi Nichi Shimpō*, July 16, 1925; "Nōkō yakyūdan kaeru: Sōryoku to kyuusoku de naichi no hitotachi o odoroka" [Nōkō baseball team returning home: Base running and pitching astonish the Japanese people], *Nichi Nichi Shimpō*, July 31, 1925.

58. Nōkō yakyūdan kaeru: Sōryoku to kyūsoku de naichi no hitotachi o odoroka."

59. Yu, *Taiwan bangqiu bainianshi*, 29; Yu, *Playing in Isolation*, 16.

60. Ye, *Lin Guixing yu tade shidai*, 38–42.

61. Ye, *Lin Guixing yu tade shidai*, 16.

62. Yu, *Playing In Isolation*, 16–18.

63. Morris, *Colonial Project, National Game*, 17–24.

64. Rubinstein, *Taiwan*, 228.

65. Morris, *Colonial Project, National Game*, 30–31.

66. Tierney, *Tropics of Savagery*, 47, 51–54.

67. As Melissa Brown illustrates in an interesting investigation of ethnic identity over time in eastern Taiwan, where late twentieth-century Hoklo Taiwanese rejected the aboriginal Taiwanese past of their communities, the division between aboriginal Taiwanese and the various ethnic groups united by Chinese cultural universalism is the more pertinent. Brown, *Is Taiwan Chinese?*, 67–94.

68. By 1942 the Japanese authorities claimed there were 10,335 aboriginal Taiwanese students in the colonial education system. Official photographs now showed aboriginal children dutifully taking part in calisthenics, sumo, and military drills. Taiwan Sotokufu Keimukyōku, *Takasago zoku no kyōiku*, 31, appendix.

69. Shepherd, "The Island Frontier of the Ch'ing," 119–29.

70. In mainland China, for example, Sun Yat-sen led a nationalist movement alongside the intellectual charge for a nation-state centered on the collective body of Han Chinese society, a construct that both facilitated a transition to a more Western-influenced form of national government and undermined the claims of the ever more unpopular Manchu court to rule. See Duara, *Rescuing History from the Nation*, 33–48.

71. Liang Qichao, the great reformer of the Late Qing period and central figure in Chinese intellectual transitions from a hoped-for constitutional monarchy under a reformed Qing throne to the more overtly modernizing republican structure, displayed an increased interest (and subsequent influence) in Social Darwinism after his exile to Japan following the Hundred Days

Reform of 1898. Willcock and Liang, "Japanese Modernization and the Emergence of New Fiction in Early Twentieth Century China," f10, 824n10.

72. Yu, *Playing in Isolation*, 17–19. Yu quotes governor Eguchi of Hualian complaining that aboriginal Taiwanese suffered from low self-esteem and struggled in front of the large crowds attending baseball games. It is possible he was upset that his team lost convincingly, 5–1. See "Takao yakyū sen" [Gaoxiong baseball game], *Nichi Nichi Shimpō*, September 28, 1924.

73. Knapp, "Chinese Frontier Settlement in Taiwan," 43–45.

74. The academic curiosity among Japanese imperialists surrounding "savages" such as those found in Taiwan was in some ways a mirror image of similar attitudes in the West. See Steere, "Formosa," for a late nineteenth-century discussion of the "savages of Formosa."

75. In 1931 Pingdong hosted a tournament series among four teams playing under the auspices of the Aboriginal Union. The Yigong team was victorious, with three victories and no defeats. "Daiichi kai Takasogo Renmei taikai" ([First Aboriginal Union meeting]), in Yukawa, *Taiwan yakyū shi*, 30, appendix.

76. The Kanō team almost immediately set out on a victorious tour of Taiwan upon the return from Japan. See, for example, "Kanō gun wo mukahe" [Welcoming the Kanō team], *Nichi Nichi Shimpō*, September 28, 1931, for coverage of another crushing victory (by a score of 8–2) in Taizhong.

77. "Nihon ni nakoe o todokashita" [The sound of the name roared in Japan], *Nichi Nichi Shimpō*, September 1, 1931. The article points out that the nine victorious Kanō starters basked in the cheers from their hometown of Jiayi and made an emotional return to the city.

78. "Aboriginal Children Attending Class and Playing," *Taiwan Memory*, ID no. 002414623, circa 1920.

79. Young aboriginal Taiwanese children in bright, clean baseball uniforms drew an entirely different picture from the typical group portrait of alien savages so popular with Japanese ethnographers. See Yuanzhumin Zhunbei Shoulie, "Aborigines Preparing for the Outdoor Hunt," *Taiwan Memory*, ID No. 0000359156, 1921.

80. This is in sharp contrast to the exclusivist quest for accepted standards of modernity characteristic of mainland China's approach to the formation of a modern nation-state. The "commitment to modernity" among the Nationalists supported an attack on rural religion in early twentieth-century China, eliminating cultural forms that rang a discordant note in the progress of the nation-state. See Duara, "Knowledge and Power in the Discourse of Modernity," 75–80.

81. See, for example, Hiromatsu, *Saikin Taiwan shi*, 71–72. Hiromatsu includes a brief description of the aboriginal Taiwanese (including some tribal divisions) among a broad collection of information regarding Taiwanese features, from plains and mountain ranges to air pressure.

82. All nineteen of the education centers dedicated to teaching aboriginal Taiwanese children had athletic grounds on the premises. Taiwan Sotokufu Keimukyōku, *Takasago zoku no kyōiku*, 15.
83. Huang Dongzhi and Qiu, *Ameizu de bangqiu*, ix.

4. The Road to Kōshien

1. Kelly, "Kōshien Stadium," 483–88.
2. Guthrie-Shimizu, *Transpacific Field of Dreams*, 95–98.
3. See Cain and Hopkins, *British Imperialism*, 372–77.
4. Young, *Beyond the Metropolis*, 3–11, 85–91.
5. Workman, *Imperial Genus*, 167–75.
6. Li, *Reinventing Modern China*, 33–52.
7. Fitzgerald, *Awakening China*, 180–85.
8. The acquisition of Taiwan proved the first step in a journey from imperialism mimicking European regional dominance to pan-Asianism. See Duara, *Sovereignty and Authenticity*, 246–48.
9. Brown, *Is Taiwan Chinese?*, 53–56.
10. Kleeman, *Under an Imperial Sun*, 231–33.
11. Fine, *With the Boys*, 15.
12. The growth in the presence of baseball in the lives of Taiwanese children echoed that of Japanese children, who had long been exposed to the promotion of baseball as both a natural outlet for their athletic skills and a fine way of improving their health. See Mizushima Tetsuya, "Foreword."
13. "Ototoi no nanboku yakyū shiai" [Day before yesterday's north/south baseball game], *Nichi Nichi Shimpō*, January 4, 1920, 3.
14. Kanda, *Gakkō to katei*, 20.
15. "Keisō yakyū sen" [Keiō-Waseda baseball match], *Nichi Nichi Shimpō*, March 9, 1922.
16. "Yakyū yōgo" [Baseball terms], *Nichi Nichi Shimpō*, August 4, 1922.
17. "Kinō no yakyū sen" [Yesterday's baseball game], *Nichi Nichi Shimpō*, September 11, 1922; "Hibuta o kiru yakyū sōhasen honjitsu hakkai shiki kyokō" [Struggle begins for baseball championship, opening ceremony today], *Nichi Nichi Shimpō*, May 20, 1923; "Shōnen yakyū daikai muika Shin Kōen de" [Youth baseball tournament at New Park on the sixth], *Nichi Nichi Shimpō*, May 5, 1923.
18. Yu, *Taiwan bangqiu bainianshi*, 13–14.
19. "Chūgakkō yakyū yhiai" [Secondary school baseball game], *Nichi Nichi Shimpō*, April 25, 1908.
20. See, for example, "Shimotsuki tai Gakushū yakyū shiai" [Baseball game between Eleventh Month Club and Tutors' Association], *Nichi Nichi Shimpō*, December 3, 1907.

21. See "Daiichi kai yakyū rengō shiai" ([The first baseball combined games]), *Nichi Nichi Shimpō*, August 11, 1908. Teams from the Eleventh Month Club, Colonial High School, and the High School Association were among those that participated.

22. *Shōnen*—literally "juveniles" or "young boys"—appears as a ubiquitous prefix for all articles in the *Nichi Nichi Shimpō* discussing youth baseball and is heavily used by other Chinese- and Japanese-language sources. "Tainan: Shōnen yakyū shiai" [Tainan: Young boys' baseball game], *Nichi Nichi Shimpō*, December 7, 1920.

23. "Shōnen yakyū daikai" [Young boys' baseball tournament], *Nichi Nichi Shimpō*, December 7, 1920.

24. Tainan shōnen yakyū daikai" [Tainan boys' baseball tournament], *Nichi Nichi Shimpō*, December 14, 1920.

25. "Shōgakusei to yakyū nyūjyō ryō" [Baseball admission prices for elementary school students], *Nichi Nichi Shimpō*, January 8, 1921.

26. "Shō kokumin no yakyū shiai" [Young citizens' baseball game], *Nichi Nichi Shimpō*, April 4, 1921.

27. Nishiwaki, *Taiwan chuutō gakkō yakyū shi*, 6–7.

28. "Daiyamondo yakyū senshu" [Diamond baseball athletes], *Nichi Nichi Shimpō*, June 2, 1921; "Honjitsu yakyū sen: Tokufudan tai isen" [Today's baseball game: Government team vs. medical students], *Nichi Nichi Shimpō*, June 8, 1921.

29. "Kōgyōgun taishousu" [Industrial team's large victory], *Nichi Nichi Shimpō*, June 5, 1921; "Kinō no yakyū Sen: Chūgakugun daishōsu" [Yesterday's baseball game: High school team is victorious], *Nichi Nichi Shimpō*, June 8, 1921.

30. Nishiwaki, *Taiwan chūtō gakkō yakyū shi*, 8–10.

31. Tsurumi, *Japanese Colonial Education in Taiwan*, 81–85.

32. Youth games continued to be held at school facilities in addition to the parks in Taipei, Taizhong, and Tainan; e.g., "Taichu yakyū sen" [Taizhong baseball match], *Nichi Nichi Shimpō*, September 26, 1917, 3, describing a game held at the Taizhong elementary school fields.

33. Yu, *Playing in Isolation*, 19. Not only did the Kanō team emerge without any official input or support, but Yu also argues that the prolonged success of the team challenged Japanese assumptions of local Taiwanese inferiority in playing the game.

34. Rantei, *Gakkō kashū*, 32–33.

35. Eigakui, *Eibun tegami no kakikaku*, 48–49.

36. Yoshioka, *Undō manga shū*, 90–109.

37. Greater Japan Youth Baseball Association, *Saishin shōnen yakyū kisoku*.

38. Hōchi Shimbun Sha, *Undō kyōgi rekōdo bukku*, 1–4.

39. Nishiwaki, *Taiwan chūtō gakkō yakyū shi*, 106.

40. "Shōnen yakyū enki" [Youth baseball postponed], *Nichi Nichi Shimpō*, April 26, 1922.
41. "Shōnen yakyū daikai" [Youth baseball tournament], *Nichi Nichi Shimpō*, May 6, 1922.
42. "Yakyū sōha ha kinō dainichi ji sen o kaimaku" [Second baseball tournament opened yesterday], *Nichi Nichi Shimpō*, May 29, 1922.
43. "Shōnen yakyū daikai: Muika Shin Kōen de" [Youth baseball tournament: At New Park on the sixth], *Nichi Nichi Shimpō*, May 5, 1923; "Shōnen yakyū to gakusei sumō" [Youth baseball and student sumo], *Nichi Nichi Shimpō*, May 14, 1923.
44. "Takao shōnen yakyū daikai" [Gaoxiong youth baseball tournament], *Nichi Nichi Shimpō*, June 4, 1923.
45. "Takao: Shōnen yakyū sen" [Gaoxiong: Youth baseball match], *Nichi Nichi Shimpō*, June 15, 1923.
46. As late as 1930 the Taiwanese intellectuals of the *Taiwan Minbao* newspaper complained that although baseball might seem the most popular Taiwanese sport, one was actually more likely to find local Taiwanese athletes playing tennis. Significant evidence refutes this claim, and the article would seem more a reaction to political climates in Taipei than anything else, as comments on sport in the newspaper are extremely limited. See "Taiwan ren de yundong: Wei zenme bu zhen?" (Taiwanese sport: Why no invigoration?), *Taiwan Minbao*, January 1, 1930, 14.
47. "Chūtō gakkō yakyū sōha sen" [Secondary-level schools' baseball competitive games], *Nichi Nichi Shimpō*, July 2, 1923.
48. Nishiwaki, *Taiwan chūtō gakkō yakyū shi*, 15–16.
49. *Nichi Nichi Shimpō*, July 18, 1923, 9.
50. "Yon chūtō gakkō yakyū sen inshō" [Four secondary schools' baseball game impressions], *Nichi Nichi Shimpō*, July 18, 1923, 7.
51. "Taihoku Daiichi Chūgakkō Yakyū Senshu" [Taipei No. 1 High School athletes], *Nichi Nichi Shimpō*, August 7, 1923.
52. Nishiwaki, *Taiwan chūtō gakkō yakyū shi*, 17.
53. "Bei ichichū senshu honjitsu kaebei" [Taipei No. 1 athletes return to Taipei], *Nichi Nichi Shimpō*, August 25, 1923.
54. "Zen koku chūtō gakkō yakyū daikai: Taiwan yosenkai no shutsujyoukō" [National secondary school baseball tournament: Taiwan's nominated entrant school], *Nichi Nichi Shimpō*, July 24, 1925.
55. "Zentō chūtō gakkō yakyū yosen daikai" [All-island secondary school baseball preliminary tournament], *Nichi Nichi Shimpō*, July 27, 1925.
56. "Zen Koku Chūtō Gakkō Yakyū Daikai no Kōshien ni ukeru taihoku kōgyō no nain" [Kōshien of the National Secondary School Baseball Tournament receives the Taipei Industrial School nine], *Nichi Nichi Shimpō*, August 26, 1925.
57. Nishiwaki, *Taiwan chūtō gakkō yakyū shi*, 33.

58. Yu, *Taiwan bangqiu bainianshi*, 34–36.
59. "Nanbu Chūtō yakyū sen: Kanshū geni sanzen" [Southern Secondary School baseball game: Audience of three thousand], *Nichi Nichi Shimpō*, July 17, 1932.
60. Yu, *Taiwan bangqiu bainianshi*, 34.
61. "Zentō chūtō gakkō yakyū shiai o yokkakan chūkei hōsō" [All-Island Secondary School Baseball Tournament games broadcast over four days], *Nichi Nichi Shimpō*, July 19, 1930.
62. "Chūchū no rikisen oyobasu" [Taichung teams fight with all their might], *Nichi Nichi Shimpō*, July 21, 1930.
63. "Kagayaku yūshō hata wa futatabi taihoku ichichū no ten ni" [Shining championship flag in Taipei No. 1 High School's hands a second time], *Nichi Nichi Shimpō*, July 24, 1930; Nishiwaki, *Taiwan chūtō gakkō yakyū shi*, 110.
64. "Shōnen yakyū shutsujyō no senshu shōtai sawakai" [Youth baseball participating athletes invited to tea party], *Nichi Nichi Shimpō*, August 1, 1930; "Shōnen yakyū daikai kumiawase kettei" [Youth baseball tournament events decided], *Nichi Nichi Shimpō*, August 2, 1930.
65. "Shōnen yakyūdan raibei" [Youth baseball team comes to Taipei], *Nichi Nichi Shimpō*, August 1, 1930.
66. "Saigō no shō yakyū sen" [Latest youth baseball games], *Nichi Nichi Shimpō*, August 5, 1930; Sentō Shōnen Yakyū sen gahō" [All-Island Youth Baseball game pictorial], *Nichi Nichi Shimpō*, August 3, 1930. One of the photographs featured a favorite of *Nichi Nichi Shimpō* photographers when covering youth baseball games: an adult umpire towering over a diminutive catcher; "Taihoku shōnen yakyū daikai hido enkō" [Taipei Youth Baseball Tournament dates revised], *Nichi Nichi Shimpō*, June 14, 1929.
67. "Quandao shaonian yeqiu bisai gongxuexiaotuan duode jinbiao neidiren guanzhong biaoshi buman" [All-Island Youth Baseball game, common school wins silver, Japanese crowds unsatisfied], *Taiwan Minbao*, August 11, 1929, 3.
68. "Zentō yakyū taikai" [All-island baseball tournament], *Taiwan Jiho*, October 1928, 38.
69. For example, see the match between players representing the Taiwan Sugar Factory and the Tainan Post Office: "Tainan no yakyū shiai" [Tainan baseball match], *Nichi Nichi Shimpō*, February 9, 1914. Such events appear frequently in the *Nichi Nichi Shimpō* archives in the late 1910s. Kwok, "Dance and Cultural Identity among the Paiwan Tribe of Pingtung County, Taiwan," 37.
70. The game grew more slowly on Taiwan's east coast, but Hualian soon became a hub for the holding of tournaments similar to those throughout the rest of the Taiwanese baseball community. The Hualian Athletic Association formed in 1922, with a major baseball tournament established in 1925, held twice a year in spring and autumn after 1930. See Yu, *Taiwan bangqiu bainianshi*, 20.

71. Yu, *Taiwan bangqiu bainianshi*, 35.

72. Nishiwaki, *Taiwan chūtō gakkō yakyū shi*, 228.

73. "Taichū ni ukeru zentō chūtō yakyū daikai" [Taizhong receives all-island secondary school tournament], *Nichi Nichi Shimpō*, January 5, 1933. In this instance the coverage of the game was completely overshadowed by photographs and articles on the same page covering the second game of Keiō University's 1933 visit to Taiwan.

74. Yu, *Taiwan bangqiu bainianshi*, 34–37. Taipei High School is not to be confused with Taipei No. 1 High School.

5. Kanō

1. Yu, *Playing in Isolation*, 19–20.

2. Morris, *Colonial Project, National Game*, 36–38.

3. Xie and Xie, *Taiwan bangqiu yibainian*, 46.

4. Yu, *Taiwan bangqiu bainianshi*, 40.

5. Xie and Xie, *Taiwan bangqiu yibainian*, 43.

6. "Taichu Shōgyō katsu" [Taizhong Commercial wins], *Nichi Nichi Shimpō*, July 15, 1928.

7. "Tainan yakyū riigu sen" [Tainan baseball league game], *Nichi Nichi Shimpō*, October 1, 1928, 5.

8. Lin Huawei and Lin Meijun, *Dianzang Kanō*, 5.

9. "Zentō Chōtō Gakkō Yakyū sōha sen" [All-Island Secondary School Baseball contest], *Nichi Nichi Shimpō*, July 11, 1929; "Chōtō Gakkō Yakyū Daikai daiichinichi senseki" [Secondary School Baseball Tournament first day results], *Nichi Nichi Shimpō*, July 21, 1929, 7.

10. Lin Huawei and Lin Meijun, *Dianzang Kanō*, 5.

11. Lin Huawei and Lin Meijun, *Dianzang Kanō*, 5.

12. Yu, *Taiwan bangqiu bainianshi*, 42; "Kanō tsuini Hokushu o hobotte" ([Kanō Defeats Taipei Commercial at last]), *Nichi Nichi Shimpō*, July 24, 1931, 7.

13. Lin Huawei and Lin Meijun, *Dianzang Kanō*, 18.

14. Yu, *Taiwan bangqiu bainianshi*, 31–32.

15. "Kanō shucchin ni shigeki sareta" [Kanō entry is encouraged], *Nichi Nichi Shimpō*, August 13, 1931, 3.

16. See, for example, "Zenkoku Chōtō Gakkō yakyū sen: Nagano shō" [National Secondary School baseball game: Nagano wins], *Nichi Nichi Shimpō*, August 14, 1931, 7.

17. Kanō's first game was a 3–1 victory over Kanagawa Industrial and Commercial School. See Yukawa, *Taiwan yakyū shi*, 431; "Kōshien kanshuu no jinki o atsumeta Kanōgun" [Kōshien crowd's mood captured by Kanō team], *Nichi Nichi Shimpō*, August 17, 1931.

18. Yukawa, *Taiwan yakyū shi*, 431–32.

19. "Zenkoku Chōtō Gakkō yakyū: Sapporo Shōgyō o yaburi" [National Secondary School baseball: Sapporo Commercial School defeated], *Nichi Nichi Shimpō*, August 19, 1931, 7.

20. "Kōshien no Chōtō yakyū: Junkesshōni haeru" [Kōshien Secondary School baseball: Into the semifinal], *Nichi Nichi Shimpō*, August 20, 1931, 7.

21. "Kanō kazen taishō shite" [Kanō achieves expected victory], *Nichi Nichi Shimpō*, August 21, 1931.

22. "Chūkyōni taishite: Kanō ikubun no tsuyomi" [Kanō has slight advantage against Chūkyō], *Nichi Nichi Shimpō*, August 21, 1931, no1.

23. "Funtō mo kōnaku: Kanō tsuini sekihai" [Brave effort not enough: Kanō finally loses], *Nichi Nichi Shimpō*, August 22, 1931.

24. Tobe, "Taiwan yakyū no rūtsu," 181–82.

25. "Wu Tōshu no chichi" [Pitcher Wu's father], *Nichi Nichi Shimpō*, August 22, 1931.

26. Yukawa, *Taiwan yakyū shi*, 435–36.

27. "Kanō chiimu no takasago shusshinsha" [Kanō team's aboriginal members], *Nichi Nichi Shimpō*, August 23, 1931.

28. Yukawa, *Taiwan yakyū shi*, 436.

29. "Kagi Nōrin Kōtsuudan: Ryō chiimu hare no kaetai" [Jiayi Agriculture and Forestry, Transportation teams: Both teams return safely], *Nichi Nichi Shimpō*, August 31, 1931.

30. "Kanō yakyūdan: Tainan de kangei o uku" [Kanō baseball team: Welcomed in Tainan], *Nichi Nichi Shimpō*, September 2, 1931, 3.

31. "Kanō funtō no ato" [Kanō efforts marked], *Nichi Nichi Shimpō*, September 16, 1931.

32. Yu, *Taiwan bangqiu bainianshi*, 47.

33. Suzuki Akira, *Takasagozoku ni sasageru*, 184. The other team to reach the Kōshien finals was Dalian Commercial School in Manchuria. It reached the finals in 1926.

34. Yu, *Playing in Isolation*, 20.

35. Tobe, "Taiwan yakyū no rūtsu," 181.

36. Xie and Xie, *Taiwan bangqiu yibainian*, 43.

37. Chen Xiaoya, *Kanō 1*, 2–11.

38. Steven Phillips, *Between Assimilation and Independence*, 25.

39. Chen Xiaoya, *Kanō 3*.

40. Ma, *Kanō*.

41. Ma, *Kanō*.

42. Zhou Wanyao, foreword to Liu Wan-lai, *Yi ge lao Kanō de huiyi*.

43. Liu Wan-lai, *Yi ge lao Kanō de huiyi*.

44. Jiang Mingshan, *Nizhuansheng*, 62–65.

45. Xie, *"Guoqiu" dansheng qianji*, 207–9.

46. Morris, *Colonial Project, National Game*, 48–51.

6. Chiang's China and Taiwanese Baseball

1. Fong, "Hegemony and Identity in the Colonial Experience of Taiwan," 173–78.
2. Xie, *"Guoqiu" dansheng qianji*, 387–89.
3. Steven Phillips, *Between Assimilation and Independence*, 52–55.
4. Chang Te-tsui, "Land Utilization in Taiwan," 363.
5. Roy, *Taiwan*, 84–85.
6. Chen Ping, "Policy on the Selection and Implementation of a Standard Language as a Source of Conflict in Taiwan," 102.
7. The Japanese, who referred to Taipei as the "civilized city," actively modernized the city's architecture beyond the construction of colonial government buildings, including the manipulation of Taipei city streets into a grid system more befitting modern modes of transport. See Lo, "A Palimpsest of 'Faits Urbains' in Taipei," 69–70.
8. Sandel, "Linguistic Capital in Taiwan," 529.
9. Roy, *Taiwan*, 95–96.
10. Not that the transition would be smooth; local elites and the arriving Nationalists competed with each other for control of the immediate postwar narrative and the depiction of the colonial legacy therein. See Steven Phillips, "Between Assimilation and Independence."
11. Jeremy E. Taylor, "The Production of the Chiang Kai-shek Personality Cult."
12. I refer here to Michael Billig's use of "flagging" in his discussion of daily performances of nationalist allegiance; far from the "banal" signposts that Billig discusses, the cult of personality surrounding Chiang was often overt and self-consciously celebratory. See Billig, *Banal Nationalism*, 93–103.
13. See, for example, Alan Bairner's discussion of the Irish categorization of sport into Gaelic, British, and universal in *Sport, Nationalism, and Globalization*, 28–30.
14. "Zhongshi yihujuan yibing liedui zouyue songjunzhong" [Middle City each household gives one cake, people line up with music to send to the army], *Lianhe Bao*, September 16, 1951.
15. "Xuetong bangqiu zuori bimu: Taipingxiao huo guanjun" [Children's baseball games finished yesterday: Taiping School wins first place], *Lianhe Bao*, September 25, 1951.
16. Yu, *Playing in Isolation*, 29.
17. Morris, *Colonial Project, National Game*, 58. Morris relates an interview with Taiwanese baseball coach Jian Yongchang in 2004, when he asked the coach about official attempts to regulate language use on the field during baseball tournaments. Jian replied, "There's no Mandarin in baseball."
18. Jay Taylor, *The Generalissimo*, 507–8.
19. Chou and Nathan, "Democratizing Transition in Taiwan," 277–78.
20. Osborne, "MacArthur and Asia."
21. Gaddis, *The Cold War*, 130–31.

22. "Tiyu duanbo: Zhongmei bangsai" [Sports in brief: China-America baseball contest], *Lianhe Bao*, September 21, 1951, 3.

23. "Zhongmei bangqiusai zuo biaozhan shiji" [China-America baseball contest, fierce battle yesterday lasted ten innings], *Lianhe Bao*, September 22, 1951, 3.

24. "Sheluman shifou zhengxuan jike jieshao" [Truman reveals whether or not he will run], *Lianhe Bao*, January 26, 1952, 4.

25. Truman, "The President's News Conference of January 24, 1952," in Truman, *Public Papers of the Presidents of the United States*, 121.

26. "Zhongmei jinian bangsai ming xiawu kaiqiu" [China-America anniversary baseball game first pitch tomorrow afternoon], *Lianhe Bao*, May 15, 1953, 3.

27. "Soft ball" baseball games should not be confused with the modern game of softball. These "soft ball" games differed from baseball only in the use of a softer, rubber ball. The game had traditionally been the domain of girls and young women during the colonial period.

28. "Zhongmei hezuo jinian bangsai jinri kaiqiu" [China-America cooperation anniversary game commences today], *Lianhe Bao*, May 16, 1953, 3.

29. "Zhongmei hezuo bangqiusai" [China-America cooperation baseball game], *Lianhe Bao*, May 27, 1953, 3.

30. "Zhongmei hezuo bangqiusai ding zhoumo juxing" [China-America cooperation baseball game confirmed for weekend], *Lianhe Bao*, June 18, 1953, 3.

31. "Zhongmei bangqiusai zuori jiemu" [China-America baseball contest started yesterday], *Lianhe Bao*, June 21, 1953, 3.

32. See Morris, *Colonial Project, National Game*, 59–64.

33. Gaddis, *We Now Know*, 61.

34. Chun, "From Nationalism to Nationalizing, 53.

35. See, for example, Soares, "Our Way of Life against Theirs."

36. "Zheng fei bangshou hui sheng men" [Baseball players who defeated the Philippines to appear at provincial tournament], *Lianhe Bao*, October 27, 1951, 3.

37. "Taiwan bangxie singqi kaihui taolun gaizu wenti shiying shijie zuzhi" [Taiwan Baseball Association confirms date of meeting to discuss reorganization issue, adopt world organization], *Lianhe Bao*, September 11, 1952, 3.

38. "Guoji bangqiu sai wo jueding canjia" [ROC confirmed to participate in international baseball games], *Lianhe Bao*, December 30, 1952, 1.

39. "Taiwan bangqiudui jinqi cheng fu fei" [Taiwan baseball team begins schedule in Philippines today], *Lianhe Bao*, April 19, 1953, 3.

40. "Taibangdui zuori fu fei" [Taiwan baseball team in Philippines yesterday], *Lianhe Bao*, April 20, 1953, 3.

41. Morris, *Colonial Project, National Game*, 60.

42. "Taibang zai fei sheng meihaijun" [Taiwan baseball team in Philippines defeats American Navy], *Lianhe Bao*, May 4, 1953, 3.

43. Chan, "The 'Two-Chinas' Problem and the Olympic Formula."

44. "Yazhou Bangqiu Sai Mingtian Kaimu" ([Asian Baseball Championship Opening Ceremony Tomorrow]), *Lianhe Bao*, December 17, 1954, 3.

45. "Yazhou bangqiusai bimu feilubin duokui" [Asian baseball championship finishes, Philippines secure victory], *Lianhe Bao*, December 27, 1954, 3.

46. "Wo yazhou bangqiudui" [China Asian baseball team], *Lianhe Bao*, January 11, 1955, 3.

47. "Yazhou bangsai wo sheng feidui" [Asian baseball championships, China defeats Philippines team], *Lianhe Bao*, December 12, 1955, 3; "Yazhou bangqiusai wodui sheng han" [Asian baseball championships, China defeats South Korea], *Lianhe Bao*, December 19, 1955, 3.

48. Morris, *Colonial Project, National Game*, 76–78.

49. The Chinese Communist Party (CCP) chose to reject such overtures; Beijing and London established diplomatic relations in 1972.

50. Guy, "Governing the Arts, Governing the State," 512–17.

51. "The First Visit of This Chinese Company to Our City," *Irish Independent*, October 10, 1957.

52. "Opera and Acrobatics," *Irish Independent*, October 19, 1957.

53. The February 28 Incident, often referred to in Taiwan simply as "228," resulted in the deaths of possibly as many as ten thousand people and the stymying of a nascent Taiwanese movement toward political autonomy. See Steven Phillips, "Between Assimilation and Independence," 292–96.

54. During the colonial period Japan turned Taiwan from an adequate provider of sugar for the domestic Chinese market into "one of the more significant sugar producers in the world." Galloway, "The Modernization of Sugar Production in Southeast Asia," 11–15.

55. Tsurumi, *Japanese Colonial Education in Taiwan*, 126–27.

56. Lin Ting-kuo, "Cong (guanyuan xiansheng riji) kan linxiantang de tiyu huodong," 796–97. Specifically, as noted above, the Japanese attitude that exercise was pivotal in the cultivation of personal health and that daily activity was a key component differed greatly from the cultural understandings of health in Taiwan before 1895.

57. The Chinese revolution is of course a topic for much debate. I reference here Lucien Bianco's analysis of the CCP's success in *Origins of the Chinese Revolution*.

7. Echoes of Empire

1. "Liang wei daqishi dou shi lao qiumi" [Two chess masters are knowledgeable ballgame fans], *Lianhe Bao*, August 21, 1967, 3.

2. Morris, *Colonial Project, National Game*, 72–78.

3. Oh Sadaharu, *Jidong!*, 3–5.

4. Brownell, *Training the Body for China*, 37–56.

5. Morris, *Colonial Project, National Game*, 54–57, offers an interesting argument in favor of baseball's utilization as a re-Sinicizing tool by the GMD.

6. Xie and Xie, *Taiwan bangqiu yibainian*, 74–76.

7. Yu, *Playing in Isolation*, 26–28.

8. Kelly, "Japan," 23.

9. Yu, *Playing in Isolation*, 91–96.

10. Morris, *Colonial Project, National Game*, 73.

11. Oh looks back on 1964 with particular fondness, recalling his hitting a home run off legendary pitcher Kaneda Masaichi. Kaneda joined the Yomiuri Giants a year later, and Oh would regularly remind the older player of this moment as they took their training laps. Oh, *Jidong!*, 103–4, 232–38.

12. Sima Sangdun, "Fengmi riben de bangqiu xuanshou Wang Zhenzhi" [Baseball player Oh Sadaharu is fashionable in Japan], *Lianhe Bao*, April 1, 1965, 2; "Luri bangqiu mingshou Wang Zhenzhi gushi" [Baseball star in Japan, Wang Zhenzhi's story], *Lianhe Bao*, September 4, 1965, 7.

13. "Tianya hechu wu fangcao mingyi haiwai si qiaobao" [Sky is the limit for these four overseas Chinese], *Lianhe Bao*, March 16, 1965, 3.

14. Li Yong, "Yi bang wei zhenfu sangdao wan zhongzheng ying mei qiuwang" [The bat overwhelms the island, masses welcome baseball star back], *Lianhe Bao*, December 5, 3.

15. "Shenjia zhi duoshao" [Know the value of the body], *Lianhe Bao*, December 5, 1965, 3; Bangxia wu sanhe zhijiang leishang you bamian weifeng" [Triple is no prize, a lion at the plate], *Lianhe Bao*, December 5, 1965, 3.

16. "Huiguo xinqing qingsong bu shi lai zhao nuyou" [Mood on visiting the country is relaxed, not looking for a girlfriend], *Lianhe Bao*, December 5, 1965, 3.

17. "Qiuwang jinji duwei duishou wang feng pimi" [Baseball king golden cock standing on one leg for those who hope to be invincible], *Lianhe Bao*, December 5, 1965, 3.

18. Oh Sadaharu and Faulkner, *Sadaharu Oh*, 32–34.

19. "Jinji duli yu qingting dianshui" [Golden cock standing on one leg and dragonfly with a little water], *Lianhe Bao*, December 6, 1965, 3.

20. Morris, *Colonial Project, National Game*, 74.

21. "Wang Zhenzhi de da he ai" [Oh Sadaharu's play and love], *Lianhe Bao*, December 6, 1965, 3.

22. "Wang Zhenzhi jin fanguo, xie xinniang du miyue" [Oh Sadaharu returns today accompanying his wife on honeymoon], *Lianhe Bao*, December 3, 1966, 3. Also cited in Morris, *Colonial Project, National Game*, 75.

23. Oh Sadaharu and Faulker, *Sadaharu Oh*, 54–55.

24. Oh Sadaharu and Faulker, *Sadaharu Oh*, 16–18; Oh Sadaharu, *Jidong!*

25. Oh Sadaharu, *Jidong!*

26. Oh Mito, *Gan en sui yue*, 62–80.

27. "Huandao tiyu" [Physical education around the island], *Lianhe Bao*, November 19, 1953.
28. "Riben daxue bangqiu guanjun Zao dao tian bangqiu dui yuezhong laitai fangwen" [Japanese university baseball champions Waseda baseball team visit Taiwan the middle of this month], *Lianhe Bao*, December 1, 1953.
29. "Zaodaotian daxue bangqiudui zaitai saicheng quanbu paiding" [Waseda University baseball team Taiwan game schedule confirmed], *Lianhe Bao*, December 2, 1953.
30. "Riben zaoda bangqiudui laitai tiaozhan zhenrong jiexiao" [Japan Waseda baseball team lineup for Taiwan challenge matches announced], *Lianhe Bao*, December 4, 1953.
31. "Riben zaodaotian daxue bangqiudui laitaidui zhiyuandian jianglu" [Record of personnel of Japanese Waseda University baseball team to visit Taiwan], *Lianhe Bao*, December 8, 1953.
32. "Zaodaotian bangqiudui laitai bisai: Kaishi shoupiao" [Waseda baseball team Taiwan games: Tickets on sale], *Lianhe Bao*, December 9, 1953.
33. "Rizaodaotian Bangqiudui Mingchen Kedi Taibei" [Japanese Waseda baseball team to arrive tomorrow morning], *Lianhe Bao*, December 16, 1953.
34. "Riben zaoda bangqiudui ding jinchen feiditai" [Japanese Waseda baseball team arrived in Taiwan this morning by plane], *Lianhe Bao*, December 17, 1953.
35. "Zhongri bangqiu youyi bisai: Zaodadui qikai de sheng" [China-Japan baseball friendship game: Waseda team hits the ground running], *Lianhe Bao*, December 20, 1953.
36. "Zhongri bangqiu youyisai: Zaodadui zuozai chuan jieyin" [China-Japan baseball friendship game: Yesterday the Waseda team recorded another triumph], *Lianhe Bao*, December 21, 1953.
37. "Zhongri bangqiusai: Zaodadui sanzhan sanjie" [China-Japan baseball game: Waseda team is three for three], *Lianhe Bao*, December 22, 1953.
38. "Zhongri bangsai zaoda zai jie" [Waseda triumphs again in China-Japan baseball game], *Lianhe Bao*, December 27, 1953.
39. "Zhongri bangqiusai: Zuozai zhongshi jiao feng zaoda zai sheng tailian" [China-Japan baseball game: Waseda defeated United Taiwan again in Taizhong yesterday], *Lianhe Bao*, December 28, 1953.
40. "Zhongri bangsai fiqi huihe: Tailian chuchuan jiebao" [Seventh China-Japan baseball game: United Taiwan records first victory], *Lianhe Bao*, December 30, 1953.
41. "Heibaiji" [Black and white collection], *Lianhe Bao*, December 19, 1953.
42. "Rizaoda bangqiudui jieshu fangwen tai saicheng" [Japanese Waseda baseball team concludes scheduled games on Taiwan visit], *Lianhe Bao*, January 7, 1954.
43. Morris, *Colonial Project, National Game*, 70–71.
44. Yu, *Playing in Isolation*, 25–36.
45. Yu, *Playing in Isolation*, 25–26.
46. Kleeman, *Under an Imperial Sun*, 237–48.

8. Hongye

1. Donald Shapiro, "Little League Team's Title Triumph Raises Morale in Taiwan," *New York Times*, August 30, 1971, 41.
2. "Taiwan Wins Little League Final, 12 to 3," *New York Times*, August 29, 1971, S2.
3. "Taiwan Wins on 9 in Ninth," *Washington Post*, August 29, 1971, 39.
4. Morris, "Taiwan," 73–74.
5. Liu Dui Hakka County Records Committee, *Liu Dui Hakka Sociocultural Development and Evolution Research*, 483.
6. Sundeen, "A 'Kid's Game'?," 253–57.
7. "Tiyu huodong: Xinzhu xun" [Physical education activity: Xinzhu reports], *Lianhe Bao*, May 26, 1952, 6.
8. "Tiyu huodong: Xinzhu xun" [Physical education activity: Xinzhu reports], *Lianhe Bao*, May 30, 1952, 6.
9. "Gedi qiuxun: Taizhong xun" [Ball reports from all locations: Taizhong reports], *Lianhe Bao*, March 19, 1952, 5.
10. "Yun shaonian bangsai: Ding xiayue juxing" [Yunlin youth baseball games confirmed for next month], *Lianhe Bao*, April 27, 1952, 5.
11. "Bangqiu, lanqiu: zuori zhangguo" [Baseball, basketball: Results of yesterday's games], *Lianhe Bao*, May 8, 1953, 3.
12. "Taiwan zheng fei bangqiudui: Zuowan zaiyu guilai" [Taiwan defeats Philippine baseball team: Victorious team returned last night], *Lianhe Bao*, May 16, 1953, 3; "Quansheng Yingshi Bangqiusai: Caisi zeng jinbei" [All-Province Hard Ball Baseball Competition: Chase donates cup], *Lianhe Bao*, May 31, 1953, 3.
13. "Dongjing de biaoqing" [The look and feel of Tokyo], *Lianhe Bao*, August 12, 1954, 2.
14. "Qingnian huodong: Chengji pingding" [Student activities graded and judged] *Lianhe Bao*, March 30, 1956, 3.
15. "Zhuoqiu jin biaosai: Mingtian chouqian. Shizhangbei nubang manshang guanjun" [Table tennis gold medal game: Lots drawn tomorrow. Manshang champions of women's Mayor's Cup], *Lianhe Bao*, June 23, 1959, 3.
16. "Kongjun bangqiu jinglu" [Air force baseball tour], *Lianhe Bao*, August 2, 1959, 3.
17. "Yixian bangqiu sai: Zuo kaishi juezhu" [Yilan County baseball game: Contest began yesterday], *Lianhe Bao*, August 26, 1966, 6.
18. "Zhongshi siqian qingnian canjia shuqi huodong" [Four thousand Taizhong young people participate in summer activities], *Lianhe Bao*, July 27, 1965, 7.
19. Jiang Tianhui, *Jiayi shizhi*, 695.
20. Liu Dui Hakka County Records Committee, *Liu Dui Hakka Sociocultural Development and Evolution Research*, 474–75.
21. Xie and Xie, *Taiwan banqiu yibainian*, 98.
22. Yu, *Taiwan bangqiu bainianshi*, 110.

23. "Tongxin bang: Xiaoxiao de jie dada de wenqing" [Sympathy bat: Little ones' hunger [and] grown-ups' warmth of feeling], *Lianhe Bao*, April 27, 1965, 3.

24. "Taidong Hongye guoxiao bangqiudui huode rexin renshi zizhu" [Taidong Hongye elementary school baseball team secures financial support from passionate people], *Lianhe Bao*, May 15, 1968, 6.

25. "Yichang bangqiusai sanzhi quanleida Hongye jiezuo guanzhong hecai" [Three home runs in one baseball game, Hongye masterpiece, audience applauds], *Lianhe Bao*, May 18, 1968, 5.

26. "Hongye bangqiu yijun jueqi zhenxing tiyu haode kaishi" [Hongye baseball distinguished team stands out, developed physical education a good start], *Lianhe Bao*, May 20, 1968, 6.

27. "Beishi zhongxue leisai" [Taipei high school ballgame], *Lianhe Bao*, May 11, 1967, 5; "Yixian shaonian bangsai mingci yi pingding" [Yilan County youth baseball competition participants already confirmed], *Lianhe Bao*, January 4, 1966, 6.

28. "Quansheng xuetong bangsai zuo zai Pingdong jiemu" [Provincial students' baseball games opened yesterday in Pingdong], *Lianhe Bao*, April 19, 1967, 2.

29. "Hongye bu fu zhongwang guoxiao bangsai chengwang" [Hongye bears the expectations of the crowd to become elementary school baseball champions], *Lianhe Bao*, May 22, 1968, 6.

30. "Taidong xiao jiang yi [Bang] xiang manshan [Hongye] ya Chuiyi" [Taidong little ones in first place, (Bat) County mountain people (Hongye) crush Chuiyi], *Lianhe Bao*, May 22, 1968, 3.

31. If anything, the state took the opportunity to present the successes of this young team of humble origin as symbolic of Taiwan's postwar economic "miracle." See Morris, *Colonial Project, National Game*, 85–86.

32. "Bu duan gengyun bi you shouhuo" [Achieving results requires continuous cultivation], *Lianhe Bao*, May 15, 1968, 6.

33. "Xiao shiqing, da qishi!" [Small matter, large inspiration!], *Lianhe Bao*, May 23, 1968, 2.

34. Yu, *Playing in Isolation*, 37–38.

35. Morris, *Colonial Project, National Game*, 81–86.

36. Yu, *Playing in Isolation*, 41–44.

37. "Hongye dui fang benbao, Wang Yiwu zeng shoutao" [Hongye team visits this paper, Wang Yiwu donates gloves], *Lianhe Bao*, May 23, 1968, 3.

38. "Ri shaonian bangqiudui jieshou fanghua yaoqing" [Japanese youth baseball team accepts invitation to visit China], *Lianhe Bao*, June 14, 1968, 6.

39. See Yu, *Playing in Isolation*, 40, and Morris, *Colonial Project, National Game*, 83.

40. "Hongye duiyuan bei zhimao ming dingti" [Hongye reserve players named], *Lianhe Bao*, June 19, 1968, 6.

41. "Hongye zuo fang Zhongshi" [Hongye visited Taizhong yesterday], *Lianhe Bao*, June 21, 1968, 6.

42. "Ri Aihe bangdui jin fanghua" [Japanese Aichi baseball team visits China today], *Lianhe Bao*, July 5, 1968, 6.
43. "Hongye renxuan qiuyuan dingqi beilai jixun" [Hongye players confirm dates for focused training in Taipei], *Lianhe Bao*, July 12, 1968, 6; "Hongye zaisheng" [Hongye wins again], *Lianhe Bao*, July 31, 1968, 6.
44. "Liuxing bang, zhui yun tui, hongye fanfei" [Popular baseball, chasing the clouds, Hongye takes flight], *Lianhe Bao*, August 26, 1968, 3.
45. "Boli shushang: Hongye zhansheng yihou" [Attending glass school: After the Hongye victory], *Lianhe Bao*, August 26, 1968, 9.
46. Liu Dui Hakka County Records Committee, *Liu Dui Hakka Sociocultural Development and Evolution Research*, 483–484.
47. Zhonghua Shaonian Bangqiudui Fendoushi Bianyi Weiyuanhui, *Zhonghua Shaonian Bangqiudui fendoushi*, 133.
48. Zhonghua Shaonian Bangqiudui Fendoushi Bianyi Weiyuanhui, *Zhonghua Shaonian Bangqiudui fendoushi*, 42.
49. Zhonghua Shaonian Bangqiudui Fendoushi Bianyi Weiyuanhui, *Zhonghua Shaonian Bangqiudui fendoushi*, 57–61.
50. Yu, *Playing in Isolation*, 44–47.
51. Morris, "Taiwan," 73–74.
52. Roy, *Taiwan*, 158–64; Morris, *Colonial Project, National Game*, 105–8
53. Roy, *Taiwan*, 183–202.
54. Ian Buruma, "Taiwan's New Nationalists," 86.
55. Yu, *Playing in Isolation*, 64–71.
56. Morris, *Colonial Project, National Game*, 123–24.
57. Yu, *Playing in Isolation*, 115–43.
58. In particular, see Yu, *Playing in Isolation*, 37–63. In Yu's view the Hongye success and the irregularities that dogged Taiwanese youth baseball during that successful period and afterward caused the decline of amateur baseball in Taiwan.
59. Sun Chen, "Investment in Education and Human Resource Development in Postwar Taiwan," 96–97.
60. Huang Ying-che, "Were Taiwanese Being 'Enslaved'?"
61. See in particular Xie Shiyuan's concluding comments in Xie, *"Guoqiu" dansheng qianji*, 428–31.

Conclusion

1. Thorn, *Baseball in the Garden of Eden*, xi.
2. Kiberd, *Inventing Ireland*, 289.
3. Brown, *Is Taiwan Chinese?*, 235–50.
4. Ching, "Colonial Nostalgia or Postcolonial Anxiety."
5. Reaves, *Taking in a Game*, 138–40.
6. Yu, Junwei, *Playing in Isolation*, 14.

7. "Ototoi no nanboku yakyū shiai" [Day before yesterday's north/south baseball game], *Nichi Nichi Shimpō*, January 4, 1920, 3.

8. "Chū Gakkō Dan No Ōshō" [Taizhong Middle School Association Championship], *Nichi Nichi Shimpō*, September 23, 1919, 7. At this time notices of games involving high school and middle school students began to gradually increase. This article describes the success of the Tainan Middle School team in a trip to Jiayi, defeating the local team in both games of a two-game series.

9. McAnallen, "'The Greatest Amateur Association in the World'?," 157, 165–72, 181.

10. Gmelch, "Afterword," 308.

11. Morris, "Taiwan," 66.

12. Xie and Xie, *Taiwan bangqiu yibainian*, 74–75; Yu, *Playing in Isolation*, 29.

13. Cal Clark discusses the emergence of the politics of this cultural symbolism at the turn of the century in the early post-democratization era. See Clark, "Taiwan Enters Troubled Waters."

14. Yu, *Taiwan bangqiu bainianshi*, 26; Yu, *Playing in Isolation*, 37–63.

15. Yu, *Playing in Isolation*, 50.

Bibliography

Archives

Amos Alonzo Stagg Papers, Box 63, University of Chicago
Baseball Hall of Fame and Museum Library, Tokyo, Japan
National Central Library, Taipei, Taiwan

Published Works

Aichiken Shōgyō Gakkō Kōyūkai. *Aishou sōkan bango*. Nagoya: Aichiken Shōgyō Gakkō Kōyūkai, 1923.

Alden, D. L., J. B. E. M. Steenkamp, and R. Batra. "Brand Positioning through Advertising in Asia, North America, and Europe: The Role of Global Consumer Culture." *Journal of Marketing* 63, no. 1 (1999): 75–87. doi:10.2307/1252002.

Al-Khaizaran, Huda Yoshida. "The Emergence of Private Universities and New Social Formations in Meiji Japan, 1868–1912." *History of Education* 40, no. 2 (2011): 157–78.

Allen, Joseph R. "I Will Speak, Therefore, of a Graph: A Chinese Metalanguage." *Language in Society* 21, no. 2 (1992): 189–206.

———. "Taipei Park: Signs of Occupation." *Journal of Asian Studies* 66, no. 1 (February 27, 2007): 159.

Ambaras, David R. "Social Knowledge, Cultural Capital, and the New Middle Class in Japan, 1895–1912." *Journal of Japanese Studies* 24, no. 1 (1998): 1–33.

Anderson, Benedict. *Imagined Communities: Reflections on the Origin and Spread of Nationalism*. London: Verso, 1983.

Asahi Shinbun Sha. *Kakushu undō kyōgi kisoku zenshū*. Osaka: Asahi Shinbun Sha, 1926.

Bairner, Alan, ed. *Sport and the Irish: Histories, Identities, Issues*. Dublin: University College Dublin Press, 2005.

———. *Sport, Nationalism, and Globalization: European and North American Perspectives*. New York: State University of New York Press, 2001. SUNY Series in National Identities.

Baker, Aaron, and Todd Boyd, eds. *Out of Bounds: Sports, Media, and the Politics of Identity*. Bloomington: Indiana University Press, 1997.

Baker, William J. *Playing with God: Religion and Modern Sport*. Cambridge MA: Harvard University Press, 2007.

Barclay, Paul D. "Cultural Brokerage and Interethnic Marriage in Colonial Taiwan: Japanese Subalterns and Their Aborigine Wives, 1895–1930." *Journal of Asian Studies* 64, no. 2 (2005).

Bianco, Lucien. *Origins of the Chinese Revolution, 1915–1949*. London: Oxford University Press, 1971.

Billig, Michael. *Banal Nationalism*. London: Sage Publications, 1995.

Billings, Andrew C., Michael L. Butterworth, and Paul D. Turman. *Communication and Sport: Surveying the Field*. Los Angeles: Sage Publications, 2012.

Blackwell Publishing on behalf of the Royal Geographical Society. "Formosa." *Geographical Journal* 2, no. 5 (November 1893): 441–43.

Block, David. *Baseball before We Knew It: A Search for the Roots of the Game*. Lincoln: University of Nebraska Press, 2005.

Brookes, Rod. *Representing Sport*. New York: Oxford University Press, 2002.

Brown, Melissa J. *Is Taiwan Chinese?* Berkeley: University of California Press, 2004.

———. "Reconstructing Ethnicity: Recorded and Remembered Identity in Taiwan." *Ethnology* 40, no. 2 (2001): 153–64. doi:10.2307/3773928.

Brownell, Susan. *Training the Body for China: Sports in the Moral Order of the People's Republic*. Chicago: University of Chicago Press, 1995.

Bryant, Howard. *Juicing the Game: Drugs, Power, and the Fight for the Soul of Major League Baseball*. New York: Viking, 2005.

Burk, Robert F. *Much More Than a Game: Players, Owners, and American Baseball since 1921*. Chapel Hill: University of North Carolina Press, 2001.

Buruma, Ian. "Taiwan's New Nationalists." *Foreign Affairs* 75, no. 4 (1996): 77–91. doi: 10.2307/20047660.

Cain, P. J., and A. G. Hopkins. British Imperialism: 1688–2000. New York: Routledge, 2001.

Carr, E. H. *What Is History?* London: Macmillan, 1961.

Chai, Winberg. "The Transformation of the Mass Media in Taiwan since 1950: Introduction." *Asian Affairs* 27, no. 3 (2000): 133–40.

Chan, Gerald. "The 'Two-Chinas' Problem and the Olympic Formula." *Pacific Affairs* 58, no. 3 (1985): 473–90.

Chang, P. H. "China's Relations with Hong Kong and Taiwan." ANNALS of the American Academy of Political and Social Science 519, no. 1 (1992): 127–39. doi :10.1177/0002716292519001010.

Chang Te-tsui. "Land Utilization in Taiwan." *Land Economics* 28, no. 4 (November 1952): 362–68.

Chen Chiukun. "From Landlords to Local Strongmen: The Transformation of Local Elites in Mid-Ch'ing Taiwan, 1870–1862." In Rubinstein, *Taiwan: A New History* (2007), 133–62.

Chen Ping. *Modern Chinese: History and Sociolinguistics*. New York: Cambridge University Press, 1999.

Chen Ping. "Policy on the Selection and Implementation of a Standard Language as a Source of Conflict in Taiwan." In Chen and Gottlieb, *Language Planning and Language Policy*, 95–110.

Chen Ping, and Nanette Gottlieb, eds. *Language Planning and Language Policy: East Asian Perspectives*. New York: Routledge, 2001.

Chen Xiaoya. *Kanō 1: Mogui Shunlian*. Taipei: Weiliu Chubanshiye, 2014.

———. *Kanō 3: Yiqiu Ruhun*. Taipei: Weiliu Chubanshiye, 2014.

Ching, Leo T. S. *Becoming "Japanese": Colonial Taiwan and the Politics of Identity Formation*. Berkeley: University of California Press, 2001.

———. "Colonial Nostalgia or Postcolonial Anxiety: The Dosan Generation in between 'Restoration' and 'Defeat.'" In *Sino-Japanese Transculturation: From the Late Nineteenth Century to the End of the Pacific War*, edited by Richard King, Cody Poulton, and Katsuhiko Endo, 211–26. Lanham MD: Lexington Books, 2012.

Chou Yangsun, and Andrew J. Nathan. "Democratizing Transition in Taiwan." *Asian Survey* 27, no. 3 (1987): 277–99.

Chun, Allen. "From Nationalism to Nationalizing: Cultural Imagination and State Formation in Postwar Taiwan." *Australian Journal of Chinese Affairs*, no. 31 (1994): 49–69.

Clark, Cal. "Taiwan Enters Troubled Waters: The Elective Presidencies of Lee Teng-Hui and Chen Shui-Bian." In Rubinstein, *Taiwan: A New History* (2007), 496–535.

Cohen, Benjamin J. *The Question of Imperialism*. New York: Basic Books, 1973.

Cohen, Paul A. *History in Three Keys: The Boxers as Event, Experience, and Myth*. New York: Columbia University Press, 1997.

Cole, Robert. "Ersatz Octobers: Baseball Barnstorming." In *Baseball History 4: An Annual of Original Baseball Research*, ed. Peter Levine. Westport CT: Meckler, 1991.

Cronin, Mike, William Murphy, and Paul Rouse, eds. *The Gaelic Athletic Association 1884–2009*. Dublin: Irish Academic Press, 2009.

Cumings, Bruce. "Power and Plenty in Northeast Asia: The Evolution of U.S. Policy." *World Policy Journal* 5, no. 1 (1987): 79–106. doi:10.2307/40209074.

Curtis, Michael, ed. *Orientalism and Islam: European Thinkers on Oriental Despotism in the Middle East and India*. Cambridge: Cambridge University Press, 2009.

Dietschy, Paul, and Richard Holt. "Sports History in France and Britain: National Agendas and European Perspectives." *Journal of Sport History* 37, no. 1 (2010): 83–98. http://muse.jhu.edu/journals/journal_of_sport_history /v037/37.1.dietschy.html.

Dirlik, Arif. "Chinese History and the Question of Orientalism." *History and Theory* 35, no. 4 (1996): 96–118.

Doak, Kevin M. "What Is a Nation and Who Belongs? National Narratives and the Ethnic Imagination in Twentieth-Century Japan." *American Historical Review* 102, no. 2 (April 1997): 283–309. doi:10.2307/2170825.

Dreifort, John E., ed. *Baseball History from Outside the Lines: A Reader*. Lincoln: University of Nebraska Press, 2001.

Duara, Prasenjit. "Knowledge and Power in the Discourse of Modernity: The Campaigns against Popular Religion in Early Twentieth-Century China." *Journal of Asian Studies* 50, no. 1 (1991): 67–83.

——. *Rescuing History from the Nation: Questioning Narratives of Modern China*. Chicago: University of Chicago Press, 1995.

——. *Sovereignty and Authenticity: Manchukuo and the East Asian Modern*. Lanham MD: Rowman and Littlefield, 2003.

Duke, Benjamin. *The History of Modern Japanese Education: Constructing the National School System, 1872–1890*. New Brunswick NJ: Rutgers University Press, 2009.

Duus, Peter. *The Abacus and the Sword: The Japanese Penetration of Korea, 1895–1910*. Berkeley: University of California Press, 1995.

——. *Party Rivalry and Political Change in Taisho Japan*. Cambridge MA: Harvard University Press, 1968.

Eifers, James E. *The Tour to End All Tours: The Story of Major League Baseball's 1913–1914 World Tour*. Lincoln: University of Nebraska Press, 2003.

Eigakui Enshūkyoku. *Eibun tegami no kakikaku*. Tokyo: Uta Sha, 1907.

Erbaugh, Mary S. "The Secret History of the Hakkas: The Chinese Revolution as a Hakka Enterprise." *China Quarterly* 132 (February 12, 1992): 937.

Erikuchi Toshisaburō. *Zentō yūryō seinendan jiseki*. Taipei: Taiwan Sotokufu, 1926.

Eskildsen, Robert. "Of Civilization and Savages: The Mimetic Imperialism of Japan's 1874 Expedition to Taiwan." *American Historical Review* 107, no. 2 (2002): 388–481.

——. "Taiwan: A Periphery in Search of a Narrative." *Journal of Asian Studies* 64, no. 2 (2005): 281–94.

Fair, Laura. *Pastimes and Politics: Culture, Community, and Identity in Post-Abolition Urban Zanzibar, 1890–1945*. Athens OH: Ohio University Press, 2001.

Fairbank, John King. *China: A New History*. Cambridge MA: Harvard University Press, 1992.

Fine, Gary Alan. "Small Groups and Culture Creation: The Idioculture of Little League Baseball Teams." *American Sociological Review* 44, no. 5 (1979): 733.

———. *With the Boys: Little League Baseball and Preadolescent Culture*. Chicago: University of Chicago Press, 1987.

Fine, Gary Alan, and Sherryl Kleinman. "Rethinking Subculture: An Interactionist Analysis." *American Journal of Sociology* 85, no. 1 (1979): 1.

Fitts, Robert K. *Banzai Babe Ruth: Baseball, Espionage, and Assassination during the 1934 Tour of Japan*. Lincoln: University of Nebraska Press, 2012.

———. *Remembering Japanese Baseball: An Oral History of the Game*. Carbondale: Southern Illinois University Press, 2005.

———. *Wally Yonamine: The Man Who Changed Japanese Baseball*. Lincoln: University of Nebraska Press, 2008.

Fitzgerald, John. *Awakening China: Politics, Culture, and Class in the Nationalist Revolution*. Stanford: Stanford University Press, 1996.

Fong Shiaw-Chian. "Hegemony and Identity in the Colonial Experience of Taiwan, 1895–1945." In *Taiwan under Japanese Colonial Rule, 1895–1945: History, Culture, Memory*, edited by Liao Ping-hui and David Der-wei Wang. New York: Columbia University Press, 2006.

The Formosan Native Tribes: A Genealogical and Classificatory Study, vol. 1. Taipei: Taihoku Imperial University, Institute of Ethnology, 1935.

Franks, Joel S. *The Barnstorming Hawaiian Travelers: A Multiethnic Baseball Team Tours the Mainland, 1912–1916*. Jefferson NC: McFarland, 2012.

Fujimoto Shigeo. "Trans-Pacific Boy Scout Movement in the Early Twentieth Century: The Case of the Boy Scout Movement in Osaka, Japan." *Australasian Journal of American Studies* 27, no. 2 (2008): 29–43.

Gaddis, John Lewis. *The Cold War*. New York: Penguin Books, 2005.

———. *We Now Know: Rethinking Cold War History*. Oxford: Oxford University Press, 1997.

Galloway, J. H. "The Modernization of Sugar Production in Southeast Asia, 1880–1940." *Geographical Review* 95, no. 1 (2005): 1–23.

Gardella, Robert. "From Treaty Ports to Provincial Status, 1860–1894." In Rubinstein, *Taiwan: A New History* (2007), 163–200.

Gems, Gerald R. "Anthropology Days, the Construction of Whiteness, and American Imperialism in the Philippines." In *The 1904 Anthropology Days and Olympic Games: Sport, Race, and American Imperialism*, edited by Susan Brownell, 189–216. Lincoln: University of Nebraska Press, 2008.

Gluck, Carol. *Japan's Modern Myths: Ideology in the Late Meiji Period*. Princeton NJ: Princeton University Press, 1985.

Gmelch, George. "After the Game." *NINE: A Journal of Baseball History and Culture* 14, no. 1 (2005): 152–54.

———. "Afterword: Is Baseball Really Global?" In Gmelch, *Baseball without Borders*, 305–13.

———, ed. *Baseball without Borders: The International Pastime*. Lincoln: University of Nebraska Press, 2006.

———. "Jim Mann: 3N2 Baseball." *NINE: A Journal of Baseball History and Culture* 16, no. 1 (2007): 156–65.

Gold, Thomas B. "Civil Society and Taiwan's Quest for Identity." In Harrell and Huang, *Cultural Change in Postwar Taiwan*. Taipei: SMC Publishing, 1994.

———. "Taiwan Society at the Fin de Siècle." *China Quarterly* 148, (February 12, 1996): 1091. doi:10.1017/S0305741000050566.

Gordon, Leonard. "Japan's Abortive Colonial Venture in Taiwan, 1874." *Journal of Modern History* 37, no. 2 (June 1965): 171–85.

Goto Chinpei. *Hawai hojin yakyushi: Yakyu ippyakunensai kinen*. Vol. 9: *Shoki zai hokubei nihonjin no kiroku. Hawai hen*. Tokyo: Bunsei Shoin, 1940.

Gotō, Shimpei. Preface to *Japanese Rule in Formosa*, by Yosaburo Takekoshi. London: Longmans, Green, 1907.

Grasmuch, Sherri. *Protecting Home: Class, Race, and Masculinity in Boys' Baseball*. New Brunswick NJ: Rutgers University Press, 2005.

Greater Japan Youth Baseball Association. *Saishin Shōnen Yakyū Kisoku*. Kobe: Mitsumura Insatsu Kabushi Kaisha, 1921.

Gripentrog, John. "The Transnational Pastime: Baseball and American Perceptions of Japan in the 1930s." *Diplomatic History* 34, no. 2 (2010): 247–73. doi:10.1111/j.1467-7709.2009.00848.x.

Guha, Ramachandra. *A Corner of a Foreign Field: The Indian History of a British Sport*. London: Picador, 2002.

Gurtov, Melvin. "Taiwan: Looking to the Mainland." *Asian Survey* 8, no. 1 (1968): 16–20.

Guthrie-Shimizu, Sayuri. *Transpacific Field of Dreams: How Baseball Linked the United States and Japan in Peace and War*. Chapel Hill: University of North Carolina Press, 2012.

Guttmann, Allen. *From Ritual to Record: The Nature of Modern Sports*. New York: Columbia University Press, 1978.

———. *Games and Empires: Modern Sports and Cultural Imperialism*. New York: Columbia University Press, 1994.

Guttmann, Allen, and Lee Thompson, eds. *Japanese Sports: A History*. Honolulu: University of Hawaii Press, 2001.

Guy, Nancy. "Governing the Arts, Governing the State: Peking Opera and Political Authority in Taiwan." *Ethnomusicology* 43, no. 3 (1999): 508–26.

Harney, John. "Youth Baseball and Colonial Identity in Taiwan, 1920–1968." *NINE: A Journal of Baseball History and Culture* 22, no. 1 (Fall 2013): 20–43.

Harrell, Stevan, and Chun-chieh Huang, eds. *Cultural Change in Postwar Taiwan*. Taipei: SMC Publishing, 1994.

Harrison, Mark. *Legitimacy, Meaning and Knowledge in the Making of Taiwanese Identity*. New York: Palgrave Macmillan, 2006.

Hiromatsu Yoshimi. *Saikin Taiwan shi*. Taipei: Taihoku Nichi Nichi Shimpo Sha, 1924.

Hirose Kenzo. *Nihon no yakyushi*. Tokyo: Nihon Yakyusi Kankokai, 1964.

Hōchi Shimbun Sha. *Undō kyōgi rekōdo bukku*. Tokyo: Undō Sōsho Kankōkai, 1922.

Holmes, Michael, and David Storey. "Who Are the Boys in Green? Irish Identity and Soccer in the Republic of Ireland." In *Sport and National Identity in the Post-War World*, edited by Dilwyn Porter and Adrian Smith. New York: Routledge, 2004.

Hopkins, A. G., ed. *Global History: Interactions between the Universal and the Local*. New York: Palgrave Macmillan, 2006.

Hsiao A-chin. *Contemporary Taiwanese Cultural Nationalism*. London: Routledge, 2000.

Huang Dongzhi and Qiu Weicheng. *Ameizu de bangqiu: Shenti wenhua yu rentong*. Nantou, Taiwan: Guoshiguan Taiwan Wenxianguan, 2012.

Huang Ying-che. "Were Taiwanese Being 'Enslaved'? The Entanglement of Sinicization, Japanization, and Westernization." In *Taiwan under Japanese Colonial Rule, 1895-1945: History, Culture, Memory*, edited by Liao Ping-hui and David Der-wei Wang, 312-26. New York: Columbia University Press, 2006.

Huizinga, Johan. *Homo Ludens: A Study of the Play-Element in Culture*. Boston: Beacon Press, 1955.

Iriye Akira. *Japan and the Wider World: From the Mid-Nineteenth Century to the Present*. New York: Longman, 1997.

Izumino Seiichi. *Wang zhenzhi: Quanleida wang*. Translated by Wenbin Chen. Taipei: Shui Niu Chu Ban She, 1972.

James, C. L. R. *Beyond a Boundary*. Durham NC: Duke University Press, 1993.

Jao Jui-Chang and Matthew McKeever. "Ethnic Inequalities and Educational Attainment in Taiwan." *Sociology of Education* 79, no. 2 (2006): 131-52.

Jiang Mingshan, ed. *Nizhuansheng: Taiwan bangqiu tezhan*. Tainan, Taiwan: Guoli Taiwan Lishi Bowuguan, 2014.

Jiang Tianhui, ed. *Jiayi shizhi*. Jiayi, Taiwan: Jiayi City Government, 2002.

Johnson, Chalmers. MITI *and the Japanese Miracle: The Growth of Industrial Policy, 1925-1975*. Stanford: Stanford University Press, 1982.

Judt, Tony, and Denis Lacorne, eds. *The Politics of Language: Language, Nation, and State*. New York: Palgrave Macmillan, 2004.

Kabushikigaisha DNP Fumitoshi Sentaa, ed. *Waseda Daigaku 125 nen*. Tokyo: DaiNihon Insatsu Kabushikigaisha, 2007.

Kanda Tatsujirō, ed. *Gakkō to katei*. Tainan, Taiwan: Tainan County South Gate Elementary, 1929.

Kano Tadao. *Taiwan san kōzan kochō*. Taipei: National Taiwan Library Archive, 1930.

Kaplan, Robert B. *Language Planning and Policy in Asia, 1: Japan, Nepal and Taiwan and Chinese Characters*. Bristol, UK: Multilingual Matters Press, 2008.

———. *Language Planning from Practice to Theory*. Bristol, UK: Multilingual Matters Press, 1997.

Karlin, Jason G. "The Gender of Nationalism: Competing Masculinities in Meiji Japan." *Journal of Japanese Studies* 28, no. 1 (2002): 41–77. doi:10.2307/4126775.

Katz, Paul R. *When Valleys Turned Blood Red: The Ta-pa-ni Incident in Colonial Taiwan*. Honolulu, University of Hawaii Press, 2005.

Katz, Paul R., and Murray A. Rubinstein, eds. *Religion and the Formation of Taiwanese Identities*. New York: Palgrave Macmillan, 2003.

Kelly, William W. "Is Baseball a Global Sport? America's 'National Pastime' as Global Field and International Sport." *Global Networks* 7, no. 2 (2007): 187–201.

———. "Japan: The Hanshin Tigers and Japanese Professional Baseball." In Gmelch, *Baseball without Borders*, 22–42.

———. "Koshien Stadium: Performing National Virtues and Regional Rivalries in a 'Theatre of Sport.'" *Sport in Society* 14, no. 4 (2011): 481–93.

———. "Samurai Baseball: The Vicissitudes of a National Sporting Style." *International Journal of the History of Sport* 26, no. 3 (2009): 429–41.

Kiberd, Declan. *Inventing Ireland: The Literature of the Modern Nation*. London: Vintage Books, 1995.

Kleeman, Faye Yuan. *In Transit: The Formation of the Colonial East Asian Cultural Sphere*. Honolulu: University of Hawaii Press, 2014.

———. *Under an Imperial Sun: Japanese Colonial Literature of Taiwan and the South*. Honolulu: University of Hawaii Press, 2003.

Knapp, Ronald G. "Chinese Frontier Settlement in Taiwan." *Annals of the Association of American Geographers* 66, no. 1 (March 1976): 43–59.

Kwok, Madeline. "Dance and Cultural Identity among the Paiwan Tribe of Pingtung County, Taiwan." *Dance Research Journal* 11, nos. 1/2 (1978–1979).

Li Huaiyin. *Reinventing Modern China: Imagination and Authenticity in Chinese Historical Writing*. Honolulu: University of Hawaii Press, 2012.

Lin Huawei and Lin Meijun, eds. *Dianzang Kanō, jianong bangqiu, 1928–2005*. Taipei: Executive Yuan Physical Education Committee, 2005.

Lin Ting-kuo. "Cong (guanyuan xiansheng riji) kan linxiantang de tiyu huodong." In *Riji yu Taiwan shi yanjiu xiace*, 791–40. Taipei: Academia Sinica, 2008.

Liu Dui Hakka County Records Committee. *Liu Dui Hakka Sociocultural Development and Evolution Research: Art and Culture Edition*. Pingdong: Liudui Cultural Education Foundation, 2001.

Liu Wanlai. *Yi ge lao Kanō de huiyi: Dalin zhi zi Liu Wanlai zixu*. Taipei: Yulan Wenhua, 2015.

Lo Shih-wei. "A Palimpsest of 'Faits Urbains' in Taipei." *Journal of Architectural Education* 52, no. 2 (November 1998): 68–75.

Ma, Chih-hsiang, dir. *Kanō*. Taiwan, 2014.

McAnallen, Donal. "'The Greatest Amateur Association in the World'? The GAA and Amateurism." In *The Gaelic Athletic Association 1884–2009*, edited by Mike Cronin, William Murphy, and Paul Rouse. Dublin: Irish Academic Press, 2009.

Minakami Takitarō. *Kaigara tsuihō*. Tokyo: Tōkōkaku Shoten, 1925.

Minichiello, Sharon A., ed. *Japan's Competing Modernities: Issues in Culture and Democracy, 1900-1930*. Honolulu: University of Hawaii Press, 1998.

Ministry of National Defense, ROC. *US MAAG-Taiwan: An Oral History*. Taipei: Military History and Translation Office, Ministry of National Defense, 2008.

Mizushima Tetsuya. Foreword to *Saikin kōshiki shōnen yakyū kisoku*. Tokyo: Dai Nippon Shōnen Yakyū Kyōkai Ensan, 1922.

Moeran, Brian. "Individual, Group and Seishin: Japan's Internal Cultural Debate." *Man*, New Series, 19, no. 2 (June 1984).

Morris, Andrew D. *Colonial Project, National Game: A History of Baseball in Taiwan*. Berkeley: University of California Press, 2011.

———. "Taiwan: Baseball, Colonialism, and Nationalism." In Gmelch, *Baseball without Borders*, 65-88.

Myers, Ramon H., and Mark R. Peattie, eds. *The Japanese Colonial Empire, 1895-1945*. Princeton NJ: Princeton University Press, 1984.

Niese, Joe. "Voyage to the Land of the Rising Sun: The Wisconsin Badger Nine's 1909 Trip to Japan." *NINE: A Journal of Baseball History and Culture* 22, no. 1 (2013): 11-19.

Nishiwaki, Yoshitomo. *Taiwan chūtō gakkō yakyū shi*. Himeji: Onokōsoku Insatsu Kabushiki Kaisha, 1996.

Norman, Jerry. *Chinese*. New York: Cambridge University Press, 1988. Cambridge Language Surveys.

Obojski, Robert. *The Rise of Japanese Baseball Power*. Radnor PA: Chilton Book Company, 1975.

Oh Mito. *Gan en sui yue: Wang zhenzhi muqin de gushi*. Translated by Wang Qinglin. Taipei: Zhonghua Ribaoshe Chubanbu, 1985.

Oh Sadaharu. *Jidong! Wode yeqiu rensheng*. Translated by Nuling Ling Huang. Taipei: Yushanshe, 2012.

———. *Wang zhenzhi huiyi lu*. Translated by China Times (*Zhonghua Shibao*). Taipei: Shi Bao Wen Hua Chu Ban Shi Ye You Xian Gong Si, 1981.

Oh Sadaharu, and David Faulkner. *Sadaharu Oh: A Zen Way of Baseball*. New York: Vintage Books, 1985.

Okumura Yoshitarō. *Daigaku shiriizu: Waseda Daigaku*. Tokyo: Mainichi Shimpo Sha, 1971.

Osborne, John. "MacArthur and Asia." *Life*, September 25, 1950.

Peattie, Mark R. "Japanese Attitudes towards Colonialism, 1895-1945." In Myers and Peattie, *The Japanese Colonial Empire, 1895-1945*, 80-127. Princeton NJ: Princeton University Press, 1984.

Phillips, Claude S., Jr. "The International Legal Status of Formosa." *Western Political Quarterly* 10, no. 2 (June 1957).

Phillips, Steven E. *Between Assimilation and Independence: The Taiwanese Encounter Nationalist China, 1945-1950*. Stanford: Stanford University Press, 2003.

——. "Between Assimilation and Independence: Taiwanese Political Aspirations under Nationalist Chinese Rule, 1945-1948." In Rubinstein, *Taiwan: A New History* (2007), 275-319.

Pomeranz, Kenneth. *The Great Divergence: China, Europe, and the Making of the Modern World Economy*. Princeton NJ: Princeton University Press, 2000.

Rantei Shōin. *Gakkō kashū*. Tokyo: Hōkō Kai, 1910.

Rawnsley, Gary D., and Ming-Yeh Rawnsley. "Public Television and Empowerment in Taiwan." *Democratization and Communication in Asia* 78, no. 1 (2005): 23-38.

Reaves, Joseph A. *Taking in a Game: A History of Baseball in Asia*. Lincoln: University of Nebraska Press, 2002.

Roden, Donald. "Baseball and the Quest for National Dignity in Meiji Japan." *American Historical Review* 85, no. 3 (June 1980): 511-534.

Rowe, David. *Sport, Culture and the Media: The Unruly Trinity*, 2nd ed. Maidenhead, Berkshire: Open University Press, 2004.

Roy, Denny. *Taiwan: A Political History*. Ithaca: Cornell University Press, 2003.

Rubinstein, Murray A., ed. *Taiwan: A New History*. London: M. E. Sharpe, 1999. Expanded edition, 2007.

Said, Edward. *Orientalism*. New York: Vintage Books, 1979.

——. "Orientalism Reconsidered." *Cultural Critique*, no. 1 (Autumn 1985).

Sandel, Todd L. "Linguistic Capital in Taiwan: The KMT's Mandarin Language Policy and Its Perceived Impact on Language Practices of Bilingual Mandarin and Tai-gi Speakers." *Language in Society* 32, no. 4 (September 2003): 523-51.

Shepherd, John R. "The Island Frontier of the Ch'ing." In Rubinstein, *Taiwan: A New History* (2007), 107-32.

Shimahara, Nobuo K. *Adaptation and Education in Japan*. New York: Praeger, 1979.

Soares, John. "Our Way of Life against Theirs: Ice Hockey and the Cold War." In *Diplomatic Games: Sport, Statecraft, and International Relations since 1945*, edited by Heather L. Dichter and Andrew L. Johns, 251-96. Lexington KY: University Press of Kentucky, 2014.

Steere, J. B. "Formosa." *Journal of the American Geographical Society of New York* 6 (18/4): 302-34.

Stronach, Bruce, and Magofuku Hiromu. "'They Must Be Judged as Japanese Institutions. . . .'" *Change* 16, no. 6 (1984): 10-11, 46.

Sun Chen. "Investment in Education and Human Resource Development in Postwar Taiwan." In Harrell and Huang, *Cultural Change in Postwar Taiwan*, 91-110.

Sun Jing. "Japan-Taiwan Relations: Unofficial in Name Only." *Asian Survey* 47, no. 5 (October 7, 2007): 790-810. doi:10.1525/as.2007.47.5.790.

Sundeen, Joseph Timothy. "A 'Kid's Game'? Little League Baseball and National Identity in Taiwan." *Journal of Sport and Social Issues* 25, no. 3 (August 2001): 251-65.

Suzuki Akira. *Takasagozoku ni sasageru*. Tokyo: Chūau Kōron Sha, 1986.

Suzuki Hiroshi. *Hyakunenme no kikyō*. Tokyo: Shōgakkan, 1999.

Suzuki Shogo. "Learning the Competence and Skill to Be a 'Civilized' State: State Reinvention in Japan." In Suzuki Shogo, *Civilization and Empire: China and Japan's Encounter with European International Society*. New York: Routledge, 2009.

Swinhoe, Robert. "Notes on the Island of Formosa." *Journal of the Royal Geographical Society of London* 34 (1864): 6–18.

Taiiku Dōshikai. *Kyōgi kinsoku to renshūhō*. Tokyo: Taiiku Dōshikai, 1923.

Taiwan Sotokofu Keimukyōku. *Takasago zoku no kyōiku* [Education of the aborigines of Taiwan]. Taipei: Taiwan Sotokofu Keimukyōku, 1942.

Tanaka, Stefan. *Japan's Orient: Rendering Pasts into History*. Berkeley: University of California Press, 1993.

Taylor, Jay. *The Generalissimo: Chiang Kai-shek and the Struggle for Modern China*. Cambridge MA: Harvard University Press, 2009.

Taylor, Jeremy E. "The Production of the Chiang Kai-shek Personality Cult, 1929–1975." *China Quarterly* 185 (2006): 96–110.

Teng, Emma Jinhua. *Taiwan's Imagined Geography: Chinese Colonial Travel Writing and Pictures, 1683–1895*. Cambridge MA: Harvard University Asia Center, 2004.

Thomas, Julia Adeney. "Naturalizing Nationhood: Ideology and Practice in Early Twentieth-Century Japan." In Minichiello, *Japan's Competing Modernities*, 114–32.

Thorn, John. *Baseball in the Garden of Eden: The Secret History of the Early Game*. New York: Simon and Schuster, 2011.

Thurston, Anne F. "Taiwan: The Little Island That Could." *Wilson Quarterly* 20, no. 3 (1996): 52–67. http://www.jstor.org/stable/40259327?seq=1#page _scan_tab_contents.

Tierney, Robert. *Tropics of Savagery: The Culture of Japanese Empire in Comparative Frame*. Berkeley: University of California Press, 2010.

Tobe Yoshinari. "Taiwan yakyū no rūtsu: Nokodan ni hajimatte Nihon o sekken shita yakyūshi." In *Besubōrojii 5 (Yakyū bunka gakkai) ronsō daigo gō*. Japan: Yakyū Bunka Gakkai, 2004.

Tobita Suishu, ed. *Waseda Daigaku yakyubu hyakunenshi*. Tokyo: Waseda Daigaku Yakyubu, 1950.

Truman, Harry S. *Public Papers of the Presidents of the United States: Harry S. Truman: Containing the Public Messages, Speeches and Statements of the President, January 1, 1952, to January 20, 1953, 1952–53*. Washington DC: U. S. Government Printing Office, 1966.

Tsurumi, E. Patricia. "Education and Assimilation in Taiwan under Japanese Rule, 1895–1945." *Modern Asian Studies* 13, no. 4 (1979): 617–41.

Tsurumi, E. Patricia. *Japanese Colonial Education in Taiwan, 1895–1945*. Cambridge MA: Harvard University Press, 1977.

Uhalley, Stephen, Jr. "Taiwan's Response to the Cultural Revolution." *Asian Survey* 7, no. 11 (1967): 824–29.

Wakabayashi, Bob Tadashi. *Anti-Foreignism and Western Learning in Early-Modern Japan: The New Theses of 1825*. Cambridge MA: Harvard University Press, 1986.

Walton, W. H. Murray. "Among the Mountains and Head-Hunters of Formosa." *Geographical Journal* 81, no. 6 (June 1933): 481–497.

Wang, Di. *Street Culture in Chengdu: Public Space, Urban Commoners, and Local Politics, 1870–1930*. Stanford: Stanford University Press, 2003.

Waseda Daigaku. *Waseda Daigaku shichijūn nenshi*. Tokyo: Waseda Daigaku Shimuraka Insatsu Sho, 1952.

Wei, Jennifer M. *Language Choice and Identity Politics in Taiwan*. Lanham MD: Lexington Books, 2008.

Westad, Odd Arne. *Decisive Encounters: The Chinese Civil War: 1946–1950*. Stanford: Stanford University Press, 2003.

Whiting, Robert. *The Chrysanthemum and the Bat: Baseball Samurai Style*. New York: Dodd, Mead, 1977.

———. "The Samurai Way of Baseball and the National Character Debate." *Asia-Pacific Journal: Japan Focus*, 2006. http://www.japanfocus.org/-Robert-Whiting/2235/article.html.

———. *You Gotta Have Wa*. New York: Macmillan, 1989.

Willcock, Hiroko, and Liang Qichao. "Japanese Modernization and the Emergence of New Fiction in Early Twentieth Century China: A Study of Liang Qichao." *Modern Asian Studies* 29, no. 4 (October 1995): 817–40.

Winn, Jane Kaufman, and Tang-chi Yeh. "Advocating Democracy: The Role of Lawyers in Taiwan's Political Transformation." *Law and Social Inquiry* 20, no. 2 (1995): 561–99.

Workman, Travis. *Imperial Genus: The Formation and Limits of the Human in Modern Korea and Japan*. Berkeley: University of California Press, 2015.

Xie Shiyuan. *"Guoqiu" dansheng qianji: Rizhi shiqi Taiwan bangqiushi*. Taipei: Guoli Taiwan Lishi Bowuguan, 2012.

———. *Rizhi shiqi Taiwan bangqiu koushu fangtan*. Tainan, Taiwan: Guoli Taiwan Lishi Bowuguan, 2012.

Xie Shiyuan, and Xie Jiafen. *Taiwan bangqiu yibainian*. Taipei: Guoshi Chuban, 2003.

Ye Boqiang. *Lin Guixing yu tade shidai*. Hualian, Taiwan: Hualian Xian Wenhuaju, 2014.

Yoshioka Torihei. *Undō manga shū*. Osaka: Chūau Undō Sha, 1924.

Young, Louise. *Beyond the Metropolis: Second Cities and Modern Life in Interwar Japan*. Berkeley: University of California Press, 2013.

———. *Japan's Total Empire: Manchuria and the Culture of Wartime Imperialism*. Berkeley: University of California Press, 1998.

Yu Junwei. *Playing in Isolation: A History of Baseball in Taiwan*. Lincoln: University of Nebraska Press, 2007.

——, ed. *Taiwan bangqiu bainianshi: Xuan dong sui yue*. Taipei: Zhonghua Min-
guo Bangqiu Xiehui, 2006.

Yukawa Mitsuo. *Taiwan yakyū shi*. Taipei: Taiwan Nichi Nichi Shimpo Sha, 1932.

Zarrow, Peter. *After Empire: The Conceptual Transformation of the Chinese State,
1885–1924*. Stanford: Stanford University Press, 2012.

Zhonghua Shaonian Bangqiudui Fendoushi Bianyi Weiyuanhui, ed. *Zhonghua
Shaonian Bangqiudui Fendoushi*. Taipei: Republic of China History and Culture Publishing House, 1972.

Zeiler, Thomas W. *Ambassadors in Pinstripes: The Spalding World Baseball Tour and
the Birth of the American Empire*. Lanham MD: Rowman and Littlefield, 2006.

Index

www.ingramcontent.com/pod-product-compliance
Lightning Source LLC
Chambersburg PA
CBHW020337100426
42812CB00029B/3167/J